PRAISE
MICHELE BORBA'S

No More Misbehavin'

"Michele Borba offers insightful, realistic, and straightforward advice that is sure to get immediate results."
—Sally Lee, Editor-in-Chief, *Parents Magazine*

"This will be the only discipline book you'll ever need to raise good kids."
—from the Foreword by Jack Canfield, coauthor, *Chicken Soup for the Soul* and *Chicken Soup for the Parent's Soul*

"A sensitive, thoughtful, eminently practical book that will help parents help their children change behaviors that will improve the child's, and the entire family's, well-being and happiness. A wonderful contribution!"
—Alvin Rosenfeld, M.D., child psychiatrist and coauthor, *The Over-Scheduled Child*

"The most complete toolkit for coping with behavior I have ever seen. Destined to be a classic for all parents and teachers, *No More MisBehavin'* is powerful and practical."
—Annie Leedom, founder and president, www.parentingbookmark.com

"Based on the good old-fashioned idea that kids who behave are happier than those who don't, *No More Misbehavin'* shows parents exactly how to turn their love into *action* with a step-by-step plan for permanently removing bad behaviors. Excellent!"
—Elaine Hightower, coauthor with Betsy Riley, *Our Family Meeting Book: Fun and Easy Ways to Manage Time, Build Communication and Share Responsibility Week by Week*

"Michele Borba's new book provides parents with an innovative strategy for dealing with children's challenging behaviors. Her suggestions are practical, doable, and proven. Any parent looking for concrete solutions for troubling kid behaviors need look no further. Simply outstanding!"

—Naomi Drew, author,
Hope and Healing: Peaceful Parenting in an Uncertain World

"This book offers hands-on, practical, and effective solutions to everyday problems that all parents encounter from time to time. These strategies are guaranteed to reduce your parenting headaches and help you enjoy your kids! I'll certainly be recommending this book to the parents with whom I work."

—Dr. Jane Bluestein, author,
Parents, Teens and Boundaries: How to Draw the Line
and *The Parent's Little Book of Lists:*
DOs and DON'Ts of Effective Parenting

"*No More Misbehavin's* clear, no-nonsense advice will be a blessing to parents paralyzed by stubborn childhood behaviors ranging from biting to bullying to heel-dragging in the face of chores. This step-by-step, here's-how manual is almost like having Michele Borba as your personal parenting trainer."

—Tom Lickona, author,
Educating for Character and *Raising Good Children*

Building Moral Intelligence

"A much-needed antidote to the waves of incivility, intolerance, and insensitivity sweeping through our nation's youth culture. Dr. Michele Borba offers parents a treasure trove of ideas for building the most neglected intelligence around: our kids' moral intelligence. I'd like to see a copy of this book in every home across America!"

—Thomas Armstrong, author,
7 Kinds of Smart, Multiple Intelligences in the Classroom,
and *Awakening Your Child's Natural Genius*

"Michele Borba is an inspiring educator, an experienced parent, and a terrific writer. She has identified the core issues for parenting moral kids and presented them with passion, wit, and enormous practicality. Her new book gives us solid empirical research but also specific day-to-day activities that will really make a difference in our children's lives."
—Michael Gurian, author, *Boys and Girls Learn Differently, The Wonder of Boys, The Good Son,* and *A Fine Young Man*

"While many people in public life decry the lack of character and moral development among our kids, few take this concern further, into the realm of practical steps to address the issue in the lives of real children and youth. Michele Borba has done so in her book *Building Moral Intelligence.* As one whose work takes him into prisons to interview kids who kill, I can testify to the need for adults to cultivate moral intelligence—and the consequences when we don't. This book is a tool for parents to use in the struggle."
—James Garbarino, author, *Lost Boys: Why Our Sons Turn Violent and How We Can Save Them*

"This smart and helpful book integrates much of what we know about raising moral children. I especially like the book's constructive way of pulling together a wide range of theoretical approaches and coming up with a wealth of sensible child-rearing tips."
—William Damon, professor and director, Stanford University Center on Adolescence

"This how-to guide to teaching children moral intelligence fills a deep need. It is practical, filled with excellent activities, and based on solid research."
—Kevin Ryan, director emeritus, Boston University Center for the Advancement of Ethics and Character

"This is perhaps the best written guide for parents and educators concerned with the deep character and moral intelligence of their children or students. It is wise, literate, and valuable."

—Peter Scharf, director, Center for Society,
Law and Justice at the University of New Orleans,
and author, *Growing Up Moral*

"Michele Borba articulates the core traits that build and promote responsible citizenship among the young and old alike. Creating safe schools begins with responsible behavior. Dr. Borba explains in clear, concise, and effective ways how to make that happen. Her book is a 'must read' for parents, educators, and community leaders."

—Ronald D. Stephens, executive director,
National School Safety Center

Parents Do *Make a Difference*

"Michele Borba's new book is invaluable. Drawing on a lifetime of rich experience, the author understands parents' concerns and speaks to them wisely and compassionately. Best of all, she spells out what parents need to know in easily accessible language and easily learnable stages."

—Nathaniel Branden, author,
The Six Pillars of Self-Esteem and *A Woman's Self-Esteem*

"Packed with helpful suggestions and insights, this book is a wonderful guide to help kids become winners."

—Louise Hart, author, *The Winning Family:
Increasing Self-Esteem in Your Children and Yourself*
and *On the Wings of Self-Esteem*

"Dr. Michele Borba's years of research and experience make her uniquely qualified as an expert in the field. The many practical and creative suggestions offered here are sound, effective ways of developing successful human beings. I'm certain that this outstanding book will become an extremely valuable guide and resource for both parents and teachers."

—Robert W. Reasoner, president, International Council for Self-Esteem, and retired school superintendent

"*Parents Do Make a Difference* is able to address the core issues of parenting. Cross-culturally, Dr. Michele Borba has brought valuable insights to teaching professionals. Her parenting ideas have also been widely adopted by parent educators in Hong Kong."

—Ivan Yiu, assistant community services secretary for children and youth, Tung Wah Group of Hospitals, Hong Kong

"Every child arrives in life with a birthright to healthy self-esteem and to be welcomed, nurtured, and inspired by parents who abide by the practices Michele Borba recommends in this book. Applying these principles would quickly help the world become a much healthier and happier place."

—Senator John Vasconcellos, 13th District, California State Senate

"Finally, a 'cookbook' for parents and educators on how to raise successful kids. My seminar attendees have asked me for years, 'Wouldn't it be terrific if children could be exposed to these principles of self-esteem?' Michele, you've done it. The world needs your recipes for success—what a difference they'll make in our kids' futures!"

—Bob Moawad, chairman and CEO, Edge Learning Institute, and past president, National Association for Self-Esteem

"Michele Borba has done it again—she's written another must-have, must-read book! Parents of children will ask, 'Why didn't they have this when my kids were younger?' and then buy it for their grown kids so the grandkids will be raised sensibly. I highly recommend this book to anyone who cares about kids."

—Hanoch McCarty, coeditor,
A 4th Course of Chicken Soup for the Soul,
and coauthor, *Acts of Kindness*

"This book is loaded with practical, proven ideas for teachers and parents to use in their efforts to be the best influence they can be. Children of all ages will be helped to develop skills they need to be their personal best in the new millennium."

—Dorothy Rouse, board member and former teacher,
Los Gatos Union School District, Los Gatos, California

"By applying the strategies from *Parents Do Make a Difference* I experienced such stunning success with a severely disturbed foster child that it caused an astonished juvenile court judge to label her transformation 'miraculous.' He even led his courtroom to a round of applause for her success and credited her rehabilitation to Dr. Borba's techniques. One could only imagine how using these techniques could profoundly impact the lives of all children."

—Dawn Hamill, foster child advocate

"I strongly endorse Michele Borba's new book, *Parents Do Make a Difference.* Grounded in solid research, her message has the potential to truly help parents help their children be more successful in school and in life."

—Richard Herzberg, executive director,
Bureau of Education and Research

Nobody Likes Me, Everybody Hates Me

Nobody likes me
Everybody hates me
Guess I'll go eat worms
Long, thin, slimy ones
Short, fat, juicy ones
Itsy, bitsy, fuzzy,
wuzzy worms

Nobody Likes Me, Everybody Hates Me

The Top 25 *Friendship Problems* and How to Solve Them

Michele Borba, Ed.D.

JOSSEY-BASS
A Wiley Imprint
www.josseybass.com

Published by Jossey-Bass
A Wiley Imprint
989 Market Street, San Francisco, CA 94103-1741   www.josseybass.com

Jossey-Bass books and products are available through most bookstores. To contact Jossey-Bass
directly call our Customer Care Department within the U.S. at 800-956-7739, outside the U.S. at
317-572-3986, or fax 317-572-4002.

Jossey-Bass also publishes its books in a variety of electronic formats. Some content that appears in
print may not be available in electronic books.

Library of Congress Cataloging-in-Publication Data

Borba, Michele.
    Nobody likes me, everybody hates me : the top 25 friendship problems
and how to solve them / Michele Borba.
        p. cm.
    Includes bibliographical references.
    ISBN 0-7879-7662-8 (alk. paper)
    1. Friendship in children. 2. Child rearing. I. Title.
    BF723.F68B67 2005
    155.4'18—dc22   2004021982

Printed in the United States of America
FIRST EDITION
PB Printing   10 9 8 7 6 5 4 3 2

Contents

ACKNOWLEDGMENTS   XV

PART ONE
Why Do Friends Matter So Much to Your Kid?   1

Why Friendship Matters   5
15 Essential Skills That Friends Help Friends Acquire   6

Why Are Kids Having Friendship Problems Today?   7
Ten Reasons Why Our Kids Are Having
a Friendship Crisis   8

How Strong Are Your Child's Friendship Skills?   10
The Friendship-Building Skills Quiz   12

How to Use This Book to Teach Your Child
Friendship-Building Skills   15
Friendship Issues and Friendship-Building Skills   16
Six Steps to Teaching Your Child New
Friendship-Building Skills   17

25 Friendship Issues and Friendship Skill Builders   17
The Ten Worst Things Parents Can Do
for Their Children's Social Lives   23

PART TWO
Friendship Begins at Home   27

How to Organize a Playgroup   29
Basic Playgroup Dynamics   29
Getting Started   30

Arranging a Schedule   32

Resources   32

How to Arrange Play Dates   33

Solving the Most Common Play Date Problems   35

Friendship Activities for Older Kids   36

Kids with Similar Interests   37

Groups with Similar Interests   37

Potential Clubs and Group Activities   38

Classes   39

Travel Programs   39

Helping Your Child Be a Good Host   40

What *You* Should Do When Kids
Come to Your House   43

Be Sure to Have the Right Supplies   44

Set Clear House Rules   46

Address Discipline Problems Effectively   47

Friendship Skill Builder Books   48

PART THREE
The Top 25 Friendship Problems and How to Solve Them   51

1 Argues   53

2 Bad Friends   62

3 Bad Reputation   73

4 Bossy   82

5 Bullied and Harassed   90

6 Cliques   103

7 Clueless   113

8 Different   122

9 Doesn't Share   131

10 Fights   142

11 Gossips   151

12 Hot Tempered 160

13 Insensitive 171

14 Jealous and Resentful 183

15 Left Out 194

16 New Kid 203

17 Peer Pressure 212

18 Shy 221

19 Siblings 231

20 Sleepovers 242

21 Tattletale 250

22 Teased 258

23 Tiffs and Breakups 268

24 Too Competitive 279

25 Too Sensitive 289

FINAL WORDS
An Invitation to the Party 299

REFERENCES 303
ABOUT THE AUTHOR 319

To Annie Leedom,
who is the best definition of a friend.
Thank you!

Acknowledgments

There are so many "behind the scenes" folks to whom I am indebted for helping and supporting me with this book. In particular I would like to express my heartfelt gratitude to these wonderful people.

To the committed folks at Jossey-Bass and Wiley for their incredible support on all five of the books we've worked on together: Debra Hunter, Paul Foster, Jennifer Wenzel, Erik Thrasher, Lori Sayde-Mehrtens, Karen Warner, Michele Jones, Seth Schwartz, Carol Hartland, Sara Long, and Paula Goldstein. Thanks also to the Canadian Wiley group, especially Meghan Brousseau, P. J. Campbell, and Jennifer Smith, for always making those jaunts to Toronto so much fun. It's a privilege to work with such a professional publishing team.

To Alan Rinzler, my editor (who I swear is the best in the business), for once again helping me develop the idea and conceptualize an organization, and then supporting me each and every step along the way. It's an honor to work with him.

To Joelle DelBourgo, my agent, for her stellar competence and warm friendship, and for lending an ear at always just the right time. Believe me, every writer should have this woman in her corner.

To the staff of *Parents* magazine, especially senior editor Diane Debrovner, for the honor of serving on their advisory board and the opportunity of speaking with many of their writers about several of the friendship issues in this book.

To Andrea Bauman, deputy editor of *Redbook,* for her "stretching" assignments and fabulous editorial advice that have helped me with my craft in more ways than she'll ever know.

To the hundreds of teachers and parents throughout the world who have so openly shared their concerns about the upsurge in peer cruelty and the pain of rejection and social incompetence. Thank you.

To the numerous people whose work has contributed enormously to my thinking about the development of children's friendship and social skills, including Robert Selman, Kenneth Rubin, Nancy Eisenberg, Arnold Goldstein, Fred Frankel, William Damon, Michael Thompson, Zick Rubin, Maurice Elias, and Steven Tobias. I only hope I have interpreted their work accurately and given it the credit it deserves.

To a few loyal souls who have always been there for me professionally and have become such valued friends: Annie Leedom, president of www.netconnectpublicity.com, for always offering much-appreciated encouragement and for designing the absolutely best Internet publicity campaigns; Steve Leedom, president of www.nowimagine.net, for creating and updating my websites, www.behaviormakeovers.com, www.moralintelligence.com, and www.micheleborba.com; Adrienne Biggs, of Biggs Publicity, for her support and creative publicity leads; Jamie Broadhurst, for continuing to offer such great advice and encouragement; and Dottie DeHart, of Rocks-DeHart Public Relations, for teaching me not only "Publicity 101" but also how to handle any (and I do mean *any*) interview confidently.

And finally to my own cheering section: Craig, my best friend, partner, and continual supporter; Dan and Treva Ungaro, parents extraordinaire; Lorayne Borba, my eternally optimistic mother-in-law; and my sons, Jason, Adam, and Zach. It's an honor being your mom and (now that you *finally* grew up) your friend.

PART 1

Why Do Friends Matter So Much to Your Kid?

The friends thou hast, and their adoption tried,
Grapple them to thy soul with hoops of steel.

—William Shakespeare; *Hamlet*

Dear Dr. Borba,

I'm concerned about my nine-year-old son lately: he just doesn't seem happy for some reason. He's a very smart, good-looking kid, and has just about everything money can buy. My wife and I want so much for him to be successful in life, so we've really put a strong emphasis on education and continually stressed the importance of his grades. We provide him with all kinds of tutors: tennis, a personal coach, and music—knowing how important it is to have a great résumé for college. But now I wonder if I've made a mistake. He has little time for friends, and when he is with a group of his peers he somehow doesn't seem to be at ease like the other kids. Am I wrong in putting all the emphasis on my son's grades? Just how important are friends?

—Jake B., a concerned dad from Seattle, Washington

I have the good fortune to work with parents and educators all over the world—conducting workshops, trainings, keynote addresses, facilitations, conferences, listening sessions. I have a very busy website where thousands of parents write me with their questions and concerns every day. I am also on the advisory board of *Parents* magazine, so editors and writers call me about the articles they're writing on topics of greatest concern to their readers.

The one thing I hear about every day from moms and dads, teachers and writers everywhere is kids' problems with friends. It seems like friendship and peer relationships are the single most crucial and widespread kid issue on everyone's mind today. I hear about bullying, aggression and violence, rejection, cliques, gossiping, unhealthy competition, backstabbing, ostracizing, one-upping. In the past these problems were more common among middle schoolers and teens, but now I'm seeing this with younger and younger kids.

Everyone needs friends—but especially kids. How many friends our kids have isn't the issue. What's important is making sure they have at least one or two good, "true blue" buddies.

FRIENDSHIP CRISIS NEWS ALERT

What's going on here? Just how bad is it? How are kids really getting along? Well, consider this:

- A nationwide survey found that 43 percent of students said they were afraid to go to the school bathroom for fear of being harassed by a classmate.
- By some estimates, one in seven American schoolchildren is either a bully or victim. In some cases, the same child is a bully one day and a victim the next.
- The National Education Association reports that every day, 160,000 children skip school because they fear being attacked or intimidated by other students.
- A national survey reveals that more than two-thirds of school police officers say younger children are acting more aggressively.
- A 1998 national survey conducted by the Josephson Institute of Ethics found that almost one in every four middle school and high school males said he had hit a peer in the past twelve months "because he was angry."
- According to the Education Foundation of the American Association of University Women, four out of five adolescents in sixteen hundred public schools across the country said sexual harassment (bullying with sexual overtones) is widespread.
- Researchers from Northeastern University surveyed thirty Massachusetts high schools and found that one-third of students reported that they had been victims of one or more hate-based crimes.
- A survey of 991 kids ages nine to fourteen revealed troubling facts about peer pressure: 36 percent of the

middle schoolers surveyed feel pressure from peers to smoke marijuana, 40 percent feel pressure to have sex, 36 percent feel pressure to shoplift, and four out of ten sixth graders feel pressure to drink.

- A recent *New York Times* article cited the new kid trend of "cyberspace bullying" as spiraling an "unprecedented degree of brutality" in spreading vicious gossip and insults about peers.

And it isn't getting any better.

Of course the prime reason a kid says friends are important is for fun and companionship. But, in fact, there are a number of reasons why friendship matters. The latest research tells us that friendships are far more significant in our kids' lives than we ever thought before. Friends not only influence our children in the here and now but also lay the groundwork for adult relationships, health and well-being, the careers they choose, their self-esteem, whom they choose as their life partner, and how they parent their own kids.

I'm not forgetting that of course your child is unlike any other. Your child *is* special, with her own unique and lovable temperament and personality. And the last thing we want to presume is that there's any possibility or even value in trying to change who our kids are way deep down. Can you imagine an Archbishop Desmond Tutu morphing into a Donald Trump? Or a Laura Bush–type morphing into a Madonna? Kids are all different, and God bless them.

Nevertheless, no matter how different his or her personality and temperament may be, each and every one of our kids really needs friends: shy friends, assertive friends, sensitive friends, friends who are leaders or followers, those who are kindhearted and lovable, those who are funny or daring. Different strokes for different folks. *Everyone* wants, needs, and must have friends. And although we never want to even try changing our children's basic identity, we can definitely help them learn what they must to do so that they'll always have those precious friends they need so much.

Let's face it: friends have a great deal to do with our kids' happiness and well-being. It's through friendships that our kids will learn how to navigate the rough waters of their social development. So let's take a closer look at the true value of friends and friendships in our kids' lives.

WHY FRIENDSHIP MATTERS

Why does my daughter need so many friends? I'm her best friend. There's no one who can love her as much as I do and be a more positive influence.

—Erin W., a mom from Topeka, Kansas

My son has no time for friends. With all the competition to get into the top schools these days, he needs to focus on grades and getting all the extra tutoring he needs to stay ahead of the pack. He can have time for friends when he gets out of school.

—Rob L., a dad from Newport Beach, California

I don't want my kids to have friends. Kids today have no values. All they care about is bad music, cheap-looking clothes, and trying to be cool. I don't want that kind of influence on my child.

—Susan P., a mom from New York City

I'm not allowing my daughter to stay overnight at some stranger's house. And I can't believe any other parent with half a brain would either. How do we know what's going on over there?

—Seth B., a dad from Chattanooga, Tennessee

Sound familiar? Can you really blame parents for feeling this way? Have you ever felt that way yourself? This is definitely a tough time to be raising kids.

The fact is, though, that kids must have friends around their own age. Parents are parents and friends are friends. Parents can never provide the kind of social, moral, emotional, and cognitive experiences that friends can. Only friends can lead the way to selflessness, trust, loyalty, intimacy, and love. Only friends can help kids survive and prosper in the world, both personally and professionally. As a moral, ethical, and spiritual force in our lives, friendship is the key. And without friendships our kids are at higher risk for mental health problems, juvenile delinquency, depression, anxiety, failed marriages, and poor job performance.

Just so we get this straight, let's consider what our kids get out of friendships.

15 Essential Skills That Friends Help Friends Acquire

Call them life skills or good old "people skills"—there's no doubt that some of the most important lessons our kids will learn don't happen in a classroom but with a kid or two in the sandbox, carpool, jungle gym, summer camp, or soccer field, or just sitting together on the bedroom floor. These lessons don't need workbooks, a new laptop, or a personal coach, and success in achieving them is not indicated on test scores. Here are just a few of the critical skills that kids learn from their friends:

1. Solving problems and resolving conflicts
2. Making decisions and distinguishing between right and wrong
3. Handling teasing and verbal barbs, developing comebacks
4. Learning to assert themselves and stand up for what they believe

5. Understanding different points of view and nurturing empathy
6. Developing identity by seeing themselves in relation to others
7. Learning to cooperate, take turns, get along in a group, and share
8. Regulating emotions and developing self-control
9. Learning humility, being modest, and recognizing their shortcomings
10. Developing trust and loyalty
11. Acquiring confidence and courage in stressful groups and situations
12. Communicating feelings, opinions, and needs
13. Taking responsibility, owning up to mistakes, and making apologies
14. Bouncing back and acquiring resilience
15. Having fun, laughing, and keeping things in perspective

WHY ARE KIDS HAVING FRIENDSHIP PROBLEMS TODAY?

Okay, so we agree that friends and friendships are important— even crucial to our kids' happiness and development. So what? My mom and dad didn't worry so much about this. What's the big fuss? Why can't kids just work things out for themselves? Why is there a big story on the friendship crisis every time we pick up a magazine or newspaper? Why are all the teachers and counselors so worried and even attending new seminars on bullyproofing and social skill development?

Here's why: things aren't what they used to be. Times have changed. The world our kids live in is radically different from the one we knew when we were growing up. We're living in the age of Columbine and 9/11. As parents today we are facing an atmosphere of fear and anxiety about our children's safety. Every day we're barraged by reports of violence, abduction, abuse—it's terrifying. Not only that, it seems like there's less and less money and fewer resources available to meet our kids' social needs.

As a result, kids today are overcontrolled and over-scheduled. Even sandbox and recess may be eliminated for budgetary and disciplinary reasons. There's "no time for play." Doors are locked. The neighborhood is gone. So are the parks. Families are more mobile. Society has become lonelier, and face-to-face interactions are replaced by text, e-mail, and fax.

At the same time, because of the demographic explosion of baby boomer children, there are more kids competing for fewer spots in the "best" schools and eventually the job market. So ambitious parents are scared that their kids won't be properly educated and that friendship problems or having the "wrong friends" will ruin their kids' chances of success.

But let's take a closer look at how things have changed since we were growing up and why kids today are having such a problem with this crucial aspect of their lives.

Ten Reasons Why Our Kids Are Having a Friendship Crisis

There's not just one new development that has changed things overnight, but instead a gradual erosion of friendship-building conditions and skills. Here are just a few signs of this decline:

- *"Who's got time?"* Our kids are hurried and harried, and so are we. Every minute of our day seems to be jammed up, tightly crammed, and overscheduled. Who's got even a minute for friends?
- *"It's everyone for himself."* It's all about win-win-win at any cost. Cooperating and looking out for the underdog is out. Our kids today are putting too much value on being selfish, unscrupulous, and greedy. There's no room for caring about the other guy.
- *"Recess will be cancelled today."* There's so much anxiety

about academic achievement and improving schools' ranking to qualify for state and federal funding that anything so frivolous as recess, sandbox, or other unstructured times when our kids could learn valuable friendship skills is out the window.

- *"All I need is batteries."* Kids today are more isolated, spending hours alone with their video games, DVD players, computers, and TV. Who needs anyone else in their lives? Why make the effort and have potential problems with friends when you have your own remote control?

- *"Double-bolt that door."* Parents must be prudent and cautious about where their children go and whom they go with. But we shouldn't teach our kids to fear people automatically and to always be so leery of strangers. Keep in mind that the media tend to focus on sensational stories that give us a false impression that the number of crimes by strangers against children has risen dramatically, when in fact it hasn't. 🛑 **The FBI says that the number of serious child kidnappings actually has not risen—it's just that we're more aware of them because of media coverage. The number one perpetrators of kid abduction aren't strangers but family members. So don't get swept away by the culture of fear.** 🛑

- *"How long is your buddy list?"* Communicating via text mail or e-mail may be fine and dandy, but there's no substitute for the value of face-to-face interaction. Many kids today lead such micromanaged, overscheduled lives that those cherished times for real human interaction are few and far between.

- *"Didn't you hear that whistle?"* Play today is superorganized, adult led, and hypercompetitive. Kids' football, soccer, ice hockey, baseball, and basketball are all modeled after professional adult sports. With so much adult supervision, there's no opportunity for kids to form their own teams, make their own rules, learn to settle conflicts and disputes, and just play for fun without worrying about pleasing their parents, winning that trophy, or getting that scholarship.

- *"Pack your bags."* Did you know that the U.S. population is one of the most geographically mobile in the world? Over a five-year period, 46 percent of Americans move at least once. This makes it really tough for kids suddenly thrust into a unfamiliar neighborhood with new schools, new kids, new cultural norms. After moving a few times, your child may stop trying to make new friends because she knows it can't last.

- *"People suck."* Sitcoms celebrate the nasty put-down. Reality TV pushes humiliation. Role models inspire us to be mean and selfish. The cold, cruel world we so often see in the media desensitizes our kids, destroys their faith in the value of friendship, and discourages them from pursuing the warmth of companionship and selfless devotion.

- *"Who needs manners?"* Without the opportunities and conditions for friendship, our kids are simply not learning the essential social skills we all grew up with. Like "please," "thank you," "excuse me." Like "What do you think?" "Now it's your turn," and "I love your new haircut." We're living in an age of incivility, and this breakdown of courtesy, respect, and good manners is leaving our kids poorly prepared to develop the intimate and empathic relationships that are so crucial for their happiness and fulfillment. In fact, nine out of ten Americans feel that the breakdown of common courtesy and civility has become a serious problem in this country.

HOW STRONG ARE YOUR CHILD'S FRIENDSHIP SKILLS?

The first step to increasing your child's friendship quotient is to assess what his interpersonal strengths and weaknesses are right now. The better you understand how your child gets along

FRIENDSHIP TIP

What Makes a Good Friend?
Here is a brief "quiz" to help your child assess his current relationships. Although no friendship is perfect, if your child can't say yes to most of these comments, it may be time to "move on."

- ☐ My friend sticks up for me if other kids talk about me.
- ☐ My friend and I have fun being together.
- ☐ When something good (or bad) happens, I want to share it with my friend.
- ☐ My friend and I may disagree, but we talk things through.
- ☐ My friend and I look out for one another.
- ☐ My friend and I can share secrets with one another.
- ☐ My friend and I know all about one other and like each other just the same.
- ☐ My friend makes me feel better if I'm sad.
- ☐ We both want to be with each other.
- ☐ My friend and I can trust one another.
- ☐ My friend encourages me to do what's right.
- ☐ My friend makes me feel good about myself.

with others and can identify the social skills he lacks, the better you'll be to help him become socially competent. So the next time your child is around other kids, watch a little closer. Here are a few hints:

- Be honest. Take a good look at your kid's friendship-making skills and how he relates to others.

- Observe your kid interacting with his peers without his being aware that you're watching. Bring a newspaper or book to pretend to read while you really watch to see how your child interacts.
- Watch him also in different social settings—for instance, on the playground, in a backyard, at an athletic event, in school, with one child and with a group of kids, with younger kids and with older kids.
- Also watch kids who your child would say are well liked. Tune in to their friendship-making skills. What do they do that helps them be popular? And what are they doing that your child is *not* doing?
- Talk to other parents about what skills they think are important in helping kids make and keep friends. Also talk to others who know and care about your child. What is their take on the situation?
- Take notes and write down your findings.

The Friendship-Building Skills Quiz

Here's a list of behaviors often displayed by children needing a boost in friendship-building skills. Check off the one box for each friendship issue that best describes your child's behavior. You might compare your notes with others who know your child well. To score the quiz, give 2 points for Regularly, 1 point for Sometimes, and 0 for Rarely. If your child scores 75 to 100, she may have serious friendship-building issues, and need immediate intervention. A score of 55 to 75 shows problems to work on. A score of under 55 is still cause for concern, but don't call the fire department yet. Remember that if you checked Regularly for some of the more serious and dangerous issues (such as "acts like a bully," "acts dangerously," "too aggressive," or "mean and cruel"), you need to take immediate steps. Whatever your child's score, taking this quiz will help you understand the strengths and weaknesses of her friendship-building skills. And there's always room for improvement.

Regularly	Sometimes	Rarely	
☐	☐	☐	Doesn't share or take turns
☐	☐	☐	Acts like a poor loser
☐	☐	☐	Doesn't cooperate; works alone
☐	☐	☐	Shows little empathy for others' feelings
☐	☐	☐	Lacks the skills to play games
☐	☐	☐	Is too competitive
☐	☐	☐	Can't read social cues
☐	☐	☐	Acts like a "know-it-all"
☐	☐	☐	Acts too maturely for the group
☐	☐	☐	Hoards toys and doesn't share
☐	☐	☐	Has poor manners
☐	☐	☐	Is reckless; acts dangerously; takes unhealthy risks
☐	☐	☐	Is impulsive; charges ahead without thinking
☐	☐	☐	Constantly compares self to friends—"She has more"
☐	☐	☐	Is mean and cruel
☐	☐	☐	Stands too close or too far from kids
☐	☐	☐	Acts bossy: always wants her own way
☐	☐	☐	Uses a sulky, unhappy expression
☐	☐	☐	Is too critical or judgmental
☐	☐	☐	Interrupts; doesn't listen to others

☐	☐	☐	Doesn't know how to initiate, maintain, or end a conversation
☐	☐	☐	Doesn't know how to join a group; hangs back
☐	☐	☐	Doesn't use eye contact
☐	☐	☐	Quits before the game is over
☐	☐	☐	Gets upset and angry easily
☐	☐	☐	Uses a whiny, unfriendly, or loud voice
☐	☐	☐	Switches rules midstream
☐	☐	☐	Lacks genuine interest in others
☐	☐	☐	Sees things only from her view
☐	☐	☐	Doesn't enjoy socializing with other kids
☐	☐	☐	Manages conflicts inappropriately
☐	☐	☐	Is too aggressive or acts like a bully
☐	☐	☐	Doesn't compromise or negotiate
☐	☐	☐	Is too argumentative
☐	☐	☐	Doesn't apologize or make amends
☐	☐	☐	Doesn't know how to solve problems or conflicts
☐	☐	☐	Doesn't encourage or support others
☐	☐	☐	Has a negative outlook on the world in general
☐	☐	☐	Lacks a sense of humor
☐	☐	☐	Can't tolerate frustrations

☐	☐	☐	Is impatient; wants instant gratification
☐	☐	☐	Can't regulate strong emotions or aggressive urges
☐	☐	☐	Feels sorry for herself
☐	☐	☐	Teases or puts down others
☐	☐	☐	Gossips maliciously
☐	☐	☐	Is insensitive and tactless; doesn't consider others' feelings
☐	☐	☐	Is too sensitive; cries easily
☐	☐	☐	Can't take criticism
☐	☐	☐	Uses other kids' stuff without asking
☐	☐	☐	Boasts and brags
☐	☐	☐	Uses annoying and attention-getting behaviors

Total Score _____

HOW TO USE THIS BOOK TO TEACH YOUR CHILD FRIENDSHIP-BUILDING SKILLS

Have you ever stopped to watch well-liked kids interact with their peers? Some kids just seem to make friends easily. They're invited to all the birthday parties, attend the sleepovers, are chosen first for teams, and are sought after as everyone's friend. If we could peek into their future, we'd see them continuing to succeed socially throughout their school years, as well as for the rest of their lives. It quickly becomes apparent that they know exactly what to say and do to gain acceptance from others. We also know that the ability to make friends is not inherited, but involves a number of skills that can all be learned.

Friends obviously play an enormous role in our kids' lives. Our real parenting goal should not be to try to produce popular kids but to help them gain the confidence they'll need to deal successfully with any social situation. After all, that's a major part of what life is all about. The good news is that friendship-making skills can be taught. By using this book to teach your kid one new friendship-building skill at a time, you can help him make and keep friends.

Friendship Issues and Friendship-Building Skills

Throughout this book you'll read the terms *friendship issues* and *friendship-building skills* again and again. So what are friendship issues, and what are friendship-building skills?

Friendship issues are the common problems that kids face in peer relationships, such as cliques, gossiping, being left out, and being bullied and harassed. This book addresses the top twenty-five friendship problems that children face. Each time I conducted a training or workshop, I asked the participants to write down what they considered to be the biggest hot-button friendship problems they saw in action every day (such as cliques, gossiping, being left out, and being bullied). A list of the top 25 Friendship Issues and Friendship Skill Builders appears on the following page.

In Part Three of this book there is a chapter for each of the top twenty-five issues with specific ideas, strategies, and steps to take in solving your child's particular friendship issue. And within each chapter is the one essential Friendship Skill Builder that is indispensable for overcoming this particular problem. When you read the chapter, you can choose a variety of tips and strategies from all those presented, but the one thing I strongly recommend you focus on teaching your child is that one Friendship Skill Builder. Of course, new skills take time to learn, so the more you practice the skill with your child, the more likely he will be able to use it with his friends— and the more likely his particular friendship issue will improve.

Six Steps to Teaching Your Child New Friendship-Building Skills

Here are the six key steps to teaching your child new friendship-building skills to boost his social competence.

Step 1. Identify Your Child's Most Important Friendship Issues. Look at the Everyday Behaviors column in the chart below and see which best fit the problems your child is having. Note the recommended Friendship Skill Builder for each issue and then turn to the appropriate chapters that explain how to teach each of them to your child.

25 FRIENDSHIP ISSUES AND FRIENDSHIP SKILL BUILDERS

Everyday Behaviors	Friendship Skill Builder	Page Number
☐ *Argues:* constantly bickering; disagreeable attitude; alienates friends	Resolving Conflicts So Everyone Is Satisfied	55
☐ *Bad friends:* chooses kids with risky behaviors and different values	Staying out of Trouble	65
☐ *Bad reputation:* ostracized; subject of rumors and gossip; rejected from social groups and gatherings	Using Good Manners and Courtesy	76
☐ *Bossy:* "Little Dictator"; "her way or the highway"; doesn't listen to or consider friend's needs or desires	Respecting a Friend's Point of View	85
☐ *Bullied and harassed:* verbally or physically abused or	Using Assertive Body Language	93

repeatedly harassed in a
mean-spirited manner;
unable to defend or stick
up for himself

☐ *Cliques:* always the outsider;   Learning How   105
never included in the group;   and Where to
on the fringe   Fit In

☐ *Clueless:* can't tell how friends   Recognizing   115
are feeling; turns friends off   How Your Friends
without knowing it   Are Feeling

☐ *Different:* excluded or   Improving Your   125
ostracized because of major   Likability
characteristics, often visible,
that are unlike those of the
other kids

☐ *Doesn't share:* doesn't take   Choosing Fairly   134
turns; hoards toys; won't share;
overly possessive of his things

☐ *Fights:* physically aggressive;   Expressing Your   145
pushes, pokes, bites, hits, and   Feelings and
hurts others   Needs Without
Violence

☐ *Gossips:* spreads rumors;   Taking   153
talks about other kids behind   Responsibility
their backs; loses friends   and Making
through backstabbing   Amends

☐ *Hot tempered:* loses control;   Tuning in to   163
shouts and screams at friends;   Body Temper
gets ticked off by the littlest   Alarms
things; his angry outbursts
cause kids to be annoyed,
resentful, or even fearful

☐ *Insensitive:* doesn't consider a friend's feelings; doesn't listen; doesn't see things from the friend's point of view; lacks empathy; is sometimes mean or cruel — Showing You Care by Listening — 174

☐ *Jealous and resentful:* never satisfied with who she is or what she has; always feels that she can't keep up with the other kids; judges her worth based only on her friends — Appreciating Your Personal Best — 186

☐ *Left out:* put down, ostracized, not chosen, excluded — Bouncing Back Gracefully — 197

☐ *New kid:* doesn't know anyone in the class, on the team, or in the neighborhood; has difficulty breaking into a new social scene — Making New Friends — 205

☐ *Peer pressure:* submissive; follows the crowd; doesn't stand up to peers; loses confidence and status as equal — Standing Up for Yourself — 215

☐ *Shy:* avoids other kids; clingy and dependent; uncomfortable or nervous and anxious away from home — Making Eye Contact — 223

☐ *Siblings:* friction, arguments, tears, and hurt feelings; feeling of resentment or favoritism — Solving the Problem Between You Without an Adult — 234

☐ *Sleepovers:* afraid to leave; wants to come home — Being Away from Home with Confidence — 245

☐ *Tattletale:* tells bad stuff about friends that gets them in trouble — Knowing What and When to Tell — 253

☐ *Teased:* can't handle it when friends poke fun; feels picked on; overreacts to playful banter — Delivering Comebacks — 261

☐ *Tiffs and breakups:* always arguing; overly possessive with a close friend; and can't "let go"; has lost a close pal — Apologizing and Making Amends — 270

☐ *Too competitive:* winning is everything; constantly compares performance, achievement, appearance, abilities to other kids; overly frustrated when losing to others; judging herself not as good as others — Respecting What's Great About Your Friends — 281

☐ *Too sensitive:* cries easily; takes friendly teasing hard; has lots of highs and lows; extremely aware of everything going on around her; too worried about what friends think of her — Accepting Criticism — 293

Step 2. Put the Book to Work. Read the applicable chapter carefully. Study the first four sections: What's Wrong? Why Is This Happening? What Can I Say? and What Can I Do? Also note the Friendship Alerts (set off with stop sign icons) and the Friendship Tip (set off with a traffic light icon) that apply to this friendship issue. I strongly recommend that you use a highlighter pen to mark the ideas and strategies you want to try with your child. Check out the Friendship Skill Builder Books to see if there are any other resources that sound helpful for your situation.

Step 3. Coach Your Child in the New Friendship Skill Builder. Each chapter has a special boxed Friendship Skill Builder designed to help your child improve this particular friendship problem. Go over it a few times by yourself first, then find a private moment to teach the new skill to your child. Talk with her about why the friendship skill is important, then be sure she can show you how to use the skill correctly. In some cases it may be helpful to go with her to a public place such as a playground or schoolyard so that she can observe other kids actually using the skill. Seeing the friendship skill in action helps your child copy it, so she can try it on her own.

Step 4. Find Opportunities to Practice the Skill. Just telling your child about the Friendship Skill Builder is not enough. Your child needs to try out the skill with other children. The best kids for your child to practice with are kids she doesn't already know and who are younger or less skilled. Stanford University's Dr. Philip Zimbardo, the world's expert on shyness, discovered that pairing an older, "shy" child with a younger or less skilled child is an excellent technique for helping reticent kids practice learning new social skills. Your child will feel much more confident practicing any new skill with someone less skilled than himself. A younger sibling, cousin, neighbor, or even one of your friend's younger children is always a safer partner than a more self-assured, skilled, older child. A father from Albany, New York, shared a unique way he used Zimbardo's advice to help his shy twelve-year-old daughter. He found her an after-school baby-sitting job with the next door neighbor's six-year-old. Not only did she earn money, but every day she practiced with the child the friendship skills—starting a conversation, using eye contact, and so on—that she was shy about trying with kids her own age.

Step 5. Review the Practice and Offer Feedback. A critical part of teaching any new Friendship Skill Builder is evaluating the child's performance with her. As soon as you can, discuss how the practice session went, asking such questions as, How did it go? What did you say? How do you think you did? and What would you do differently next time? Don't criticize what your child didn't do; instead praise what your child did right. If your child wasn't successful, talk through what didn't go well, so she can try it differently the next time. As soon as your child feels comfortable with the skill, you're ready to teach another one. Gradually, your child's social competence will grow.

Step 6. Get to the "Go It Alone" Stage. Notice the 21-Day Friendship Follow-Up section at the end of every chapter. Be sure to fill it in conscientiously. Here are some other ways to help you reach the point where your child can use the Friendship Skill Builder without your guidance.

- *Keep a journal*—if that's your style. Some parents prefer to use a chart on the wall or an audiotape, or to track their practice sessions and their child's friendship-making progress in their Palm Pilot.
- *Consult other parents.* Don't do this alone; there's no reason to feel isolated, seeing as how every family is having similar issues.
- *Talk to teachers and counselors.* People outside your family or neighborhood may have a different perspective on your child. Seek their knowledge and insights, and ask for suggestions.
- *Start a book club.* Read this book with at least one other parent, family member, or friend. Compare notes on what works best.
- *Pass it on.* The more your child practices the Friendship Skill Builder, the quicker she'll use it without you. So let people who really care about your kid in on this so that they reinforce your efforts.

Ultimately, your goal is for your child to become confident and comfortable enough to use the Friendship Skill Builder on her own *without your guidance.*

THE TEN WORST THINGS PARENTS CAN DO FOR THEIR CHILDREN'S SOCIAL LIVES

You are influential. You *do* have a tremendous impact on your child's ability to make friends and form meaningful relationships. You can also do harm and hinder her chances. Sometimes with the best intentions and sometimes with a wrong-headed bullishness, parents can really rain on their kids' social parade. So be honest and see if anything in the list that follows just might be a little bit true for you. Come on—all of us are guilty of some of these deadly parenting sins some of the time.

1. *Set a terrible example.* Got any friends? Or are you one of those people who goes it alone? To heck with the other guy, who needs them? Do you exploit friends only for personal gain or social status, and just call them when you need a shoulder to cry on or to borrow money? Do you tell your kids to have good manners but then verbally abuse your waiter or hairdresser? Do you tell your kids not to talk about people behind their backs and then pick up the phone to gossip? Do you tell your kids they need to apologize to their friends when they're wrong and then won't say you're sorry to your kids when you've been thoughtless or rude to them? *Don't expect your kids to be a good friend unless you are.*

2. *Be a pushy stage mom (or dad).* Are you the parent who dresses your daughter in the latest runway fashions and insists she try out for cheerleading squad in hopes that she'll become "Little Miss Popular"? Do you insist that your shy and retiring son have a huge and extravagant birthday

party at the local sports coliseum and invite all the "top" people, even though he'd rather invite his one close friend to spend the night? Have you tried to make play dates for your kid from a list of names on the social page? *Don't think you can muscle your kid into friendships that only you care about.*

3. *Act like a micromanaging drill sergeant.* Do you orchestrate or supervise every minute of your child's time with his friends? Are you the kind of parent who doesn't trust your child to share, solve his own problems, use good manners, or get along when he's out of your sight? Do you hover on the sidelines at every play date or social event, worrying or constantly darting back and forth with some suggestion or concern? *Don't hyper-parent or prevent your child from gaining his own friendship experiences and skills.*

4. *Make your home as sterile as an operating room.* Do your child's friends feel like they ought to wear white gloves when they come in the house? Do you insist they take off their shoes, never touch anything, and stay out of the kitchen? Do you follow them around with a bottle of disinfectant? No kidding, some parents are kid-phobic and make it impossible for friends to get together in a comfortable and relaxed environment. *Don't be so uptight about being clean and orderly that your kid and her friends can't feel relaxed around your house.*

5. *Act like a brontosaurus.* Are you a dinosaur when it comes to keeping up with the twenty-first century? Do you embarrass your kids in front of their friends by not understanding their language or their references to the media and culture? Do you insist that your kid dress like he's in the fifties or starring in the original production of *Grease?* Do you keep track of how the other kids are cutting their hair so that your kid can fit in, or do you insist she have the kind of cut you had way back when? *Don't refuse to change with the times when it comes to critical customs and attitudes that are really important to your kids and their friends.*

6. **Put on the robe and pick up the gavel.** Are you constantly criticizing the way your child tries to make friends? Do you deliver solemn judgments on manners or courtesy, the way she apologizes, or how she tries to be a host? Do you eavesdrop on his conversations with friends and tell him what he should have said? Do you render "right or wrong" verdicts when she has a tiff or breakup with a friend? *Don't be so critical that you discourage your child from taking each small step toward learning new friendship skills.*

7. **Stick that nose in the air.** Are your kids' friends never quite good enough for your standards? Are you always worried they're going to damage your child in some way or get him in trouble? Do you disrespect, ignore, or yell at your kid's friends, never taking the time to sit down and find out who they really are? *Don't dismiss your child's friends without appreciating what it is about them that your child values.*

8. **Be your kid's "bestest" buddy.** Are you more concerned about having your kid like you than you are about setting appropriate boundaries and limits? Do you worry so much about making your kid popular that you lower your standards to make your home the most permissive spot in the neighborhood? Do you dress down, try to talk "cool," or stay up on all the latest stuff so your kid's friends think you're really great? *Don't forget that you're the parent and need to keep up the standards and structures within which your child can make good friends.*

9. **Chuck in that towel.** Are you thinking, What's the big deal? No one had to help you with finding and keeping friends, so why should you bother? Let the kid find her own ways with others. Never mind trying to teach good manners, assertiveness, kindness, compromise, or conflict resolution. Let the school do it. *Don't assume that there's anyone better or more responsible than you for supporting your kid's efforts to learn friendship skills—or that she can do it without you.*

10. *Live in a little house of horrors.* Do you believe that friendship begins at home? Do you treat everyone in your family with love and respect? Do your children want to bring friends home? Are they proud of you, and do they look up to you as their role model? How do you resolve conflicts with your spouse? Do you listen and have empathy for each other? Do you put your family above everything and really enjoy being with one another? *Don't expect your children to make friends and bring them home if your house is an unhappy place.*

Now that we've seen why friendship matters, why kids are having problems building friendships today, and what the specific friendship-building skills are that you can help your child learn, let's take a closer look at how to make your home "friendship friendly."

PART 2

Friendship Begins at Home

A friend is a person with whom I may be sincere. Before him I may think aloud.
—Ralph Waldo Emerson

One of the best ways to help your kid make and keep friends is to encourage regular activities and events in your home. After all, friendship does begin at home. Play dates in your home are also great opportunities to get to know your kid's friends and their parents and to monitor your child's behavior with other kids, so you'll have a better handle on how to boost her social competence. They're also a great way for your child to learn friendship-making skills. Not only that, but there's nothing better than hearing the sound of giggles, secret whispers, and encouraging cheers around the house. It's a wonderful thing to fill your home with joy and love. In fact, it almost makes up for all those five-day-old half-eaten pizzas, broken windows, scratched DVDs, and stains on your new couch.

Whether your child is a toddler, preschooler, or preteen, there are specific things you can do to make your home a place where kids want to come and where your child has every chance to form important and long-standing friendships. This part of *Nobody Likes Me* will help you make your home "kid friendly," a place for fun and for fond memories, a safe haven, a place where conflicts are reduced and where play dates, play-groups, sleepovers, and parties run smoothly. Best yet, your home will be the special spot to which your kid's friends not only want to be invited but also love coming back.

Zick Rubin, author of *Children's Friendships,* tells us three critical reasons why it's essential that parents *do* find time for kids to play with friends. Only friends can fulfill these needs that are so essential in helping our children acquire social competence.

1. Friends provide opportunities for learning critical friendship-making skills.
2. Friends help our children develop a strong sense of who they are.
3. Friends enhance a sense of group belonging.

In fact, although kids can learn many critical skills from their parents, it is only through interacting with their peers that they learn how to survive among equals in the real world. The sooner you start giving your children time to be with friends the better, so let's begin with the youngest kids and see how we as parents can help them make and keep friends.

HOW TO ORGANIZE A PLAYGROUP

A playgroup is a small group of preschool-age children who get together once or twice a week to play and do activities together. The members generally alternate hosting the playgroup in their home, with the hosting parent planning activities and supervising the children. The goal here is *not* to provide child care but instead to meet children's social needs. If planned well, these get-togethers can offer a number of friendship-building benefits. This is a chance for kids to be with other children in a group setting and learn to get along, participate in new activities, and develop social skills, such as taking turns, sharing, cooperating, solving conflicts, and considering the needs of others. There's another great plus: playgroups are also a chance for kids' parents to enjoy each other's company.

Although playgroups require a bit of organization and parental planning, there are so many rich social benefits for youngsters that the number of playgroups is expanding from coast to coast. Here are a few of the most important pointers in starting up a playgroup for your child so that it is successful as well as fun.

Basic Playgroup Dynamics

Playgroup dynamics vary, but here are a few factors to consider to ensure that the group is more compatible, has more fun, and helps kids develop the friendship-making skills that should be your goal.

- *Who.* Even at three years of age, children tend to play with others of the same gender. So consider the proportions of male to female and be sensitive to the balance of the group. It's easier to plan activities if the children are similar in age, skill level, and interests. Kids generally begin participating in playgroups at around three years of age, when they are usually capable of staying a brief time away from their parents. A group with children younger than three is considered a "Mommy and me" group in which the parent stays the whole time with the toddler.

- *How long.* Playgroups usually last around two hours, though you can gauge the best length once you get to know the children's needs. *Hint:* It's always better to make the session shorter than longer. Also keep in mind kids' nap schedules, which can interfere with play time, so consider kids' biological clocks.

- *How often.* Playgroups usually meet regularly once or twice a week. The goal is for the children to get to know each other and feel comfortable.

- *How big.* The general advice on this one is to keep the group size small: the younger the age of the kids, the smaller the group. For preschool-age kids the *maximum* should be six kids per adult.

Getting Started

If you already have a group of kids in mind, just invite the parents over to talk it through. Or you could find one interested mom; she'll usually be able to suggest another interested parent to get your group started. Another option is to make a few flyers describing your mission. Be sure to include your name, phone number, e-mail address, and the age of your child. Safe places to post the flyer might include your church, community center, pediatrician's office, or preschool.

Once you have a group, simply invite the parents over for a get-acquainted session. Beyond exchanging names, phone numbers, e-mail addresses, and directions to your homes, it's also a time to arrange how you will rotate playgroup sessions and how frequently you want to meet, and to discuss the kinds of activities you'd like to set up for your children. For instance, many playgroups set up a policy that the hosting parent will plan a snack or craft activity. So talk a bit about what will be expected from the hostess; you might also consider splitting the obligations. (For each session, two parents share the duties: one arranges the snack, and the other plans the activity.) Keep in mind that playgroups don't have to be held in one another's homes: some playgroups meet in a community hall or church facility.

The get-acquainted session is also a time to discuss what you agree is best for your children, and that includes listening to one another's philosophy of discipline. What do you do if a child bites or hits? Do you approve of disciplining one another's kids? How will you make sure the group is playing nicely and including all the children? *Hint:* Don't feel you have to agree on discipline—you probably won't. Finally, why not talk about the kinds of friendship skills you can encourage in your children? You might even want to start a book club in which everyone reads *Nobody Likes Me, Everybody Hates Me* or another selection about the development of friendship in children. Finally, what about setting a policy that television or video viewing is not an option, nor are more aggressive toys, such as guns and swords? If the goal is to help the children develop cooperative friendship-making skills, then turn off the TV and put away the Ninja weapons for two hours!

Each parent in the playgroup should have a roster of the names, phone numbers, and addresses of the children. Additional contact and cell phone numbers should also be on the list. All of you should have a medical release form authorizing the playgroup parent to use in case of an emergency. Also determine if any of the children have any allergies or fears (for instance, bee stings, peanuts, milk, dogs, or loud noises). You will also want to set a "no sick child" attendance policy. Finally, do remind one another to "kidproof" your homes.

Arranging a Schedule

Most children are more secure knowing what to expect, so predictable routines during playgroups are important. Although the session doesn't have to be as tightly scheduled as a preschool, some semblance of the same general routine at each session is beneficial. It's also desirable to have a combination of both active and quiet times.

- *Circle time.* This is the time when the children and parents gather in a circle for special activities. It might be a time when you sing songs, learn fingerplays, read stories about friendships, do puppet shows, or just have great "talk times" together.
- *Friendship Skill Builder.* Emphasize a different Friendship Skill Builder from this book for every group session or choose one to reinforce each month.
- *Snack time.* Midway through your session, offer healthy snacks, such as oranges, carrot sticks, apple slices, graham crackers, cheese squares, and juice or milk.
- *Craft or activity time.* Consider a simple arts and crafts activity, such as finger painting with pudding, bubble blowing, easel painting, or a simple cut-and-paste paper project.
- *Play time.* Some possible activities include sandbox, tricycles, balls, dress-up, blocks, Lego, dolls, and action figures. Keep in mind that boys and girls choose different ways to play.
- *Special outing.* Some playgroups also take children on special outings together, such as to the zoo, fire department, police station, grocery store, library, or park.

Resources

- *The Playgroup Handbook,* by Laura P. Broad and Nancy T. Butterworth (New York: St. Martin's Press, 1991). This book is full of helpful hints and detailed suggestions on planning your child's activities, as you meet and work with other parents. It provides step-by-step instructions for over two hundred easy and imaginative activities, including arts and crafts, cooking, games, exercise, and storytelling.

- *A Stay-at-Home Mom's Complete Guide to Playgroups,* by Carren W. Joye (Writers Club Press, 2000). Packed with practical advice and step-by-step instructions, this covers everything a mom needs to know to start and maintain a successful playgroup for herself and her child!
- Another valuable resource is http:www.Online.Playgroup. com.

HOW TO ARRANGE PLAY DATES

When your child has learned a few friendship skills, gets a little older, and needs less supervision, then he may be ready for a play date.

A play date is a prearranged time when your child invites one guest over and plays with her in private. Such occasions create some of the best childhood memories. They are wonderful opportunities to help kids practice essential friendship-making skills as well as build close friendships. Here are strategies to help your child arrange successful play dates at your home. 🛑 **UCLA studies find that organizing one-on-one play dates is among the best ways to build close friendships. The experience also enhances children's self-esteem. Between 55 and 90 percent of parents arrange play dates for their kids.** 🛑

- *Oversee invitations of younger kids.* Unless your child's play chum is the kid next door, you should plan play dates with your child. To prevent any misunderstandings (and disappointments), your child should ask your permission before extending an invitation. For younger kids, you'll probably be doing the inviting. Zick Rubin, author of *Children's Friendships,* suggests that for kids under five, you should arrange the play dates; for kids five to seven years, you arrange the date after consulting your child; for those eight to ten years, the child makes plans with your help; for children ten to twelve years, the child plans activities, and you finalize the date and time.

- **Seek out guests with similar interests.** Common interests are the glue that keeps friends together. They are also what attract kids to seek out each other's company in the first place. So find kids who have similar interests for your child to invite. Here's a big hint: if your child discovers he has nothing in common with this guest, it's unlikely their friendship will last long.

- **Teach your child how to use the phone.** Practice phone etiquette so that she knows how to ask if the friend is available. Tell her to say her phone number slowly and to say "please" and "thank you." She should ask the child if she'd like to come over, provide a date and time, and then ask what kinds of things she likes to do. You should then ask to speak to a parent to confirm the invitation and provide specifics. Also teach your child how to leave a *polite* message on the answering machine: "Hi, this is Richard. Please ask Kevin to call me at 731-5428. Thank you." Keep a list of friends' phone numbers handy.

Tips for More Successful Play Dates

- **Create "activity" bins.** To minimize kid conflicts and "there's nothing to do" complaints, create "activity bins" (baskets, boxes, or plastic bins) stocked with a few toys and age-appropriate activities. Contents for younger kids might include Legos, Play-Doh or clay and cookie cutters, toy cars, or dolls. Older kids' bins can have art supplies and paper, a craft set, and comic books. Lap-size baskets or canvas bags filled with "quieter" activities (such as Etch-a-Sketches, portable CD players and CDs, and books) are great sanity-savers for carpools, field trips, or long drives with kids. *Hint:* For little tykes just learning to share, provide each with a personal bin and then periodically exchange them among the kiddies.

- *Keep the TV off.* Watching television with a guest will do nothing to improve your child's friendship-making skills, let alone help the kids learn about each other.
- *Keep siblings occupied elsewhere.* This is the time when your child needs to practice social skills and develop relationships separate from siblings. So when the guest arrives, find activities to occupy other siblings' time or farm them out to grandma or another friend.

SOLVING THE MOST COMMON PLAY DATE PROBLEMS

Put any two kids together for a period of time, and a problem will inevitably arise. So of course times with friends at your home won't always go smoothly. But *if you plan ahead,* there are a few things you can do to cut down on disasters and help things go more smoothly. Here are solutions for some common problems.

Problem	*Solution*
Kids get tired of one another.	Cut down the play time. Play dates for younger kids typically shouldn't run any longer than two hours. Even bigger kids get tired.
Three's a crowd.	You're better off keeping things in twos, fours, or sixes.
Too "wound up."	Prohibit "aggressive" toys and games (video, guns, swords). They will increase aggressive behaviors. Suggest "calmer" activities following lively ones (coloring books after dodge ball). Limit sugar content!

Guest arrives too early or too late.	Be sure to have those activity bins handy and stocked with a few quiet games such as an Etch-a-Sketch or crayons and a coloring book. And to be sure this doesn't happen again, talk to the guest's parent before the event; don't put this on your kid.
Annoying sibling.	Your child needs his own friends; occupy siblings elsewhere.
Tattling.	Refuse to listen unless it's "to help the friend."
Too many kids.	Some kids' parents can begin to take advantage of your hospitality. One mom actually put a traffic light in her window: if the red light was on, neighbor kids knew they had better not come over.
Parent doesn't pick up kid.	Now's the time to turn on the TV for two tired kids; you may have to take the child home.
Parent won't leave.	Whether it's at drop-off or pickup time, set clear boundaries and move on to another activity. "Well, it was great seeing you. I've got to get started on . . ."

FRIENDSHIP ACTIVITIES FOR OLDER KIDS

Now that we've seen how playgroups and play dates for younger children can work, let's take a look at how you can help your older child make and keep friends. Kids develop independence and social maturity at their own rate, so be careful not to micromanage a child who doesn't appreciate a pushy parent interfering with their friendship agenda. Nevertheless, there are things we can do to offer options, make subtle recommendations, and help our kids organize their social lives even when they approach those tumultuous teen years. Here are some of the things we can do:

Kids with Similar Interests

Experts say that those pairs of children who become friends and stay friends—for at least some period of time—are especially likely to share similar activities, abilities, styles, interests, values, and level of physical maturity. 🛑 **Research reveals that the "Principle of Similarity" is the single greatest predictor of kids' attraction to one another as friends.** 🛑 So provide opportunities for your child to find friends based on her interests and talents.

Tune in to what your kid spends most of his time doing. Is it practicing a sport? Making music? Drawing? Learning to write software? Skateboarding? Then look around your neighborhood or community and see which other kids share the same passions. Encourage them to connect.

Groups with Similar Interests

Some of your kid's activities and passions involve more than one friend. The trick is to match your child's strengths with the kind of group activities that nurture his interests. If your child's strength is singing, you might look for a choir for him to join. If soccer is her passion, find her a soccer team to join. Or if he's a chess whiz, search for groups of kids who love to play chess, so they can play together.

Once you find similar-minded kids who share your child's unique passion, encourage them to hook up together to form a group. Remember: all it takes is one other kid to form a "club" or "activity group." The kids then meet on a rotational basis (as often as convenient) to share their interest and expand their skills. The parents can also rotate the duty of finding ways to enrich the kids' interest further when it's their turn to house the group. If the group expands, meetings could be held at a school, church, community center, museum, or other appropriate location. You'll be enhancing not only your child's natural talents, personality, and interests but also her friendship-making skills.

🛑 Studies reveal that children who regularly experience peer rejection in school usually don't find success in such organized groups as the Boy Scouts, Brownies, Rainbow Girls, or 4-H and continue to have the same rejected status. They are more likely to achieve peer acceptance in groups whose membership focuses on similar skills, interests, or abilities. 🛑

Potential Clubs and Group Activities

Here are a few possibilities for groups that concentrate on children's special interests and abilities:

- *Hobby club.* Rock collecting, butterfly catching, star gazing, stamp collecting, photography, chess, computers
- *Cultural outings.* Museums, the zoo, art classes, and cultural events
- *Sports and athletics.* Skiing, snowboarding, soccer, gymnastics, ice skating, hockey, basketball, baseball, swimming, cycling
- *Drama.* Theatres, acting, putting on backyard plays, writing a screenplay
- *Religious youth groups, church groups.* Meetings, retreats, missions
- *Music ensemble.* Creating a band, attending concerts together, taking lessons on a favorite instrument
- *Dance groups.* Jazz, folk, ballet
- *Political activism.* Getting involved with her buddies in the party and issues of their choice
- *Service projects.* Volunteering at nursing homes, Kids Care clubs, tutoring younger kids, neighborhood cleanup brigades, joining Lions Clubs of America or Kiwanis Clubs
- *Exercise groups.* Go to the gym, do yoga, purchase a kid-appealing exercise video or DVD, and have a group of kids

work out at your home to stay fit. ⬡ **Since the early 1970s, the percentage of American children and adolescents defined as overweight has more than doubled, to about 15 percent. Three out of four overweight teens remain overweight as adults.** ⬡

- *Cooking club.* Hold progressive dinners or lunches, learn new recipes, provide each kid with a recipe file to start with his own personal cookbook.

Classes

Sometimes after-school or weekend classes for kids are remedial, helping them catch up on math or science. But kids can also take classes just for the fun of it or to pursue their special interests. Here are some examples:

- Painting and drawing
- Tennis, golf, surfing, and other skilled sports
- Cooking
- Fashion design
- Photography
- Public speaking
- Acting
- Dance
- Juggling
- Writing and poetry
- Film making

Travel Programs

Having an adventure with a group of peers, be it a visit to a city or nearby state, or traveling as far as Africa or Australia, can be a tremendous bonding experience and an opportunity to form lifelong friendships. Sometimes schools arrange for such programs, sometimes churches, sports clubs, service organizations, or special companies devoted entirely to such programs, and sometimes just a group of parents who get together and plan such an adventure for their kids.

Travel programs can be focused on

- Education and apprenticeships
- Learning a special skill
- Attending a sports or academic competition
- Providing a community service
- Living with a family in another country
- Testing your endurance and outdoor survival skills
- Church missions
- Internships for research and archaeological digs
- Cultural immersion
- Nautical expeditions

HELPING YOUR CHILD BE A GOOD HOST

Being a good host is important not only for helping your child make and keep friends but also for her future success. It's also a skill that must be learned. Here are a few points of good host etiquette to teach your child:

Before Your Guest Arrives

- **Invite your friend.** Be clear about the time she should arrive and leave. Provide your phone number so that she can call if she has any questions. Let your parent talk to your guest's mom or dad to give directions and to make sure everything is set.
- **Find out your friend's interests.** Ask your friend what kinds of things he likes to do. *Hint:* One of the most important factors that make or break a friendship is whether or not the kids have common interests.
- **Clean up the play area.** Put out a few things you think your guest would like to play with.
- **Store special things.** Anything you do *not* want to share, put away before the guest arrives.

GROUP DYNAMICS BY AGE

As children age, peer groups take on a growing importance in their lives. In fact, belonging to a group provides kids with new resources that individual friendships often can't, including a feeling of group membership, support, and identity. The following are typical group behaviors that you can expect for children's different stages and ages. (This list is based on the work of Zick Rubin.)

- *Ages 1 to 2.* Interacts usually with one other toddler (if at all), and almost never in groups of three or more.
- *Ages 3 to 4.* Begins to enjoy being with groups of kids of either gender. Still favors playing in pairs, though does like to play with one friend while still in the company of others. Begins to show concern about group belonging, and membership can become important: "I'm going to *my* preschool," "This is *my* group."
- *Ages 4 to 5.* Begins to display a clear preference for playing with groups of kids of the same gender.
- *Ages 6 to 7.* Starts to value group membership and may develop a feeling of loyalty to these groups: "*my* soccer team," "*my* church group," "*my* scout troop." Groups are usually still organized by adults; nevertheless, membership can enhance kids' sense of belonging and confidence.
- *Ages 7 to 8.* Starts to identify peer groups without adults as the principle organizers. "Secret" clubs are common, and club members can go to great lengths

deciding who can (and can't) belong, as well as creating club rules, duties, and regulations.

- **Ages 9 to 12.** Group belonging becomes of major importance, and peers take on a valuable supportive role; membership is almost exclusively of the same gender. Pressure to conform to the group is fierce, and gossip, rejection, and cliques are common.

When Your Guest Arrives

- **Be friendly and greet the guest.** Welcome your guest at the door and invite him inside. If his parent is with him, greet her also. Call your mom or dad to meet the guest (and his parent).
- **Store personal belongings.** Show your guest a safe place to set anything she may have brought with her, such as a backpack, sweater, or jacket.
- **Give a brief tour.** If it's the first time the guest has been in your home, show him around. Let him see where you'll be playing, as well as your bedroom, kitchen, and bathroom. If certain rooms are off-limits, tell him: "That's my brother's room. We can't go there."
- **Ask the guest what she'd like to do.** Give your guest a few choices of things you know she'd probably like to do. "Would you like to do this, or this?" Let your guest choose the first activity. Then you can take turns.
- **Give your friend your full attention.** Don't invite or call other kids unless you and your friend have agreed on this in advance.
- **Don't be critical.** Be supportive, fun, and friendly. No one likes to hear put-downs.
- **Offer a snack.** "Would you like something to eat or drink?" Tell what you have available.

- *Walk your friend to the door.* Help him gather anything he left. Thank him for coming and say good-bye.

WHAT *YOU* SHOULD DO WHEN KIDS COME TO YOUR HOUSE

Your child is not the only one with responsibility for being a good host. Hospitality starts at the top. So keep the following points in mind:

- *Get to know the parents.* Make a point of getting acquainted with the parents of your kid's friends. Phone them just to introduce yourself, or invite them over for coffee and to "stay awhile" until your child and theirs get to know each other. Keep in mind that some parents will not allow their kids to go to a home if they have not met the parents.
- *Greet each guest.* Always take a moment to personally meet each of your children's guests. **Author and child psychologist Michael Thompson makes it a practice to do three things when his kid's friends are in his house: personally say hello; tell each one that he enjoys having her in his house; compliment the child on her behavior in front of the parent who picks up the child.**
- *Supervise "indirectly."* Of course, when it comes to very young kids you need to be present at all times. But as kids get older, gradually wean yourself away from always hovering over their every move. **In fact, research tells us that when we supervise too closely or always structure and organize our kids' play time, we're actually hindering their friendship-making capabilities. Younger kids stick to activities for less time and play less cooperatively when left entirely without adult supervision.** But when a parent stays involved from a distance and gives indirect suggestions ("Wouldn't you two like to

play in the sandbox? There's more room" instead of "Go play in the sandbox"), kids not only play cooperatively for a longer time but also have more fun. So stick your head in only periodically and let the kids enjoy each other's company alone.

Be Sure to Have the Right Supplies

Here are some all-time favorites that are good to have around to keep kids at your home content and *you* sane. Your specific choices can vary depending on the ages, stages, and interests of your kids.

- *Snacks and refreshments.* Stock up the fridge with microwavable pizzas, Popsicles, bread, sandwich meats and cheeses, and sodas or juices; set up a snack shelf with such items as microwavable popcorn, cheese spreads, graham crackers, cookies, apples, plastic (or paper) cups, plates, and napkins. Limit sugar content to avoid a household of overstimulated "critters." Teach your child how to use the microwave and make simple snacks and sandwiches. *Safety alert:* Do find out if the guest has any food allergies. For younger kids, always ask the parent. Some foods, such as peanuts, can be life threatening.
- *Clean-up supplies.* Messes and spills are inevitable, so show your child where the sponge, paper towels, garbage can, and spray cleaner are so that he can help his friend clean up any "tragedies."
- *Medical supplies.* Set aside a designated shelf or basket for adhesive bandages of varying sizes, mosquito repellant, sunburn ointment, sunscreen, antiseptic, cotton balls, and an emergency first-aid booklet (for *you*).
- *Outdoor games and activities.* Thick chalk for drawing on sidewalks, basketball and hoop, rubber balls, a plastic bat and ball (unless you have a huge backyard), Frisbees, jacks, marbles, and bubbles and wands. For younger ones: a sandbox, measuring cups, small cars, and cans to fill with water and

big paint brushes to "paint" sidewalks and fences. Keep sports equipment in baskets or plastic bins so that kids can find it and put it away. *Hint:* Unless you want to supervise constantly and use up a huge supply of adhesive bandages, limit (or prohibit) aggressive video games, toy weapons, samurai swords, and guns. Your goal should be to help your kid learn how to get along with others, and aggressive toys generally tend to make kids more hyper and less cooperative.

- *Indoor games and activities.* Crayons, felt pens, paper, coloring books; cookie cutters and clay or Play-doh in plastic tubs or bags; a plastic tablecloth to put on a table; toy cars, trucks, trains; CDs or tapes, a player, and extra batteries; board games, such as Monopoly, checkers, chess, Clue, Candyland, Chutes and Ladders; a deck of cards. An old teacher tip is to always have available "calming" activities (such as books, arts and crafts activities, and a video). On certain days, you'll be glad you did.

- *Interactive toys.* Some toys lend themselves to interactive play and can be great icebreakers to start kids talking. 🛑 **The UCLA Social Skills Training Program says the best interactive toys that encourage cooperation are ones that require at least two people to use, have simple rules, are inexpensive, don't encourage aggression, and are fun by kid standards.** 🛑 Any kind of ball, board games, marbles, pretend figures, and dolls are appropriate. Visit your child's schoolyard or a nearby park to see what kinds of outdoor games are current. Ask other parents and toy store owners for names of the hottest indoor toys for your child's age—besides video games, which are anything but interactive. Try to match activities to your child's interest and then spend the next days teaching your child how to play the game before the guest arrives. She doesn't have to be great; she just has to know the rules. Once she has learned the game, she'll be in better shape to play it with guests.

- *Time keepers.* Timing devices, such as an oven timer, stopwatch, or egg timer are great for kids who always complain that they didn't get a turn or who monopolize equipment. Teach your child how to use the device and have it available for "just in case" peer problems.

- *Just-in-case stuff.* An extra sweatshirt and sweatpants for a friend, a sleeping bag and pillow, a nightlight.

Set Clear House Rules

Now the absolutely last thing I'm suggesting is that your child's guest be met at the door with a list of your house rules. Nothing will turn a kid off faster. But kids will appreciate it if you establish guidelines that encourage cooperative behavior and safety. *And rules only need to be set as needed.* So choose those that you think best fit your kid, her friends, and your household values right here and now.

It's best to review the rules with your child *before guests arrive. Hint:* Stress to your child that *his* job is not to tell his guest all your house rules, but instead to gently remind the guest of the rule *if the situation arises in which it is needed.* You may want to help your child practice how to explain a rule to his friend in a tactful manner so it doesn't sound bossy—another huge kid turnoff. Emphasize to your child that if *he* follows the rules, his guest generally will as well. Here are some perennial favorites that help kids get along. Adapt of any these rules to fit your family's needs and values. Notice that many of these rules apply to parents, not just kids.

- *Set safety standards.* "No running in the house, and no running *ever* with sticks." "Throw only things that are meant to be thrown (no rocks, glass, sticks)." "Throw balls in the opposite direction of the house." A pool entrance and guns should *always* be locked.
- *Ask about animals.* Be sensitive to your guest's reactions to household pets. Even Little Fido can be traumatic for some kids. Some kids are fearful; others have allergies.
- *Report all injuries.* "*Any* injury—no matter how small—must be reported to an adult in the house."

- ***Don't leave without telling.*** For younger kids: "I expect you to stay on the property." For older kids: "If you leave, I want to know where you are going. Call as soon as you get there." This rule applies regardless of kids' ages.
- ***Set clear boundaries.*** Be clear about any rooms or areas in your house that are off-limits to kids. If there are any tools or equipment you don't want touched—from chain saws to the surround-sound—make sure everyone knows it. Lock any cabinet or door whose contents could be a potential hazard. Better safe than sorry.
- ***Clean up your mess.*** "The house and yard should be left the same as when your friend came over." Give kids a clean-up warning: "It's almost time for Kara to go home, so you'd better start cleaning up."
- ***Set food rules.*** "You may eat only in the kitchen [or out-doors]." "No food in the bedrooms." "Help yourself to the snacks only on the second shelf." "Please clean up anything you take out."
- ***Nothing leaves the house.*** "Any items from this house may not leave our property" (at least without *your* permission). This rule dramatically reduces potential problems.
- ***Announce "no visitors" times.*** Be clear when kids are welcomed and when they should *leave*. For instance, "No friends when there's no adult at home." "Sunday is our family time: friends can come the rest of the week." "Please tell your friends not to come over before nine o'clock."
- ***Unlock bedroom doors.*** All inside doors—except bathrooms—must be left unlocked. And a word to the wise: "Bedrooms are off-limits for entertaining members of the opposite sex."

Address Discipline Problems Effectively

Sure, it might make you feel uncomfortable to enforce discipline when kids are at your house. But you can't let inappropriate behavior slide. Here are a few discipline tips to stop the misbehavior of either your kid or his guest.

- *Step in before things get ugly.* A private, previously agreed-on signal (pulling on your ear or touching your nose) saves your child's dignity. Or you can say, "I see two kids who need to calm down" or "Looks like you two need a time-out from one another for a few minutes." Never yell.

- *Redirect.* "Why don't you two go play Monopoly?" If things get too rough, suggest a quieter activity: "Why don't you find a game to play?"

- *Be clear.* Explain your expectations and what will happen if kids don't comply. "If you don't play nicely, Kevin will have to go home."

- *Discipline privately.* If you must speak to one child, or discipline your own, do so privately. "Excuse me, I need to talk to John a minute."

- *Explain why the behavior is inappropriate.* "When you call Alexis a dummy, it hurts her feelings and makes her want to say something mean back to you." "You can tell your friend you want a turn, but you can't just grab the controller. Kids won't want to play with you." 🛑 **Children whose parents discipline by helping them understand the consequences of their actions instead of threatening a punishment or giving a verbal scolding are more popular with peers as well as less bossy and demanding.** 🛑

- *Follow through.* Don't hesitate to drive a kid home or show him the door if the misbehavior continues. "Come on back next time when you can remember the rules."

- *Talk to the parent.* Any time a child is injured, call the parent and explain. Better that she hears from you than from the child. Use your judgment as to when to talk to a parent about his child's misbehavior.

📖 FRIENDSHIP SKILL BUILDER BOOKS 📖

For Parents and Teachers

These are my favorite suggestions of books that give you a good understanding of friendship issues and the development of children's social competence.

Best Friends, Worst Enemies: Understanding the Social Lives of Children, by Michael Thompson and Catherine O'Neill Grace with Lawrence J. Cohen (New York: Ballantine, 2001). A wonderful guide to help us understand the motives and meanings of children's social behavior.

Good Friends Are Hard to Find: Help Your Child Find, Make and Keep Friends, by Fred Frankel (Los Angeles: Perspective, 1996). Invaluable friendship-making tips for being a better host, setting up safe and fun play dates, and curbing interests that prevent friendships.

The Friendship Factor: Helping Our Children Navigate Their Social World—and Why It Matters for Their Success and Happiness, by Kenneth H. Rubin (New York: Viking Penguin, 2002). Over twenty-five years of research on friendship is described in this valuable guide for parents and teachers.

The Unwritten Rules of Friendship: Simple Strategies to Help Your Child Make Friends, by Natalie Madorsky Elman and Eileen Kennedy-Moore (New York: Little, Brown, 2003). A gold mine of strategies to help kids become better friends and better hosts.

"Why Doesn't Anybody Like Me?" A Guide to Raising Socially Confident Kids, by Hara Estroff Marano (New York: Morrow, 1998). A friendly, informative book on how to help boost kids' social competence.

For Kids

A Good Friend: How to Make One, How to Be One, by Ron Herron and Val J. Peter (Boys Town, Neb.: Boys Town Press, 1998). Ten tips on getting along with others, a set of people skills that kids need for handling social situations, plus a list of behaviors to avoid so that you don't jeopardize your friendship. Ages 10 to 14.

A Smart Girl's Guide to Friendship Troubles: Dealing with Fights, Being Left Out and the Whole Popularity Thing, by Patti Kelley

Criswell (Middleton, Wis.: Pleasant Company, 2003). I like this one because it provides realistic solutions to the kinds of issues that trouble middle school–age girls. Ages 10 to 14.

Don't Slurp Your Soup, by Lynne Gibbs (Waterbird Press, 2002). Describes behaviors that help children get along with others, including table manners, introductions, phone protocol, and being a good host and a good sport. Ages 4 to 8.

PART 3

The Top 25 Friendship Problems and How to Solve Them

Friendship Issue 1

Argues

Everyday Behaviors: Constantly bickering; disagreeable attitude; alienates friends

Friendship Skill Builder: Resolving Conflicts So Everyone Is Satisfied

"Of course I'm mad. He hasn't a clue!"
"Why should I say I'm sorry? He started it."
"That's it—she can't come over anymore. We'll just end up arguing."

WHAT'S WRONG?

Arguing. Quarreling. Yelling. Door slamming. Crying. Hurt feelings. Arguments are a big part of why kids can't get along and how their friendships break up. Of course, conflict is also a part of life. 🛑 **A national survey found that 43 percent of**

53

middle school students said they have conflicts with other kids at least one or more times a day. (STOP)

One of the most essential friendship-building skills you need to teach your child is how to handle conflicts so he can survive the social jungle. Learning how to deal with all those problems that crop up is a big part of growing up and an essential life skill. The key point is that your child must learn not only how to solve problems but also how to do so in a peaceful, calm way so that all the kids involved feel like they've won. That's call a win-win scenario, and it's the best way to reduce arguments and restore friendships. Learning this skill will not only dramatically boost your child's friendship quotient but also improve harmony on the home front. And wouldn't that ever be a plus?

WHY IS THIS HAPPENING?

To figure out why your child constantly argues with friends, you need to get to the bottom of what's really going on. Why are your kid and his friends always at each other? Here are some things to consider. Check the ones that apply.

- ☐ Is this a new behavior? If so, have there been any big changes in his life lately?
- ☐ Does your child quarrel with *all* of her friends, or just certain ones? Which seem to be the most troublesome?
- ☐ Could your child be jealous or resentful of this friend? Why?
- ☐ Is your child selfish or materialistic? Are these arguments about always wanting what the other child has?
- ☐ Is he quick tempered, or does he have a problem calming himself down? (If so, also see Hot Tempered.)
- ☐ Is your child overly sensitive, and does she easily get rubbed the wrong way? (If so, also see Too Sensitive or Teased.)

- [ ] Do arguments usually crop up when your child and this pal are competing? Is he overly competitive, afraid to lose, a perfectionist, or just a poor loser? (If so, also see Poor Loser and Too Competitive.)
- [ ] Is she always coming to you or someone else to solve the problem?
- [ ] Is this about power or control? Is he domineering or bossy? (If so, also see Bossy.)
- [ ] Is this friendship on the rocks? Is this bickering just a way of breaking things off? (If so, also see Tiffs.)
- [ ] Does the bickering start up when another friend steps in? Maybe it's the old "three's a crowd" problem.
- [ ] Are you noticing that these arguments usually happen at a certain time or day of the week? Could the arguments be triggered by hunger, fatigue, stress, or frustration?
- [ ] What's the bickering all about? (A toy, where to go, what to do?) Is there an easy solution?

What is your best guess as to why your kid is always quarreling? Write it here.

_____

_____

_____

FRIENDSHIP SKILL BUILDER

Resolving Conflicts So Everyone Is Satisfied

An important secret to getting along with friends is to learn how to solve a problem together. If you can't get past the bickering, it means no one is listening and no one is satisfied. So here are the steps to solving conflicts that you can teach your child.

1. **Stop and cool off.** As soon as you feel an argument is getting nowhere, tune in to your friend's mood. Are your friend's feelings getting hurt? If you or your friend looks or sounds tense, call for a time-out. You can take a deep breath, suggest that you both stop to calm down, get a drink of water, or leave a minute and then come back. Only when you and your friend are calm can you talk about what's bugging you.

2. **Set some talking rules.** Agree to take turns as talker and listener to hear each other's side of the problem. No interrupting. No put-downs. No name-calling, insulting, or blaming. Stay calm. Tell the truth and remain respectful. Remember that you both should take a bit of responsibility.

3. **Listen carefully.** Hear your friend's point of view.

4. **Use "I messages."** When you talk, say how you feel. Say why you feel that way. Say what you want or need to make things fair. Don't say "You did this" or "You said that." Your job is to attack the problem and not your friend.

5. **Agree on what the problem is.** Both of you need to decide what you're really arguing about.

6. **Brainstorm alternatives.** Find a solution that's fair to both of you.

7. **Agree to do it and move on.** If there have been any hurt feelings, try to forgive each other and move ahead.

WHAT CAN I SAY?

- **Express sympathy.** Arguments among friends are tough for everyone—but especially so for kids. Chances are that your child, the friend, or both are hurting. Keep in mind, your goal isn't to solve the problem—that's up to them—but you can acknowledge the hurt. "I can see why you're upset." "Arguments are never fun. They get everybody hurting."
- **Don't ask why, ask what.** Asking the right questions can help your child think about what triggered the argument and might even prevent the next one. Asking "why" questions ("Why are you arguing?" "Why can't you get along?") is almost guaranteed to confuse your kid and get an "I don't know" response. Instead try "What was your quarrel about?" "What did your friend say?" "What did you do?" "What do you want to happen now?"
- **Call for time-outs.** Even a few seconds can be enough to stop a big quarrel, so help your child come up with a few things he can say to back off from an argument ready to blow. "When you feel like you and your friend are starting to argue, try to cool things off. You could say, 'You know I'm too mad to talk right now,' 'Give me a minute to cool off,' 'I need to take a walk,' or 'Let's go shoot some hoops.'"
- **Encourage them to work it out themselves.** Ask the kids involved what they plan to do to solve "their" problem. After all, real-life practice is the best way for kids to learn skills. "I know you two can solve this. If you need me, I'm in the other room, but don't leave the table until you can work this out fairly." "Let's see if you two can work this through calmly for three minutes. You've been friends far too long not to solve this."
- **Encourage learning.** If your kid has had any success so far in ending an argument, help her remember how to do it again. "That was a great idea. You should try that the next time."

- **Remind your kid to see the other side.** Kids often get so caught up in their own point of view that they lose sight of where their friend is coming from. You can help change their focus: "How does Patrick feel?" "Did you hear what he actually said?" "What would he think is fair?"

WHAT CAN I DO?

- **Find the real cause.** Usually there are deeper issues involved: What's really triggering these arguments? Is the other child getting more attention, being manipulative, or bullying? Does he have more of something? Does anyone feel she is not being listened to or being taken advantage of? Is the other kid argumentative while your kid is just trying to hold his own? Is your child too sensitive, jumping to conclusions that he is being taken advantage of or treated unfairly? Ask friends, teachers, and coaches who know your child well. Compare notes and get to the root of the issue, then commit yourself to doing one thing you can do to start turning things around.
- **Teach conflict solving.** Use the Friendship Skill Builder: Resolving Conflicts So Everyone Is Satisfied, but don't expect overnight miracles. Learning any skill takes practice, so look for real-life opportunities to practice the skill, then practice over and over. 🛑 **Forty-five percent of middle school students have conflicts one or more times each day, and 80 percent say they see kids having arguments or fights every day.** 🛑
- **Bring the friend into the new strategy.** Encourage your child to tell his buddy that he knows he's been arguing a lot lately and doesn't want it to continue because it's hurting the relationship. After all, it takes two to tango.
- **Encourage honesty.** Many kids argue because they have never learned ways to express their frustrations in a healthy manner. The trick here is to pass along an emotion vocabulary

FRIENDSHIP TIP

Major Source of Arguments
Naomi Drew, author of *The Kids' Guide to Working Out Conflicts,* surveyed the major sources of arguments among middle school students. Here they are in order of frequency:

Top conflict starters for boys:
1. Who's right and who's wrong
2. Bragging
3. Who does better at sports or in school
4. The rules of games
5. Insults and name-calling

Top conflict starters for girls:
1. Gossip, rumors
2. Having secrets told
3. Boyfriends
4. Feeling jealous or left out
5. Mean remarks behind people's backs

so she can express how she feels when she starts to get angry, nervous, anxious, irritated, frustrated, or stressed. But remind her to use "I messages" and not "you . . . you . . . you."

- *Intervene only if necessary.* If you hear an argument brewing, stay within earshot, but jump in only when emotions are too high but *before* an argument escalates. A gentle reminder might be called for, such as a private, previously agreed-on signal (like tugging on your ear). With younger kids, you might say, "I see two angry kids who need to cool down. You go to the other room, and you to the kitchen until the two of you can talk calmly and work things out."

- *Encourage making amends.* If there are hurt feelings and your child is the cause, encourage her to make amends. She can call the friend, forgive him or apologize and tell the friend she's sorry, or suggest a way the two can get beyond the hurdle and on with their relationship.
- *Emphasize patience.* Your child needs to know change isn't easy. It will take time for your child to change his habits. And it will take a bit of adjustment for his friend to realize that your kid is trying a new behavior. So keep encouraging your child—but also help him stay realistic. This will work, but does take time.

21-DAY FRIENDSHIP FOLLOW-UP

Over the next 21 days, here's what I will do to help my child learn Friendship Skill Builder: Resolving Conflicts So Everyone Is Satisfied:

_____

_____

_____

 FRIENDSHIP SKILL BUILDER BOOKS

For Parents and Teachers

Peaceful Parents, Peaceful Kids: Practical Ways to Create a Calm and Happy Home, by Naomi Drew (New York: Kensington Books, 2000). This is the must-have parenting book for raising kids who are less stressed and more cooperative and peaceful.

Tired of Yelling: Teaching Our Children to Resolve Conflict, by Lyndon D. Waugh (Athens, Ga.: Longstreet Press, 1999). A psychiatrist offers parenting solutions for defusing family tension and helping toddlers through teens learn skills of peacemaking.

Waging Peace in Our Schools, by Linda Lantieri and Janet Patti (Boston: Beacon Press, 1996). A must-read for every educator and child advocate, written by two top experts in conflict resolution.

For Kids

Matthew and Tilly, by Rebecca C. Jones (New York: Puffin Books, 1995). Matthew and Tilly figure out how to solve their conflict after having a fight. Ages 4 to 8.

Peace on the Playground, by Eileen Lucas (New York: Franklin Watts, 1991). This book helps children realize why it's important to work out conflicts and find peaceful ways to do so. Ages 4 to 7.

The Butter Battle Book, by Dr. Seuss (New York: Random House, 1984). An absolutely wonderful classic that helps kids realize how perceived differences can escalate to fighting and ultimately to war. Ages 5 to 10.

The Cybil War, by Betsy Byars (New York: Viking Penguin, 1981). Misinformation causes a conflict between two long-time best friends. Ages 9 to 12.

The Hating Book, by Charlotte Zolotow (New York: Harper-Collins, 1989). A gem if your child has hurt feelings and a fight with a best friend. The two kids eventually work out a misunderstanding and learn there are two sides to every conflict. Ages 4 to 7.

The Kids' Guide to Working Out Conflicts: How to Keep Cool, Stay Safe, and Get Along, by Naomi Drew (Minneapolis, Minn.: Free Spirit, 2004). A well-known expert on conflict resolution provides kids with practical ways to solve conflicts peacefully. An excellent resource for kids 9 to 14. Highly recommended.

Bad Friends

Everyday Behavior: Chooses kids with risky behaviors and different values

Friendship Skill Builder: Staying out of Trouble

"Why don't you like my friends? We never get in big trouble or do anything really bad."
"Why don't you trust me, Mom? Jeremy isn't such a bad kid."
"Chill, would ya? It's not like we robbed a bank or anything."

WHAT'S WRONG?

Among the most troubling questions I get from parents involve their kids' "bad friends." "What do I do if my daughter has a new friend who may be a bad influence?" "I'm dying every time my son goes to this kid's house: I know there's no parental supervision, and who knows what they may be doing?" Bad friends. They're every parent's worst nightmare. We imagine only the worst: drugs, smoking, sex, trouble with the law. What should parents *do* if they notice that their daughter is starting to hang out more with a kid whose values don't seem in sync with their own? Is there ever a time when you should forbid your son from being with a particular friend? The bottom line on this one: it's okay for your child to have friends who are different from her. After all, exposing our kids to diversity is a big part of helping them broaden their horizons, learn new skills and perspectives, and get along with others. The trick here is to figure out when the other kid's values or lifestyle is in fact reckless, self-destructive, or totally inappropriate. Consider this: Could hanging around this kid damage your child's character, reputation, or health? Keep in mind that a kid is rarely "made bad" by another kid, but the friends your kid chooses to hang around with sure can increase the odds that he may—or may not—get into trouble.

WHY IS THIS HAPPENING?

Don't be so quick to blame the "bad friends." Remember, your kid is the one who chose them. So the real question is, What's going on? Why is your kid inclined to hang out with this particular companion? Here are some questions to ask yourself:

☐ Was there anything going on at the time to trigger the relationship when it first started, such as the loss of a friend? A divorce? A move? Changing schools? Changing classes? Peer rejection?

☐ Did your kid choose this kid as a companion, or vice versa? If the other kid befriended your child first, what does your kid offer in the relationship? Companionship, your home as a place to hang out, security, food, a good time, a family to hang around? Why is this "bad kid" choosing *your* kid?

☐ Is your kid looking for excitement? Enjoying the risk?

☐ Does your child lack friends? Does he not know how to make new friends? Do you need to teach him new social skills so he can gain approval from other, more particular groups of kids?

☐ Does the companion or group give her status? Peer approval? Has she been rejected by a clique or other kids?

☐ What about protection? Is there a chance that your child is being bullied by other kids, and this kid offers him security? Are there cliques or gangs in your child's school or neighborhood?

☐ Is this about control? Is she deliberately hanging around this group knowing that you or her other parent disapproves? Is she trying to get back at you for something? Is she excited by risk? Does she seek these kids because they "push the envelope"?

What is your best guess as to why your kid has these "bad friends"? Write it down.

_____

_____

_____

WHAT SHOULD I SAY?

• *Restate your standards.* Don't make any assumptions: remind yourself what you stand for and repeat your family rules to your child. Be clear that she knows them, and be certain she is aware of the consequence if she violates them. Here are a few parental favorites: "No drugs, drinking, smoking,

FRIENDSHIP SKILL BUILDER

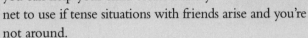

Staying out of Trouble

By teaching him the following skill, you can help your child create a safety net to use if tense situations with friends arise and you're not around.

1. *Decide if there could be trouble.* Rely on your gut instinct. If you don't feel comfortable, think there's a possibility that you or your friends could be hurt, or know that someone is doing something wrong—it's trouble. Remember, good friends never put you in danger or make you do something you don't want to do or ask you to break a rule or even the law.

2. *Decide what you should do.* Identify your options. Remember, you don't have to tell your friend what to do; just do it yourself. You do have options. You could:
   - Call your parents or another adult you know well to pick you up.
   - Try to talk your friend into doing something else.
   - Tell the friend your reason or just firmly say, "I don't want to."
   - Make an excuse, like "I have to get home. I'll get grounded."
   - Exit the scene. Say good-bye and walk out.

3. *Do what is best for you.* Remember, it's better to be safe than sorry.

or weapons." "Always call to tell me where you are." "You go only to homes where parents are there to supervise." "You don't leave one location and go to another without telling me." "Kids are allowed to come over only if there's a parent here." "You may not watch movies, listen to music, or play video games with a ___ rating." A one-time talk to your child isn't going to cut it, so plan to tell your child your rules again and again.

- *Search for the reason.* Talk to your child about her friends and ask questions that will help you understand her selection criteria. "You and your new friend are spending a lot of time together. How did you two meet? Does she like to play soccer like you? Tell me about her. Do I know her parents?"
- *Share your concerns.* Instead of judging or criticizing your kid's companion (which is guaranteed to end the conversation), describe the changes you see in *your* child. "I notice that whenever you sit next to Kevin in class, I get a call from the teacher." "Before you met Darla you never came home after curfew. Now you're late every night, and your clothes smell like cigarettes." "You've been swearing a lot lately. You never swore before you starting hanging around that group." If you're not sure you understand what's going on, ask questions. "Do your friend's tattoos have a special meaning?" "You hid Ricky's magazine when I came in your room. What exactly was it that you didn't want me to see?" "You didn't enjoy that kind of music before you met Josh. You told me you didn't approve of it. Have you noticed the change in your taste?"
- *Talk to the parent.* Do try to talk to the other kid's parent, and it's best to do so as soon as your child befriends her child. Meeting personally would be ideal, but a phone call is usually more realistic. Try your best to be positive, friendly, and open minded. Here is the gist of what you might say: "Our kids have been seeing a lot of one another, and I wanted to introduce myself. I always try to make a point of talking to the parents of all my children's friends. Since

they're spending a lot of time together, I thought we should share any rules we each have and pass on any special information." Do make sure to give the parent a phone number to contact you, and write down any she provides. If your kid has a "fit," so be it: explain that getting to know his friend's parents is part of good parenting. And if you haven't taken time to do so with his other friends, make it a policy from now on.

- *Talk to the friends.* Befriend your child's friends. Get to them and let them know you are interested in their lives. You may see a different side to your child's friends. "Would you like a soda or lemonade?" "Do you play any sports?" "How did you and Josh meet?" "Are you in any of the same classes?" "Do you have any brothers or sisters?" "I didn't know you last year. Are you new to this school?" "Can you stay for dinner?"

- *Ask "What if."* A good way to assess your kid's ability to handle peers who could be trouble is by posing "what if" questions. You make up the problem scenario, but then listen to how your child responds. Her answers will be a springboard to talk about possible problems she may face in bad company. "What if you go to a friend's house and there aren't any parents there?" "What if you're at the movies to see a show with your friends, and they say they're going to see the R-rated one instead?" "What if you're at a slumber party and your friends want to sneak out and [smoke, drink, meet boys, and so on]?" "What if your friend dared to take a shortcut through those old abandoned houses [the woods, the freeway]?"

- *Keep your relationship open and strong.* Keep the lines of communication open and your relationship warm and positive. You want to convey the message loud and clear: "I love you." "Remember, I'm always here for you." "Talk to me anytime. You have my cell number." Don't let your dislike of your child's friends hinder your relationship with your child.

WHAT SHOULD I DO?

- *Get the facts.* Talk to parents, teachers, and adults whose opinions you value. Do they know the kid and share your concerns? Do their kids hang around with him? If not, why? What do they suggest?

- *Stay in contact.* Know where your child is at all times. Make it clear that you want to hear from her immediately after school (or any activity). If your child doesn't have access to a cell phone or pager, give her a phone card and teach her how to use it. Show younger kids how to make collect phone calls. There should be no excuses.

- *Keep an open house.* Stock your refrigerator with sodas, save those pizza coupons, and make your house kid friendly so that your child's friends *want* to come to your house. In fact, worry more if your kid *doesn't* want to bring his friends over. Buy a DVD player, have the most popular video games, set up a basketball court. Besides feeling more comfortable knowing where your kid is, you'll also be able to keep your eyes and ears open to see if your concerns are really grounded.

- *Be available.* Carpool, chaperone, chauffeur, coach, and volunteer to work in the classroom or school. Keep yourself visible and get to know your kid's friends.

- *Foster new associations.* The best way to limit time spent with a potential bad friend is to find other social avenues for her to go down instead. Look for places she can make new friends, such as Boys' and Girls' Clubs, scouts, clubs, music, and sports. Arrange activities that your child really wants to do (the basketball team, guitar lessons, the art class). One of the best ways to build your child's self-esteem and help her develop a strong identity is through activities that nurture her natural strengths. So identify your kid's strengths (athletic, artistic, verbal) and match an activity to boost them.

- *Be prepared.* Teach your child what to do any time he doesn't feel comfortable or thinks there could be trouble.

If your child doesn't have access to a cell phone or pager, give him a phone card and teach him how to use it. Show younger kids how to make collect phone calls. Set up a code word that only you and your family know, such as "Robin Hood," "trick or treat," or "Jimmy called." That way, any time you are talking to your child and his friends are listening, he can say the word and you'll know he really wants to come home. Also have a "parent support" group available in which you and another friend who knows your child will agree that any time you're not available, your child will call her to pick him up (and vice versa with her kid).

- **Watch for red flags.** Keep your antennae up a little higher and tune in to your child a bit closer. Are you seeing any changes in your child's behavior that are big warning signs that the situation is becoming more serious? The key is to look for differences you've noticed in your child *since she began hanging around with this companion:* grades slipping, tears, moodiness, red eyes (drugs), alcohol or smoke smell (or cologne to possibly cover up the smell), defiant or disrespectful attitude, hiding things or acting sneaky, sleeping too much, more accidents, a complete wardrobe change that is "not your kid." Also, perhaps another parent, adult, or teacher has made a comment to you about the change or about the new companion. When in doubt, get help. Talk to a school counselor, a social worker, your pediatrician, or a mental health professional. And remember to direct your concerns to where they really count: how *your* kid acts instead of how the *other* kids behave.

- **Forbid the bad friend when serious issues emerge.** If the companion clearly is a "bad influence" and is pushing your kid into experimenting with serious behaviors, such as drug or alcohol use, shoplifting, sex, or smoking, it's time to draw a halt to the relationship. This may be easier said than done, and you might need to consider the extreme: a new school, a summer camp, a month at a relative's, a boarding school, or even moving. In some cases extreme action may really be the only option to prevent a potential tragedy.

 FRIENDSHIP TIP

The Importance of Staying Busy
A recently released report finds that one of the best ways to keep your kid out of trouble is to keep him busy during the after-school hours. The after-school hours between 2 and 6 P.M. are considered the prime time for risky behaviors with bad friends and for juvenile crimes. Keep close tabs on your kid after school; get him involved in after-school programs or sports; or enlist the help of other parents, taking turns opening your homes and making sure your children are supervised after school. If you're not home, insist that he call as soon as school is out to notify you where he is. Set clear parameters as to where he may or may not go after school, and enforce them.

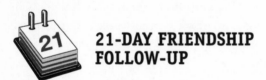 **21-DAY FRIENDSHIP FOLLOW-UP**

Over the next 21 days, here's what I will do to help my child learn Friendship Skill Builder: Staying out of Trouble:

_____

_____

_____

For Parents and Teachers

Yes, you're right. Most of these titles appear to address adolescent problems. But that's exactly why I cited them. Too often we wait until our kids are in trouble to read these books. Don't. All of them have great preventive strategies and methods to teach kids strong resistance skills and how to use good judgment.

On the Safe Side: Teach Your Child to Be Safe, Strong, and Street Smart, by Paula Statman (New York: HarperPerennial, 1995). Good, wise information and easy ways to teach our kids good judgment as they try to survive the social jungle.

Protecting the Gift: Keeping Children and Teenagers Safe (and Parents Sane), by Gavin DeBecker (New York: Random House, 1999). An empowering book by a leading expert on predicting violent behavior and on ways to keep our kids safe.

Teens in Turmoil: A Path to Change for Parents, Adolescents, and Their Families, by Carol Maxym and Leslie B. York (New York: Penguin Books, 2000). A no-nonsense guide for parents struggling with troubled sons or daughters.

The Second Family: How Adolescent Power Is Challenging the American Family, by Ron Taffel (New York: St. Martin's Press, 2001). Fascinating reading for all parents, regardless of the age of their child. The author makes a strong case for staying connected to our kids: if we don't, the counterculture and peer group may well be raising them.

When Good Kids Do Bad Things: A Survival Guide for Parents of Teenagers, by Katherine Gordy Levine (New York: Pocket Books, 1991). If your well-behaved kid has suddenly turned a bit rebellious or if you're afraid your good kid could be getting into trouble you don't even know about, this book is for you. A foster mother to nearly four hundred children, Levine has seen and handled it all. Straight talk and practical solutions for parents.

When Kids Get into Trouble (Rev. ed.), by Priscilla Platt (Toronto: Stoddart, 1990). Good reading with helpful ideas for parents.

For Kids

Stick Up for Yourself! Every Kid's Guide to Personal Power and Positive Self-Esteem, by Gershen Kaufman, Lev Raphael, and Pamela Espeland (Minneapolis, Minn.: Free Spirit, 1999). Simple ideas include real-life examples that help kids learn ways to stick up for themselves and stay out of trouble. Ages 9 to 13.

The Behavior Survival Guide for Kids: How to Make Good Choices and Stay out of Trouble, by Tom McIntyre (Minneapolis, Minn.: Free Spirit, 2003). A great book with very practical, positive, helpful suggestions to help kids learn ways to stay out of trouble. Ages 10 to 14.

The Mouse, the Monster and Me! by Pat Palmer (San Luis Obispo, Calif.: Impact, 1977). Assertiveness concepts taught in a simplified way for kids. Ages 8 to 12.

3

Bad Reputation

Everyday Behaviors: Ostracized; subject of rumors and gossip; rejected from social groups and gatherings

Friendship Skill Builder: Using Good Manners and Courtesy

"Jimmy says he won't play with me anymore because of what I did last time."
"Kelly's mom won't let me come over."
"You won't believe what they're saying about me."

WHAT'S WRONG?

A bad reputation is deadly to a kid's social image. If your child is thought to be a vicious gossip, a cheat, a clumsy oaf, a bully, a dangerous influence, hot tempered, too fast, vulgar, untrustworthy—whether it's true or not—this perception can stick like glue not only with friends but also teachers and parents. Soon word passes through the grapevine, and your child becomes the "talk" of the town. And parents do talk. Party invitations dwindle, sleepovers become infrequent, and the phone stops ringing once a child breaks the social rules or is perceived to have made a huge, huge blunder. Of course, sometimes reputations are based on erroneous gossip or rumors that just aren't true. But whatever the case, being ostracized or rejected by friends or their parents is devastating to your child and your family.

WHY IS THIS HAPPENING?

One thing for sure, your child can't turn this bad reputation around overnight. It takes time. And you need to investigate how your kid developed this terrible image or is alienating others.

If you don't have a clue, ask a few people who know your child well and whose opinion you trust. Talk to other parents at the baby-sitting co-op, day-care workers, coaches, bus drivers, teachers. Eavesdrop on what peers are saying to and about your child. Here are some possibilities of what turns people off. Is your child

☐ The victim of a misperception, misunderstanding, mistaken identity, or false rumor?

☐ Too loud, too spoiled, too pushy, too aggressive?

☐ Impolite? Does he never say please or thank you? Does he leave a mess? Is he a sloppy eater?

☐ Disrespectful toward people? Does he name-call, insult, say racist or prejudicial comments? Is he flippant or defiant toward authority figures? Does he swear, or is he vulgar?

☐ Disrespectful toward property? Does she borrow things without returning them? Does she use stuff in a friend's house without asking or putting things back?

- [ ] Too flashy? Does she use too much makeup or have a piercing of some kind (when the other kids have none)? Is she wearing her skirts too short or pants too low? Is his hair cut or worn too severely?
- [ ] A gossip, rumor monger, or backstabber?
- [ ] Untrustworthy? Has she betrayed a friend by revealing a confidence?
- [ ] A bully? Mean or cruel, or not treating the other kids nicely?
- [ ] Argumentative? Self-centered? Not sharing? Always wanting things to go his way? Thoughtless or selfish?
- [ ] A poor sport or bad loser?
- [ ] A whiner, tattler, complainer, or crybaby?
- [ ] "Too mature"? Is she choosing activities or entertainment that might be perceived by other parents as inappropriate for their kids? Are you allowing her to see movies, listen to music, or play video games that other parents restrict their kids from?
- [ ] A victim of your own reputation? Do people think you are too strict or too permissive? Do you smoke or drink too much? Do you yell or swear? Do you make lewd or inappropriate jokes?

All or any of these facts or perceptions can contribute to your child's bad reputation. What is your best guess as to why your kid developed this negative image? Write it down.

_____

_____

_____

_____

_____

_____

FRIENDSHIP SKILL BUILDER

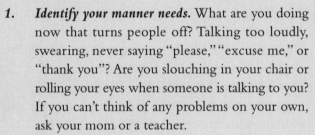

Using Good Manners and Courtesy

After that "big first impression" (see the section What Should I Do?), the thing that affects your child's reputation most is her manners. So if you want to make a positive impact on your child's image quickly, teach her to follow these steps:

1. *Identify your manner needs.* What are you doing now that turns people off? Talking too loudly, swearing, never saying "please," "excuse me," or "thank you"? Are you slouching in your chair or rolling your eyes when someone is talking to you? If you can't think of any problems on your own, ask your mom or a teacher.

2. *Agree on an A-list of replacement manners.* Start with your top five needs, and write them on index cards. Commit to one big change per week. Maybe the first week you can work on not interrupting and on saying "please," "thank you," and "excuse me."

3. *Look for opportunities to use your new manners.* This could be at home first, but eventually in public, even in a situation where you've previously done poorly.

4. *Do it.* Look at the person. Smile. Stand or sit tall. Use a friendly voice. Use the right manner to be courteous, gracious, and polite.

5. *Acknowledge any response or walk on.*

6. *Keep practicing.* Remember, everyone slips from time to time, so keep at it.

WHAT SHOULD I SAY?

- *Empathize.* "I see how angry you are about not getting invited to Joey's sleepover." "It's not fair that people think you're fast. I know how that rumor got started, and you and I know it's just not true." "Nobody likes being talked about liked that, so I can understand why you're so upset."
- *Don't make excuses.* If you're sure that your child's reputation is earned, then neither you nor your child should permit yourself to blame others. "Coach Byer was right. You were being a poor loser after the play-off game. So let's work on how you can be a better sport so people don't keep that image of you forever." "It's not fair to criticize Mrs. Rossman for banishing you from her house. You were the one who crashed Molly's scooter and left without apologizing."
- *Make your child part of the solution.* "Mrs. Jones told me you used bad words at her house, and that's why she doesn't want you at Bonny's party. How can you let her know you won't talk like that again?" "I know it makes you mad when your friends call your outfits too dark and gloomy. Is there anything you could put on or take off that would change their minds?"
- *Emphasize the time factor.* Help your child realize that this situation is not going to turn around overnight. "I know you want to fix this by tomorrow. But you need to be patient. Reputations can take time to rebuild."
- *Acknowledge efforts.* When you see your child trying to reverse a previous bad behavior and repair a damaged reputation, be sure to let him know you appreciate it. "I heard you tell Billy how you felt instead of hitting him like you did before. Good job!"

WHAT SHOULD I DO?

- *Be sure the reputation is deserved.* If your child is the victim of a misperception, misunderstanding, mistaken identity, or false rumor, take action. Get to the source, confront the mistake, and correct the false image.

- *Expect a fresh start.* Be clear with your child that a big change is needed.

- *Be realistic.* It may be impossible to change some behaviors, characteristics, or personality traits of your child. So focus only on what you can control and correct, and do your best to improve your child's reputation within that context. In some cases, the situation is irreversible, and you may have to let your child make a fresh start. If possible, switch schools.

- *Pick one bad behavior to change right away.* Reread the Why Is This Happening? section. Identify the problem that is contributing most to your kid's bad reputation. Create a plan to turn that behavior around, and stick to the plan until it does.

- *Help your child make a good first impression.* First impressions *do* make a difference, so take a serious look at the way your kid presents herself. What are the other kids wearing, and how do they do their hair? How about your kid's body language or posture? Does the way he stands push people away or signal anger or defiance? 🛑 **Research has shown that only 7 percent of our messages are actually communicated through words. The rest are expressed through facial expression, body language, and tone of voice.** 🛑 Is your child's voice tone too loud or his facial expression too grim? Is there one thing you can do to help your child make a better first impression?

- *Keep a low profile.* If your kid is really having a serious behavioral problem that will take some time to turn around, hang low and keep her out of sight while you are working on this problem.

- *Redirect bad behavior.* If your child is in public and displays the destructive behavior that has contributed to his bad reputation, halt it on the spot by making some prearranged secret signal and steer him in a different direction.

- *Find new social outlets and activities.* Encourage your child to learn a new skill or engage in some activity that involves a different group of friends. Maybe there's even a new hobby or interest to pursue: guitar lessons, ballet, gymnastics, rugby. Meanwhile, he can practice his image makeover with kids who don't know about his bad reputation, before trying it out with the old gang.

- **Be there.** Supervise more closely. Let her know you're serious. Sit and watch during practice. Talk to the teacher to tell her to please be on the alert. Volunteer to chaperone field trips, do the carpooling, help out in scouting, work in the classroom. Then be a fly on the wall—supportive but unobtrusive.

 FRIENDSHIP TIP

Using the Right Words Makes a Difference
Rosaline Wiseman, author of *Queen Bees and Wannabes,* finds that girls respond much better to the word *image* than to *reputation.* So if you talk to your daughter about what people are saying, she'll be more receptive if you say, "You know, I'm afraid you'll project the wrong image if you wear those jeans so low." Choose your words carefully.

 21-DAY FRIENDSHIP FOLLOW-UP

Over the next 21 days, here's what I will do to help my child learn the Friendship Skill Builder: Using Good Manners and Courtesy:

_____

_____

_____

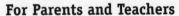

For Parents and Teachers

More Than Manners! Raising Today's Kids to Have Kind Manners and Good Hearts, by Letitia Baldrige (New York: Rawson Associates, 1997). This is a road map for guiding kids to succeed in life by enhancing decency, kind hearts, and great manners.

The Gift of Good Manners: A Parent's Guide for Raising Respectful, Kind, Considerate Children, by Peggy Post and Cindy Post Senning (New York: HarperResource, 2002). A wealth of wonderful advice is offered in this comprehensive guide by a renowned manners expert and her daughter.

When Kids Get into Trouble (Rev. ed.), by Priscilla Platt (Toronto: Stoddart, 1990). Good reading with helpful ideas for parents.

For Kids

Coping with Peer Pressure, by Leslie Kaplan (New York: Rosen, 1987). Good strategies to help kids stick up for themselves and defy peer pressure. Ages 8 to 12.

Manners, by Aliki (New York: Greenwillow Books, 1990). An assortment of different manners are cleverly illustrated. Ages 3 to 7.

Perfect Pigs: An Introduction to Manners, by Marc Brown and Stephen Brensky (Boston: Little, Brown, 1983). A simple introduction to good manners to use with family and friends at school, during meals, with pets, on the phone, during games, at parties, and in public places. Ages 5 to 9.

Table Manners for Kids (Public Media Video, 1993). A detailed narration of everything kids need to know about proper table manners. Ages 6 to 16.

The Berenstain Bears Forget Their Manners, by Stan and Jan Berenstain (New York: Random House, 1985). Mama Bear comes up with a plan to correct the Bear family's rude behavior. Ages 3 to 8.

Bossy

Everyday Behaviors: "Little Dictator"; "her way or the highway"; doesn't listen to or consider friends' needs or desires

Friendship Skill Builder: Respecting a Friend's Point of View

"It's my house, so we're doing it my way."
"You'd better do what I say or you're not invited to my party."
"Nobody gets to use this video controller except me."

WHAT'S WRONG?

Does your child anoint herself as the one in charge of the world? Does he always tell other kids what to do? Does she rarely stop to listen to the needs and opinions of others? If so, you have a "Little Dictator," and chances are that the other kids don't appreciate your son or daughter's bulldozing their agenda.

Certainly there are some pluses to being assertive and self-starting. In fact, you may spin your kid's dictatorial ways as outstanding leadership abilities. But let me tell you, the kids next door probably have quite a different reaction. "She's so bossy." "He always thinks he knows what's right." "Who wants to play with her? She'll just tell you what to do."

Someday this kid of yours may indeed make a fabulous CEO, but right now she needs to temper her "assertive spirit" so other kids will want to stick around. And it can be done. You can teach your child ways to "direct" others in a far more civil and friendly manner. You can help your child learn to consider the feelings and needs of others. Enhancing this friendship aptitude will greatly enhance future relationships as well. Thank yourself now: tempering his domineering attitude may not only boost his popularity among kids but improve his future chances in the job market.

WHY IS THIS HAPPENING?

Check the factors that may apply to your child so you can find the best ways to temper his bossiness and improve his ability to get along better with kids.

- [ ] Is she so used to being bossed and dictated to that she's merely modeling what she's experienced?
- [ ] Might someone—parent, teacher, sibling, another parent, peer, relative, coach, or yourself—be intentionally (or unintentionally) reinforcing your kid's bossiness by labeling it as assertive, confident, or outgoing, or as leadership capability?
- [ ] Could your child be covering up for insecurities or low self-esteem?
- [ ] Does she need to feel a sense of power to compensate

for being at the bottom of a pecking order among family and friends?

☐ Is she concerned about failing or faltering in front of peers? Might she be needing to control the game plan so she does what she feels is more comfortable?

☐ Has she lacked social experiences such that she really doesn't know how to get her opinions across in a friendly way?

☐ Is she hanging around kids who lack direction and need someone to "take charge"?

Read over the list carefully. Talk to others who know your child well to get their opinion and then write your best guess as to why your child is so dictatorial with friends.

_____

_____

_____

WHAT SHOULD I SAY?

- *Show how no one likes being bossed around.* The first step to curbing your child's dictatorial ways is to help him recognize how it turns kids off. 🛑 Preadolescents described by their peers as "altruistic" (or more cooperative, sharing, and caring) are also named as more popular by classmates as well as happier in their peer relationships. 🛑 "I saw a lot of unhappy faces today in the playgroup. Did you see that your friends didn't want to play with you today because you kept telling them what to do?" "Your friends didn't appreciate your picking the movie without asking what they wanted to see. Most of them said they didn't want to go."

- *Enforce sharing.* Explain taking turns to your child, why

FRIENDSHIP
SKILL BUILDER

Respecting a Friend's Point of View

Remind your child that kids want to be able to share their ideas or have an equal chance to choose what to do. In fact, the secret of being good friends is that each person's opinion counts the same. This Friendship Skill Builder will help your child learn to ask friends about their feelings and desires.

1. *Look at your friend in a friendly way.* Smile and make eye contact.
2. *Ask his opinion.* "What would you like to do?" "Do you want to go first?" "Would you like to do this, or this?"
3. *Listen without interrupting.* If the friend's idea seems fair, smile and go along with it. Remember, you can't always have your way.
4. *If the idea doesn't seem fair, suggest an alternative.* "That's one idea, but check this out." "Okay, let's do that for ten minutes, then we'll do the same with my idea. Sound fair?"
5. *Always be considerate.* Show your friends respect by allowing their opinions to count as much as yours.

it's important, and how it makes her friend feel good. And then expect the behavior. "Let's make sure to take turns when we play. You go first and then it'll be Sammy's turn and then mine. That's the house rule." "If there's anything you really don't want to share, put it away *before* your friends come. Otherwise you must let them have a turn."

- *Explain compromise.* Look for opportunities to practice compromising in real situations. "When you meet your friend halfway, it shows that you're willing to give up a little of what you want, and the other person is too."
- *Reinforce cooperation.* If your child is in the habit of dictating, change isn't always easy. Do acknowledge his efforts to be more agreeable and be sure to tell him exactly what you appreciate so he'll do it again. "I saw how you waited to hear your friend's idea. You didn't interrupt that time, and Alan appreciated getting all his words out." "I noticed how you asked Juan what game he wanted to play. That was thoughtful and considerate."
- *Set a consequence if dictating continues.* "Unless you can be less bossy, you won't be able to have Matt come over. Let's work on ways you can treat him more fairly."

WHAT SHOULD I DO?

- *Stop bossing.* Model a more moderate tone in which you ask your child's opinion, stop and consider other family members' views, and follow their lead.
- *Point out bossiness ASAP.* The minute you hear or see your kid bossing friends or siblings (or you!), tell her to stop. When in public, you might develop a quiet signal between the two of you, such as touching your nose or clearing your throat.
- *Teach decision-making methods.* Dictatorial kids always want to set the game plan, so teach your child ways to even the odds among friends. Rock, paper, scissors; drawing straws; picking a number; flipping a coin—these are old-time favorites that come in handy when kids can't decide on rules, who gets to choose what to do, or who goes first.
- *Provide a timer.* Teach younger kids to agree on a set amount of time—usually only a few minutes—for using an item. It's a great way to ensure that one kid (in other words, the

bossy one) doesn't dominate the tasks. Oven or sand timers are great gadgets for younger kids to use. Older kids can use clocks or stopwatches. When the time's up, their turn is over.

- *Emphasize consensus.* Dictators need to learn democracy, so emphasize that in your home. In fact, enforce a new rule that for certain family decisions (choice of restaurant, DVD rental, TV show, board or video game), all members should be surveyed. Your child needs to learn democracy in action so that she can apply it with her own friends.

 FRIENDSHIP TIP

Perceiving Other Kids' Needs
Research shows that to understand the concept of give and take, a child must perceive other kids' needs, interpret them accurately, and recognize that she can do something to be helpful. In addition, the child must feel competent in the situation (capable of providing what is needed). Otherwise, she won't bother to help or share.

 21-DAY FRIENDSHIP FOLLOW-UP

Over the next 21 days, here's what I will do to help my child learn Friendship Skill Builder: Respecting a Friend's Point of View:

_____

_____

_____

📖 FRIENDSHIP SKILL BUILDER BOOKS 📖

For Parents and Teachers

Parenting the Strong-Willed Child, by Rex Foreland and Nicholas Long (New York: McGraw-Hill, 1996). A program to help parents of strong-willed kids find positive and manageable solutions to their kid's difficult behavior.

Raising Your Spirited Child: A Guide for Parents Whose Child Is More Intense, Sensitive, Perceptive, Persistent, and Energetic, by Mary Sheedy Kurcinka (New York: HarperPerennial, 1992). Redefining the "difficult" kid as "spirited," Kurcinka provides tools to understand your own temperament as well as your child's. She also gives parents specific tools to help work with their kids. Also helpful is Kurcinka's *Raising Your Spirited Child Workbook.*

The Challenging Child: Understanding, Raising, and Enjoying the Five "Difficult" Types of Children, by Stanley I. Greenspan and Jacqueline Salmon (Cambridge, Mass.: Perseus Press, 1996). Calm and reassuring advice that helps parents deal with all types of difficult kids.

For Kids

Bartholomew the Bossy, by Marjorie Weinman Sharmat and Normand Chartier (New York: Atheneum, 1984). A much-loved author writes the perfect book to help young kids realize that their bossiness isn't always appreciated. Ages 4 to 8.

Bossy Anna (Silver Blades Figure Eights, No. 4), by Effin Older with Marcy Ramsey (New York: Skylark, 1996). Becoming sick of Anna's persistent bossiness, the Figure Eights tell her to mind her own business but realize when Anna stops coming to the lessons that her efforts had been helping them. Ages 4 to 8.

Franklin Is Bossy (Franklin series), by Paulette Bourgeois (Toronto: Kids Can Press, 1994). Franklin the turtle learns that no one likes a bossy friend. Perfect for kids 3 to 7.

Little Miss Bossy (Mr. Men and Little Miss series), by Roger Hargreaves (New York: Price Stern Sloan, 1998). Simple text helps youngsters realize the need to treat friends more nicely. Ages 3 to 6.

5

Bullied and Harassed

Everyday Behaviors: Verbally or physically abused or repeatedly harassed in a mean-spirited manner; unable to defend or stick up for himself

Friendship Skill Builder: Using Assertive Body Language

"Please don't make me go to school."
"There's nothing I can do, Dad. She just won't leave me alone."
"I had to give him my money. He said he'd rip my shirt if I didn't."

WHAT'S WRONG?

We usually think of bullying as physical aggression, such as punching, hitting, and shoving, but it's way beyond that. If your kid is being bullied or harassed, that means his "pal" or peers are hurting him intentionally. As a result, your child feels powerless, helpless, humiliated, shamed, and hopeless about the whole situation. A bully can attack her victim verbally (by spreading rumors, making prejudicial comments, using cruel put-downs) or emotionally (by excluding, humiliating, hazing); there is also the problem of sexual harassment. 🛑 **In one survey, 40 percent of fifth through eighth graders say they've been sexually harassed by their peers. By some estimates, one in seven American schoolchildren is either a bully or a victim. And this is not just a "big-kid" problem: little kids are suffering as well.** 🛑

The newest form of bullying includes spreading vicious rumors, tales of sexual exploits, and insults through cyberspace on I.M.s, e-mails, videos, digital photos, and personalized websites as well as sending ugly text messages via cell phones. Parry Aftab, executive director of WiredSafety.org, summed up the electronic bullying craze: "We're always talking about protecting kids on the Internet from adults and bad people. We forget that we sometimes need to protect kids from kids."

The two biggest mistakes parents make is not taking their children's complaints seriously and telling them to "toughen up," and allowing the bullying in the first place. There is *no* excuse for this behavior, and each and every one of us needs to be on the same page to stop it.

WHY IS THIS HAPPENING?

Children rarely do anything to cause them to be picked on by a mean-spirited kid, so don't blame your kid or accuse her of setting the bully off. But there are some traits that cause some kids to be targeted more often. Peter Sheras, author of *Your Child: Bully or Victim?* provides a critical clue: "The essential quality that any bully looks for in a victim is not difference but *vulnerability*—some indication that the bully can abuse this child without retaliation." Here are things that may make a child appear more vulnerable. Check ones that apply to your child.

- ☐ Has a physical weakness or disability
- ☐ Is clumsy or uncoordinated
- ☐ Is of small stature or overweight
- ☐ Is shy, too cautious, or oversensitive; cries easily
- ☐ Has a family issue that might cause embarrassment, such as a financial problem or scandal
- ☐ Lacks assertiveness or social skills that would help her stand up to a bully
- ☐ Responds to bullying by crying, whining, displaying a hot temper, tattling, or threatening
- ☐ Is "different" in some way: race, culture, speech, dress, appearance, ability, physical stature, annoying personality trait
- ☐ Lacks self-esteem or self-confidence; is anxious or insecure
- ☐ Carries material items a bully might want (electronic gadgets, pricey sneakers, "cool" jacket or backpack, cell phone, CD player)
- ☐ Has few friends or lacks friends who are reliable enough to support her or help her out
- ☐ Has been encouraged to be dependent and not stand up for himself
- ☐ Is overprotected by you

What is your best guess as to why your child is being targeted? Write your thoughts, then make a plan to change anything that *can* be changed. For instance, if your kid is targeted because of weak social skills, coach a few new ones. If his appearance is somehow "different," help him "fit in" when possible.

FRIENDSHIP SKILL BUILDER

Using Assertive Body Language
Research finds that kids who learn how to be assertive and appear more confident are less likely to be targeted by bullies. In fact, studies show it's often not how "different" your child looks or acts, but rather her insecure, victimlike posture that makes her an easy target. Here are the steps to teaching your child assertive body language.

1. *Learn to use a more confident posture.* Stand tall, hold your head high, and put your shoulders slightly back so you look more confident and less afraid. Check yourself out in the mirror.

2. *Switch off your scared look.* Turn the feelings off your face or pretend you're wearing a special bully-proof vest that bounces taunts off you. Bullies love knowing they can push your buttons, so *don't* let them think you're upset.

3. *Look at the bully.* Use a stone-faced glare or try a mean stare that looks straight through the bully. It makes you look more confident and controlled.

4. *Say no using a firm voice.* If you need to respond, use a strong, firm voice and say a short, direct message: "No." "Nope." "Cut it out." "Leave me alone." "No way." *Do not cry, whine, or insult,* and *never* threaten a bully. It only makes things worse.

5. *Leave.* Hold your head high and walk toward other kids or an adult. Don't look back. Get help if you need to. Fight only as a very last resort if you must defend yourself.

The trick is to look assertive, and that means you can't appear to be a doormat (everyone walks on you) or a steamroller (you push everyone to get what you want). You want to look somewhere in between: cool and confident.

WHAT SHOULD I SAY?

- *Take your child seriously.* Bullying is frightening and humiliating at any age, so listen to your child. Don't say, "There's nothing to be afraid of," "Just toughen up," "It'll go away," or "You're making too big a deal out of this." Instead, reassure your child that you believe her and will find a way to keep her safe. 🛑 **In one study, 49 percent of the kids said they had been bullied at least once or twice during the school term, but only 32 percent of their parents believed them.** 🛑

- *Get to the bottom of anything suspicious.* Kids often don't tell adults they're being bullied: you may have to voice your concerns. You'll get better results by asking direct questions: "You're always hungry; have you been eating your lunch?" "Your CDs are missing? Did someone take them?" "Your jacket is ripped. Did someone do that to you?"

- *Determine if it's bullying.* Bullying is different from just kidding around and teasing one another. (See Teasing.) It is always intentional and mean-spirited, and rarely happens only once. So establish that this is bullying: "Was it an accident, or did he hurt you on purpose?" "Did you do or say anything first to upset him?" "Did she mean to be mean?" "Did he do it more than once?" "Did he know that he was hurting you?" "Did she care that you were sad or angry?" "Did you tell her to stop?" "Did she keep on?" If your child is unsure that what happened was really bullying, encourage her to talk with witnesses to get their take on the situation.

- **Gather facts.** Next, you need all the facts so you can help your kid create a plan to stop the bullying. "What happened?" "Who did this?" "Where were you?" "Who was there?" "Were you alone?" "Has it happened before?" "How often?" "How does it start?" "What did you do?" "Do you think he'll do it again?" "Did anyone help you?" "Did an adult see this?"

- **Don't make promises.** You may have to protect your child, so make no promises about keeping things confidential. "I want to make sure you don't get hurt, so I can't guarantee I won't tell. Let's see what we can do so this doesn't happen again."

- **Offer specific tips for a plan of action.** Most kids can't handle bullying on their own. They need your help, so provide it.

- **Tell him to avoid the scene.** "Don't go to the park; come straight home." "I will pick you up after swimming. Don't take the bus." "Where can you play instead of by the swings?" "Is there a way you can keep your books with you so you don't have to go to your locker?" Bullying usually happens in unsupervised areas, so tell your kid to be near other kids at lunch, recess, in hallways near lockers, parks, or other open areas.

- **Encourage her to find a supportive companion.** Tell your child there's often safety in numbers. "Stay with Kevin at recess." "Sit with Josh on the bus. He'll keep an eye out for you." Kids who have even one friend to confide in can deal with the torment of bullying better than children on their own. Twenty percent of kids admit they try to stay in a group to avoid harassment.

- **Remind her not to retaliate except when unavoidable.** "Don't hit back—it will only increase the chances that you'll get hurt. Fight back *only* if you feel there are no other options and you are hurt."

- *Tell her to yell "Fire."* "If you're in danger, yell 'Fire.' People are more likely to get help."
- *Encourage him to tell a grown-up.* "Find someone you can trust; someone to back you up. If she doesn't, I will."
- *Suggest she make a strategic exit.* "Sometimes the best thing to do is leave the scene." "If you feel you could be hurt or need help, walk toward an adult, a crowd, or older kids."
- *Reinforce coming to you.* "You know you can always come to me." "I'm so glad you told me." "Let's keep talking about what to do so that you can be safe."

WHAT CAN I DO?

- *Take responsibility.* You'll be far more successful at protecting your child from becoming a reoccurring target if you nip the bullying in the bud immediately. Don't let this escalate and don't tell your child to handle this on her own.
- *Talk to other parents.* Keep a dialogue going with parents about how prevalent bullying is in your community and school. Pay special attention to anonymous I.M.s and e-mails that are flooding cyberspace. Consider enlisting school support to initiate a campaign to squelch spam bullying. 🛑 **A nationwide survey found that 43 percent of children said they were afraid to go to the bathroom for fear of being harassed. The National Education Association reports that every day, 160,000 children skip school because they fear being attacked or intimidated by other students.** 🛑 Find out if other parents' kids are being bullied, who the bullies are, where the bullying is happening, and what, if anything, they're doing to help their kids. If bullying is a problem in your neighborhood, start a Neighborhood Watch group or designate "safe houses" for kids to go

to. If bullying is happening in your child's school, create a parent group to discuss your concerns with educators or enlist the help of the PTA.

- **Identify a trustworthy adult.** Identify an adult who can help your child when you're not around. It must be someone who'll take the bullying seriously, protect your kid, and, if necessary, keep the situation confidential. It could be a secretary, teacher, neighbor, school nurse, bus driver, or even the custodian—anyone you and your child trust. Kids are more likely to seek help when they're young but are far less so by the time they reach middle school. This is also the time bullying can be most intense and the victim feels trapped and isolated.

- **Create a comeback.** Bullies rarely just go away, so offer ways to handle a bully if your kid must face him (though it's often best to avoid him altogether). Pleading ("Please stop that") or emotion-laden messages ("It really makes feel mad when you do that") rarely work. Bullies want to get their victim upset, so such comments just mean they've won. A firm, direct statement such as "Cut it out" or "Leave me alone" is usually best. Sometimes a humorous comeback can derail a bully: "Can you do this later?" "Now why would you say that?" or "Thanks for telling me." (See Teasing for other comebacks.) Once your child agrees on a strategy, you *must* rehearse it until he feels confident to use it alone. A big part of success is the ability to deliver the comeback assertively. (See the Friendship Skill Builder in this chapter, Using Assertive Body Language.)

- **Boost self-confidence.** Being bullied affects your child's self-esteem dramatically, so find ways to boost her confidence. A few possibilities include learning martial arts, boxing, or weight lifting. Find an avenue—such as a hobby, interest, sport, or talent—that your kid enjoys and in which she can excel. Then help her develop the skill so her self-esteem grows. Or encourage your child to join activities at school or in the community. This approach may help your child make new friends and gain a much-needed support group, as well as provide a safe place to go after school. The key here is to make sure the bully is not present and a caring adult can watch out for your child if necessary.

- *Step in when needed.* If there's ever the possibility that your child could be injured—step in.
- *Notify authorities.* Inform those directly responsible for your child: his teacher, coach, or day-care worker. If you do not get assurance from them, go up a level: call the principal, superintendent, or school board.
- *Keep records.* If you need to meet with school officials, the bully's parents, or law enforcement officers, keep records and evidence: torn clothing, threatening e-mail, witnesses' names and phone numbers, and details. Print out copies of all vicious I.M.s or threatening e-mails.
- *Demand confidentiality.* You don't want retaliation, so limit the number of people you tell.
- *Expect protection.* Get specifics: "What will you do to ensure my child's safety?"
- *Prevent personal contact.* Your child doesn't feel safe with this child, so no face-to-face contact should be allowed. Even apologies should be done in writing. If possible, ask that the bully not come within a certain number of feet of your child. If you can't get support, your only option may be to move your child from the class, bus, park program, day-care facility, or, in worst-case scenarios, neighborhood or school.
- *Be vigilant.* Don't be surprised if you are met with resistance or told to "toughen up" your kid. Be prepared for the bully's parents to deny your allegations. Voice your concerns and get others to join you. As Hara Estroff Marano, author of *"Why Doesn't Anybody Like Me?"* says, "There is ultimately only one way to stop bullying. And that's to establish a climate in which aggressive behavior is not tolerated—and enforce it."

FRIENDSHIP TIP

Warning Signs of Bullying

Chances are that if your child is being bullied, he won't tell you about it. So watch your child's behavior: a sudden, uncharacteristic change usually indicates that something is going on. Even the most attentive adults can miss the warnings. Research by Dorothy Espelage of the University of Illinois found that although teachers could identify 50 percent of bullies, they were able to pick out only 10 percent of their victims. Here are a few possible warning signs of bullying. Check off any symptoms that may apply to your child.

☐ Unexplained marks, cuts, bruises, and scrapes, or torn clothing

☐ Unexplained loss of toys, school supplies, clothing, lunches, or money

☐ Doesn't want to go to school; is afraid of riding the school bus; wants you there at dismissal

☐ Is suddenly sullen, withdrawn, evasive; remarks about feeling lonely

☐ Marked change in typical behavior or personality; displays out-of-character behavior

☐ Physical complaints; headaches, stomachaches, frequent visits to the school nurse's office

☐ Difficulty sleeping, nightmares; cries self to sleep, wets bed, or is overtired

☐ Begins bullying siblings or younger kids

☐ Always waits to get home to use the bathroom (afraid to use the school restroom)

☐ Is ravenous when she comes home (lunch money or lunch may have been stolen)
☐ Afraid to be left alone, or suddenly clingy
☐ Sudden and significant drop in grades

 ## 21-DAY FRIENDSHIP FOLLOW-UP

Over the next 21 days, here's what I will do to help my child learn Friendship Skill Builder: Using Assertive Body Language:

_____

_____

_____

FRIENDSHIP SKILL BUILDER BOOKS

For Parents and Teachers

And Words Can Hurt Forever: How to Protect Adolescents from Bullying, Harassment, and Emotional Violence, by James Garbarino and Ellen de Lara (New York: Free Press, 2002). Highly recommended for educators and concerned parents.

Bullies and Victims: Helping Your Child Through the Schoolyard Battlefield, by Suellen Fried and Paula Fried (New York: Evans, 1996). Must reading for parents and teachers about a very serious topic.

Facing the Schoolyard Bully: How to Raise an Assertive Child in an Aggressive World, by Kim Zarzour (Buffalo, N.Y.: Firefly Books, 2000). A thorough examination of the dynamics of bullying. Helpful suggestions are provided on how to stop the cycle of bullying, how to prevent your child from becoming a victim, and how to raise an assertive child in these aggressive times.

Girl Wars: 12 Strategies That Will End Female Bullying, by Cheryl Dellasega and Charisse Nixon (New York: Simon & Schuster, 2003). Two experts explain how to prevent behaviors that are the basis of bullying, such as teasing, cliques, and gossip.

The Bully, the Bullied, and the Bystander, by Barbara Coloroso (New York: HarperCollins, 2002). From preschool to high school: how parents and teachers can help break the cycle of violence and cruelty in our youth.

Your Child: Bully or Victim? Understanding and Ending Schoolyard Tyranny, by Peter Sheras with Sherill Tippins (New York: Fireside, 2002). Strategies to help both victims and bullies.

For Kids

Bullies Are a Pain in the Brain, by Trevor Romain (Minneapolis, Minn.: Free Spirit, 1997). This book combines humor with serious, practical suggestions for coping with bullies. Ages 8 to 13.

Don't Laugh at Me, by Steve Seskin, Allen Shamblin, and Glin Dibley (New York: Tricycle Press, 2002). A wonderful picture book accompanied by a heartfelt tune that calls for tolerance and an end to bullying. Ages 6 to 12.

How to Handle Bullies, Teasers and Other Meanies: A Book That Takes the Nuisance out of Name Calling and Other Nonsense, by Kate Cohen-Posey (Highland City, Fla.: Rainbow Books, 1996). Great for helping kids understand what makes bullies tick and how to handle them. Ages 8 to 12.

Move Over, Twerp, by Martha G. Alexander (New York: Dial, 1981). Perfect if your little one is getting picked on by those bigger critters out there. Ages 4 to 7.

No More Victims: An Underdog Who Came Out on Top Challenges You to Put a Stop to Bullying in Your School, by Frank Peretti

(Nashville, Tenn.: W Publishing Group, 2000). A powerful account written for older kids and teens urging them to stop their bullying peers.

Operation Respect.com (www.operationrespect.com). An education program founded by Peter Yarrow of the musical group Peter, Paul, and Mary to boost tolerance and respect and stop bullying. A highly recommended and invaluable resource that is making a difference in schools and communities.

Please Stop Laughing at Me! One Woman's Inspirational Story, by Jodie Blanco (Avon, Mass.: Adams Media, 2003). An inspirational memoir about how one child was shunned and even physically abused by her classmates from elementary to high school. Impossible not to be moved! For young teens.

6

Cliques

Everyday Behaviors: Always the outsider; never included in the group; on the fringe

Friendship Skill Builder: Learning How and Where to Fit In

"They all hate me. They never let me play."
"What's wrong with me?"
"Why can't I get a nose job? Please, Mom. Maybe they'll let me sit with them."

WHAT'S WRONG?

The word *clique* strikes terror in the heart of every parent. A clique is an often tightly bound group of friends who hang out together and are not too keen on extending the "welcome wagon" to newcomers. Trying to break in can be as tough as trying to make it into an exclusive country club or sorority.

Being "in" is every child's dream, and being excluded is painful. There's nothing worse than sitting alone in the cafeteria or not getting invitations. Cliques rule. They often determine how you dress, who you hang out with, who's in, who's out. Pick your child up after school and you can instantly see which kids are mingled together with heads turned toward one each other for support and which are walking alone with eyes downcast in the shadow of misery. But this isn't about trying to make your child Miss or Mister Popularity—this is about helping your child avoid a diet of put-downs and humiliation that can be disastrous to her self-esteem and instead learn essential skills for a life of getting along, forming alliances, becoming trustworthy, and learning to become close to a broad variety of friends.

WHY IS THIS HAPPENING?

If your child is being permanently or even temporarily excluded by a group he wants to belong to, there are many questions you need to ask to figure out why this is happening.

- ☐ Is this a sudden or recent exclusion?
- ☐ Has your child never been a member of any group?
- ☐ Do you think this rejection could be the result of being "really different," such as being of a different color, culture, or economic situation?
- ☐ Is this really a group *you* want your child to belong to? Are you pushing your child to belong to a group she really doesn't want to join?
- ☐ Is your child doing anything that is turning the kids off? (If so, what is it: being too pushy, too meek, too loud, too flamboyant, too boring?)
- ☐ Does your child have poor hygiene or wear unfashionable clothes?
- ☐ Is your kid brand new to the scene?

- [ ] Does your kid have a bad reputation? (If so, also see Bad Reputation.)
- [ ] Do you or your family have a bad reputation?
- [ ] Does your child have other friends whom the clique doesn't approve of? Is your daughter's boyfriend attractive to a member of the clique?
- [ ] Do the members of this group all share a common bond your child doesn't possess, such as sports, boyfriends, ethnicity, or past history?
- [ ] Is your child aspiring to belong to a group that is too high up the popularity ladder?
- [ ] Does your child lack the social skills that would help her fit in better?

What is your best guess as to why your child is having problems with cliques? Write your thoughts here, then make a plan to change anything that can be changed.

_____

_____

_____

FRIENDSHIP SKILL BUILDER

Learning How and Where to Fit In
Cliques will always be with us; there's no avoiding them. It's human nature to form friendship groups that bond together and tend to have strong feelings about who's in and who's out. But you can help your child figure out whether it's

worthwhile to get into a particular group or move on to another. Here's how.

1. **Ask yourself: "Is this the right group for me?"** Do you really admire these kids? Do they have the same interests as you? Do you feel comfortable with them, or are you barking up the wrong tree?
2. **Notice how the group looks.** Is there a special way the members dress, talk, use makeup, or wear their hair? Now look at your appearance. Is there anything you'd be willing to change? Don't think major makeover or changing who you are but one or two things to tweak, like your haircut or shoes.
3. **Pick one person to start with.** Who in this clique is the most likely candidate to become your ally? Look at the person and smile or say hello. If the person smiles back or gives a friendly greeting, take it from there.
4. **Give it time.** Keep at it. Show this person your friendly side every day. Smile. Hold open her locker door. Give a deserved compliment. Say hi. Wave hello. Offer a vacant seat. Little by little you can build this relationship into a real friendship, which can help you enter into the clique.
5. **Don't push it.** If the person you've chosen isn't friendly in return, don't sulk. Move on and choose someone else or another group altogether.

WHAT SHOULD I SAY?

- **Express empathy.** "I know how tough it must be to be shunned like this. Let's figure out what we can do about it."
- **Provide a balanced view.** "Everyone does not hate you.

What about your friend Shelley?" "Nobody has it made at first." "A lot of famous people say they were unpopular in high school, like Bill Gates, Steven Spielberg, and Christina Aguilar. You'll find your niche."

- *Don't press too hard.* "This is a tough topic. I'm here when you need me." It can be humiliating for your child to confess this kind of rejection. Just being available and supportive may be a good first step. Later she may open up.

- *Find out the facts.* "You need to help me understand what's really going on during lunch. Can you show me how it plays out in action? How does it really look?" 🛑 **Charlene C. Giannetti and Margaret Sagarese, authors of *Cliques,* interviewed hundreds of middle schoolers and found that one of the best ways for kids to open up about the problems of cliques at their school is to have them draw a map of where everyone sits in the cafeteria.** 🛑 This map will help you see where your child "fits in" and give you a sense of the social dynamics at her school.

- *Don't knock the other kids.* Yes, they're snubbing your kid, but criticizing them won't help. Your child wants their friendship, so don't say, "Those kids are stupid. Why would you want to be friends with them anyway?" Do say, "We can see those kids have their way of seeing and doing things. We just have to find a way for you to fit in."

- *Don't push too hard on being popular.* Some parents over-emphasize the need to be good looking or to be in with the in group. Ask yourself if you're not trying to compensate for your own high school experiences. Or maybe your expectations for this particular child are unrealistic. Don't say, "Oh, she's so cute! The boys are always going to want to take her out." "I can't believe you didn't get invited to that party."

- *Push harder on interests and activities.* Instead of focusing on popularity, encourage your child to develop other skills and pursuits. "Hey, you're such a great guitarist. What about forming that band you always talked about?" "I really admire the way you committed to reading to the kids at the shelter every Sunday afternoon. Do you think Kara might want to join you next time?" De-escalating the huge importance of popularity by encouraging your child to develop other aspects of her life may actually boost your child's social standing.

WHAT SHOULD I DO?

- *Talk to teachers.* Is it as bad as your kid makes it out to be? Find out the reality of cliques in your child's school by talking to those adults who are with the kids every day.
- *Don't assume your child has to be at the top of the heap.* Your child may assume that being popular makes you happy. But both of you should keep in mind that this may not be the best long-term goal.
- *Identify one ally.* One friend can be your child's social entry card. Tell your child not to aim at first for the whole group but to start with just a one-to-one relationship with someone already there.
- *Help him blend in.* Superficial as it may seem to you, having the right look, clothing, and hairstyle can be critical for being accepted by a clique. Take a good look at the crowd your child is trying to join and then make a few suggestions.
- *Try a different direction.* If your child is rebuffed by one group, encourage her to try another that may be more appropriate. Sociological studies have revealed an amazing number of different cliques and groups on a typical high school campus, including everything from athletes to geeks to arty types.
- *Encourage special strengths.* Help your child identify what's really special or unique about her, such as being a good singer, writer, musician, artist, athlete, or dedicated community worker. Use positive labels to help her reframe her-

self. Ultimately this can both increase her self-confidence and make her more attractive to new friends.

- ***Help manage frustrations.*** This kind of rejection can be very traumatic, so offer your child healthy outlets and strategies for coping. Suggest that she keep a journal, talk to a mentor, and express herself in her favorite creative way, such as through music, painting, or drawing.
- ***Watch for downslide.*** If you think your child is really having a bad time, be available. Schedule a few weekends together and plan things your child enjoys. Take him to the gym with you. Take her to lunch. Tune in to any red flags, such as poor grades, changes in eating or sleeping habits, mood swings, and anger or withdrawal, which could indicate problems he's not discussing with you. If things get really tough, consider seeking professional help.

 FRIENDSHIP TIP

Understanding the Types of Cliques
Researchers followed third- through sixth-grade students in their community for eight years and discovered that they divided themselves into four social categories based on peer status or cliques:

- *The Popular Clique* was about 35 percent of the population and the "coolest" by kid standards. Membership included the most beautiful, athletic, affluent, charming.
- *The Fringe* was made up of about 10 percent of the kids; these were the "wannabes" who copied the dress, style, and mannerisms of the most popular clique but whose membership in the group was clearly not permanent.

- *Middle Friendship Circles* consisted of about 45 percent of the kids, who formed smaller groups with their own culture and identity, most often based on unique interests (the skaters, geeks, musicians, stoners).
- *The Loners* made up about 10 percent of the population and represented children with no friends or group membership.

21-DAY FRIENDSHIP FOLLOW-UP

Over the next 21 days, here's what I will do to help my child learn Friendship Skill Builder: Learning How and Where to Fit In:

FRIENDSHIP SKILL BUILDER BOOKS

For Parents and Teachers

And Words Can Hurt Forever: How to Protect Adolescents from Bullying, Harassment, and Emotional Violence, by James Garbarino and Ellen deLara (New York: Free Press, 2002). A powerful must-read for parents and educators who want to stop cruel, vicious kid attitudes.

Behind My Back: Girls Write About Bullies, Cliques, Popularity, and Jealousy, by Rachel Simmons (New York: Harvest Books, 2004). Best-selling author of *Odd Girl Out* writes a powerful book for preteen and teen girls.

Cliques: 8 Steps to Help Your Child Survive the Social Jungle, by Charlene C. Giannetti and Margaret Sagarese (New York: Broadway Books, 2001). A fresh perspective on a wide-scale problem; details an eight-step program to help parents turn around the climate of cruelty that distresses so many kids.

Girl Wars: 12 Strategies That Will End Female Bullying, by Cheryl Dellasega and Charisse Nixon (New York: Simon & Schuster, 2003). Two experts offer strategies on how to prevent relational aggression and help girls navigate through those clique land mines.

Odd Girl Out: The Hidden Culture of Aggression in Girls, by Rachel Simmons (Orlando: Harcourt, 2002). A wake-up call about the hidden world of cruelty among girls.

Queen Bees and Wannabes: Helping Your Daughter Survive Cliques, Gossip, Boyfriends, and Other Realities of Adolescence, by Rosalind Wiseman (New York: Three Rivers Press, 2002). Useful guide and step-by-step instructions to help your daughter learn how to survive the all-too-common cruelties of growing up.

Reviving Ophelia: Saving the Selves of Adolescent Girls, by Mary Pipher (New York: Ballantine, 1994). Wonderful reading to help parents gain insight into girls' common experiences and the pain of growing up.

For Kids

Cliques, Phonies, and Other Baloney, by Trevor Romain (Minneapolis, Minn.: Free Spirit, 1998). Written for every kid who has ever felt excluded or trapped by a clique, this book blends humor with practical advice as it tackles a serious subject. Ages 8 to 13.

Mean Chicks, Cliques, and Dirty Tricks: A Real Girl's Guide to Getting Through the Day with Smarts and Style, by Erika V. Shearin Karres (Avon, Mass.: Adams Media, 2004). Terrific tips for girls, who are often very upset about the difficult social episodes they encounter. The book includes writings from girls in need of real-life, down-to-earth, objective help for tough situations dealing with peers who can be nasty and hurtful. Ages 12 to 15.

The Clique, by Cecily von Ziegesar (Boston: Little, Brown, 2004). Claire Lyons moves with her parents. Seventh grader Massie chooses to make Claire's life miserable for no other reason than that Claire's the new girl, and enlists her clique of friends, all part of the beautiful and popular crowd, to help with the harassment, catty comments, and plain mean-spiritedness. Ages 11 to 14.

The Girls, by Amy Goldman Koss (New York: Puffin, 2002). A realistic portrayal of a popular middle school clique's devolution as told through six narrators.

Friendship Issue 7

Clueless

Everyday Behaviors: Can't tell how friends are feeling; turns friends off without knowing it

Friendship Skill Builder: Recognizing How Your Friends Are Feeling

"But I didn't know he was upset."
"I didn't mean to hurt his feelings. It didn't look to me like he was ticked off."
"Why do the kids always think I don't care when I really do, Mom?"

WHAT'S WRONG?

Clueless isn't just a joke or a movie title. When it comes to friendship, it means not knowing what's really happening in terms of other kids' feelings, emotions, and interactions. It means being "emotionally unintelligent," and it's a huge disadvantage on the social front. If you can't read how your friends are really feeling, how can you offer support, know what to say or not to say, or even know when to stop doing what you're doing? Clueless kids are often perceived as insensitive, inept, or tactless. And these kids can get in trouble with friends and adults simply because they can't read the emotional cues of others. "Didn't you see that Dad was tired? How thoughtless of you to ask him to play catch!" "Couldn't you figure out that it wasn't a good time to talk to your teacher? I can't believe you're so tactless." "Didn't you know your friend was upset? That was rude! No wonder you didn't get invited to the party." This isn't funny. Clueless kids are more likely to be rejected and have serious problems making friends.

WHY IS THIS HAPPENING?

There are a number of reasons why your child may be turning her friends off without being aware of it. Here are just a few:

- ☐ Your family style doesn't encourage showing or talking about feelings.
- ☐ Your family or your child has experienced a recent illness or trauma that has left you or your child in a state of grief or anxiety.
- ☐ Your child is experiencing some emotional or neurological problem—anything from being overly shy to suffering from a learning or speech disorder.
- ☐ There may be cultural differences that make it difficult for your child to read his friends' emotions.
- ☐ Your child is doing things that annoy people, such as avoiding eye contact, talking too slowly or loudly, always touching and hugging other kids, or standing too close.
- ☐ Your child is not "getting it" when friends display strong feelings or sentiments. He doesn't recognize that a friend's

frown signals that he doesn't want to go ahead with the game even though he says yes; she doesn't compute that a friend's slumping in his chair means "Don't bother me"; he doesn't get that a friend's rolling eyes indicate he's getting annoyed.

☐ Your child uses the wrong words to express his feelings or those of his friends. She may say, "I'm really mad at you" when she's actually scared. Or she may ask a friend, "Why are you so sad?" when the child is in fact irritated and withdrawn.

What is your hunch about why your child is clueless? Write it here.

_____

_____

_____

FRIENDSHIP SKILL BUILDER

Recognizing How Your Friends Are Feeling
You can help your child's friendship-making skills by teaching her how to identify the feelings of others.

1. *Learn feeling words.* Study photographs, look at pictures in magazines, watch friends whenever you can, and begin to match feeling words with facial expressions, tones of voice, and body language. (See the activities discussed in the section What Should I Say?)

2. ***Watch your friend closely for clues.*** Look at his posture, listen to his voice, and notice his face. Is he standing straight, speaking confidently, and smiling? Is he slumped in a chair, using a voice you can hardly hear, and frowning?

3. ***Figure out how your friend is feeling.*** Is he sad, mad, frustrated, annoyed, embarrassed?

4. ***Show you understand.*** If he's happy about something, you might say, "Congratulations" and shake his hand. If it's a sad feeling, you might hug him. If she looks really stressed, ask if there's something you could do to help. Try to act in a way that best fits how your friend is feeling.

WHAT SHOULD I SAY?

- ***Explain emotional intelligence.*** "You may be having a problem understanding the clues your friends give you about how they're feeling. Kids don't always tell you whether they are sad or mad or even stressed or irritated. But they'll show you with their facial expressions, tone of voice, and posture."

- ***Play the "feeling name" game.*** Start by using words to describe how you see your child feels. "You look sad today. I can see your mouth has a huge frown." "Wow, you look really stressed. Your hands are clenched so tightly, and you're grinding your teeth." "What happened? Your eyes are glaring so it gives your face a mad look." Doing this can help your child name the correct feeling with the right word.

- ***Make an emotion scrapbook.*** Help your child collect pictures of a variety of facial expressions and paste them into a scrapbook. Be sure to include the six basic emotions: happy, sad, angry, surprised, afraid, and disgusted. Now make a game of naming the emotions with your child by asking, "How is this person feeling?" "Can you make your face look sad, too?"

- *Translate body language.* "When your friend Hannah curls up in a ball on the couch, you can be pretty sure she doesn't want you to disturb her." "If that boy puts his arm around you again, maybe it's because he likes you a lot." 🛑 **Research tells us that kids communicate through words only 7 percent of the time; the rest of their messages are sent via body language. So enhance your child's ability to understand this important form of communication.** 🛑

- *Guess people's emotions together.* Make a game out of watching other kids' expressions and body language at a playground, park, or shopping mall with your child. Try together to guess their emotional states: "How does her face look?" "He's standing with his arms crossed; how do you think he's feeling right now?" "Listen to the sound of that kid's voice. How do you think he feels?" "See how that girl is sitting next to the boy? She's frowning and folding her arms. Do you suppose she wants to be with him or not?"

- *Practice using different tones of voice.* If you notice that your child is speaking in a voice tone that is whiny, loud, sarcastic, angry, or sullen, help her realize the impact and how to modify it. "Did you see how Ryan made a frowning face when you used that whiny tone? Let's try saying the same thing a different way." "I'm going to say the same thing you just said two times. Tell me which sounds friendly and which doesn't." Rehearse the friendlier new voice tone. Tape it so she can hear it. Don't humiliate your child, but try to copy how he sounds to you. Once he gets the "right" voice, reinforce it again and again until the tone becomes a habit.

WHAT SHOULD I DO?

- *Search the photo album.* Look through an old family photo album together and find your child's "best look"—the facial expression people would want to be around. Also find an example of one you want to avoid. Take out her "best look" and tape it on her mirror or bulletin board so she can be inspired to use it.

- *Watch silent movies.* Turn off the sound on your television and watch a show or film for a few minutes together. Make a game out of trying to guess how the actors feel, using only what you see. You'll see dozens of nonverbal things people use to express their feelings. Tension behaviors might include blinking eyes rapidly, biting nails, twirling hair, clenching jaws, and grinding teeth. Withdrawal or uninterested behaviors might be folded arms, crossed legs, rolling eyes, and not facing the speaker. Expressions of interest might be nodding, smiling, leaning into the speaker, and standing or sitting close to the person.

- *Try a "switch off and on" technique.* Once child your knows the looks he should and shouldn't have, play the "switch off and on" game. Agree on a signal or special word to use in public, and if you see that sullen or angry expression on his face, use the signal to remind him to switch to that friendlier, more likable look.

- *Play "act out the emotion" charades.* Help your child learn to identify other people's feelings by asking her to show you how her friend would look if her dog died, if she were voted most popular, if her teacher caught her cheating, and so on.

- *Observe space and spacing.* Watch how close your child sits or stands in relation to her friends. If you've noticed that she's pushing too close or being too standoffish, help her learn a more appropriate distance that makes her friends more comfortable. Help her by pointing out the distance other kids maintain with their friends.

- *Play "How do I feel?" charades.* A fun, quiet car game is to have family members play "emotion" charades. Riders must try to guess the person's emotion. Just be sure to enforce the basic rule of charades: no talking. Only your face and body are allowed to express your feelings.

- *Teach good listening behaviors.* Show your child how to focus on what her friends are saying and also on nonverbal behaviors that really express their feelings, such as pouting, smiling, rolling their eyes, lowering their eyebrows, or glaring. 🛑 **Research has shown that two of the most frequently used behaviors of socially competent kids are smiling and eye contact.** 🛑

 FRIENDSHIP TIP

Nonverbal Cues

Drs. Marshall Duke and Stephen Nowicki, child psychologists at Emory University in Atlanta, found that one out of ten children, despite normal and even superior intelligence, has significant problems in nonverbal communication. This disability may explain why these kids have trouble getting along with others and just don't seem to fit in. Duke and Nowicki also discovered that the most well-liked children are very good at recognizing how their friends are feeling.

21-DAY FRIENDSHIP FOLLOW-UP

Over the next 21 days, here's what I will do to help my child learn Friendship Skill Builder: Recognizing How Your Friends Are Feeling:

_____

_____

_____

📖 FRIENDSHIP SKILL BUILDER BOOKS 📖

For Parents and Teachers

Helping the Child Who Doesn't Fit In, by Marshall Duke and Stephen Nowicki Jr. (Atlanta: Peachtree, 1992). Two psychologists offer parents, teachers, and caregivers a valuable guide to the puzzle of social rejection and its relationship to nonverbal language.

How to Raise a Child with a High EQ: A Parents' Guide to Emotional Intelligence, by Lawrence E. Shapiro (New York: Harper-Collins, 1997). A practical guide to helping children master social and emotional skills.

Problem Child or Quirky Kid? A Commonsense Guide, by Rita Sommers-Flanagan and John Sommers-Flanagan (Minneapolis, Minn.: Free Spirit, 2002). If you're wondering about your child's physical development, you can consult a medical professional. If you're worried about your child's attitudes, behaviors, feelings, or general development, finding the right information gets harder. This book gives you the advice you need to help your child—and yourself.

Teaching Your Child the Language of Social Success, by Marshall Duke, Stephen Nowicki Jr., and Elisabeth A. Martin (Atlanta: Peachtree, 1996). A wonderful reference to help you teach your children nonverbal skills so they can communicate more effectively and interact with others more successfully.

For Kids

Stone-Faced Boy, by Paula Fox (New York: Aladdin, 1968). Ridicule and rejection from classmates cause Gus to "turn off" his emotions and become "stone-faced." Ages 11 to 14.

Tobin Learns to Make Friends, by Diane Murrell (Arlington, Tex.: Future Horizons, 2001). This colorful picture book is quite effective in teaching social skills to children with autism, Asperger's Syndrome, and other pervasive developmental disorders. Follow Tobin, a train, as he learns to make friends and engage in proper social activities. Ages 3 to 8.

Friendship Issue  8

Different

Everyday Behaviors: Excluded or ostracized because of major characteristics, often visible, that are unlike those of the other kids

Friendship Skill Builder: Improving Your Likability

"They won't invite me, Mom, because I talk funny."
"I hate this school. Everyone calls me 'fag' and throws stuff at me."
"All the kids make fun of my skin. They say it looks like mud."

WHAT'S WRONG?

Let's face it: all people don't look, talk, or act the same. In our twenty-first-century society there are many kids of different colors, cultures, religions, and economic backgrounds. There are kids who have learning disabilities, are overweight, have mental or physical health problems, have visual or hearing impairments, are in wheelchairs, have different sexual orientations, are geniuses, come from infamous or dysfunctional families. What all these kids have in common is the problem of being really different and therefore marginalized by the group because they don't fit in easily. They often experience debilitating chronic rejection and as a result may suffer from anxiety, depression, and acute loneliness.

WHY IS THIS HAPPENING?

The trick here is to look beyond what makes your child different. Many children who are blatantly different from their peers still manage not only to fit in but to flourish. So the question goes beyond the obvious discrepancies of background, economic status, or disability: What is your child doing to turn the kids off? There are things that are definitely beyond your control, but for our purposes let's focus on what you *can* possibly help change. The first step is to consider how the items in the follow list apply to your child:

- ☐ Has your child come to terms with the difference between her and most of the other kids around?
- ☐ Does your kid avoid or deny the fact of his being different?
- ☐ Is your child angry and defiant about being unlike the others?
- ☐ Does she have a chip on her shoulder or blame everyone for what's unusual about her?
- ☐ Has your child withdrawn from the social scene and given up on fitting in or having friends?
- ☐ Does your child want everyone to feel sorry for her?
- ☐ Does your kid refuse to accommodate any well-intentioned efforts by wannabe friends who are trying to get closer but don't know how?

☐ Is your child openly obnoxious and disagreeable? Does he deliberately turn people off because he feels so victimized?

☐ Is your child overprotected in a way that prevents healthy relationships?

Write down what you think is the main reason your kid is having a hard time being different or being accepted by his peers.

_____

_____

_____

WHAT SHOULD I SAY?

- *Express empathy.* "I know it's really tough being the only black kid in your class." "You're right, Christmas can be a hard time if you're Jewish." This is painful stuff. So acknowledge that it will be tough and may continue to be hard the rest of her life.

- *Let your kid know if there are things he needs to change.* "If you deny your background or who you really are, your friends won't respect you." "You're always yelling at the kids; if you want them to like you, you'll need to be more courteous." "Do you think it's Jerry's fault that you have trouble reading? You can't blame him for your disability. He's trying to be helpful."

- *Focus on one thing.* The total number of changes that need to be made may seem overwhelming, so start out with just one thing and work on that before moving on. "For the next month we're going to work on controlling that anger. I know you're frustrated that you can't hear what's going on in class, but that's no reason to start hitting all the kids sitting around you." "Kevin, I know you read as well as the

FRIENDSHIP SKILL BUILDER

Improving Your Likability
Use the following script and teach the steps listed here to boost your child's likability quotient with her friends. Tell her, "You are who you are. Some things can't be changed. Be proud of your differences. Some things about you, however, you have control over and can be improved. The fact is, kids accept or reject you not only because of who you are but also because of how you act. So here are some things you can do to improve your 'likability.'"

1. *Make a good first impression.* Check your personal hygiene and style. Take a look at how the rest of the kids dress or wear their hair. Are there one or two things you could do to look cool and fit in better?

2. *Smile more.* It may seem silly, and you don't want to overdo it, but the fact is that kids are more attracted to other kids who smile. So whenever it's appropriate and you have the opportunity, flash that grin.

3. *Make eye contact.* If you find yourself in a culture or community where people favor direct eye-to-eye communication, try it. It's a good way to acknowledge someone and begin a relationship. Kids like to be acknowledged, and one way to let them know you care is to use eye contact.

4. *Use appropriate compliments.* Nobody appreciates flattery when it's not deserved. But when it's sincere, nothing can be more appealing than heartfelt praise or congratulations. So be sure not to miss a chance to say things like "Nice job!" "Great outfit!" or "Thanks for the help."

> **5.** *Use a friendly tone of voice.* You can say nice
> things, have a great smile, and make good eye con-
> tact, but unless your voice has a friendly and up-
> beat sound to it, the kids won't want to hear what
> you're saying. So listen to people who have a warm
> and welcoming tone of voice and then practice
> your own best tone of voice.
>
> It may take some time to practice and apply these skills,
> but in the long term you will probably find these very
> useful in gaining new friends.

other kids when you're called on to read out loud in class,
but the kids don't think it's funny anymore that you can
only speak Russian. From now on, it's no more class clown-
ing for you, and I'll check every day with your teacher."

- *Teach a comeback.* If your child is being teased constantly,
you might help her develop a snappy response. For example: "You're too thin." "Well, thanks for noticing. I'm trying
out for the Guinness Book of World Records." "You've got
a wheelchair!" "Yeah, where's yours?" "Hey, Four-Eyes!"
"That would sure help. I can't see well enough out of the
two I have." (See Teasing.)

WHAT SHOULD I DO?

- *Accept your child's differences.* In some cases it's easier to
have empathy and understanding for the reactions your
child is experiencing because you share his differences. You
too may be of a different culture, ethnicity, or economic
status; or perhaps you have a mood disorder, so you know
what it feels like to be shunned or rejected. In other cases,
however, your child may have a problem or disability that
you've haven't experienced. So for your child to come to
terms with his differences, you must accept them yourself.

Be sure to be clear with your child that he has your unconditional love and support.

- **Be realistic.** Remember, there are some things you can change and some things you can't. Your child may always be different, but he may not always be disliked or rejected.
- **Boost a talent.** Find the special skill or talent that your child is really good at: chess, baseball, science, singing, drawing, guitar. Every child has something to shine for—what is your child's? Find it, nurture it, and capitalize on it so it can become a way for him to gain attention and recognition and to make friends.
- **Help him fit in.** First impressions and how a child looks are two things that are not too hard to fix. No matter how different your child is, he can be well groomed, have good hygiene, be courteous, and dress in a style that fits in with the rest. And there may be other things you can do in some cases, such as making sure a child moving from another country has a chance to learn the language.
- **Find a mentor.** If there is another adult or older child nearby who shares the same difference and has an upbeat, positive attitude, seek him out. Any person who is empathic and supportive can be helpful. 🛑 **Research has proven that two-thirds of children with serious obstacles in their lives, such as learning disabilities, physical handicaps, or dysfunctional home environments, were able to compensate if they had a mentor who believed in them.** 🛑
- **Volunteer.** If your child is able, be sure to encourage him or her to do volunteer work in the community. Ideally it should be in an area that your child cares about or that matches a natural interest or talent. You might also want to pair her with a younger child who has the same differences so she can be the mentor.
- **Participate in school activities.** Any way you can engage in the school community can help your child make friends and fit in better. Get to know the teachers and other parents, volunteer to help out in class, join the PTA.

- ***Resist the urge to defend and protect.*** There may be occasions when it's necessary to intervene, but jumping in and fighting your kid's battles doesn't really help in the long run. I know this is going to be very tough, but your child has to learn to stand up for himself.

- ***Provide positive role models.*** It's often helpful for kids who are different to recognize that there are many people out there just like them who are happy and hugely successful. So find examples who match up with your kid, from Helen Keller and Jackie Joyner Kersey to Wilma Rudolph and Christopher Reeve.

- ***Be sure your child is in the most supportive environment.*** Ideally you can work with your local school and community to create an atmosphere of acceptance and tolerance of your child, but in some cases it just may be impossible, so you'll need to switch schools or move. You may want to do some research on where individuals and institutions have been supportive in the past.

- ***Get the best help.*** If your child has a physical, emotional, or mental disability, be sure to research and seek out the best possible help you can. And don't stop until you find it. If the differences have to do with culture, religion, or ethnicity, find people and organizations who emphasize pride and solidarity to support your child and your family.

 ## 21-DAY FRIENDSHIP FOLLOW-UP

Over the next 21 days, here's what I will do to help my child learn Friendship Skill Builder: Improving Your Likability:

_____

_____

_____

FRIENDSHIP TIP

Why Warmheartedness Counts
According to recent research, the quality that most at-tracts peers to a child is kindness or warmheartedness. "Even among preadolescents and young teens—kids who are keenly aware of in-groups and out-groups and the troublesome aspect of popularity-as-dominance—it is those humane and decent peers who are truly embraced." And that's a huge clue for parents: if you want your "dif-ferent" child to be liked, boost his kindness quotient by nurturing his caring side.

 FRIENDSHIP SKILL BUILDER BOOKS

For Parents and Teachers
"I Think I Can, I Know I Can!" by Susan Isaacs and Wendy Ritchey (New York: St. Martin's Press, 1989). A tool to help-ing kids learn to replace self-doubts with positive self-talk.

Nurturing Resilience in Our Children: Answers to the Most Impor-tant Parenting Questions, by Robert Brooks and Sam Goldstein (New York: Contemporary Books, 2003). More valuable ad-vice from two credible experts.

Positive Self-Talk for Children: Teaching Self-Esteem Through Af-firmations, by Douglas Blouch (New York: Bantam Books, 1993). A wonderful source that instructs parents, step-by-step, in how to help toddlers to teens turn off the negative voice within and activate the powerful "yes" voice.

Raising Resilient Children: Fostering Strength, Hope, and Optimism in Your Child, by Robert Brooks and Sam Goldstein (New York: Contemporary Books, 2001). This unique, wise book helps parents focus on their children's strengths in overcoming obstacles, not their weaknesses.

The Optimistic Child, by Martin E. P. Seligman (Boston: Houghton Mifflin, 1995). A great guide offering parents specific tools to teach kids of all ages life skills to bolster genuine self-esteem, optimism, problem solving, and hope.

For Kids

Comeback! Four True Stories, by Jim O'Connor (New York: Random House, 1992). Here are the tales of four famous athletes who overcame serious injuries or debilitating conditions through effort, perseverance, and an optimistic outlook. Ages 7 to 11.

Fortunately, by Remy Charlip (Old Tappan, N.J.: Macmillan, 1987). This is an absolute must for young readers. It's a model of changing your unfortunates and turning them into fortunates. Ages 4 to 10.

Friendship Issue 9

Doesn't Share

Everyday Behaviors: Doesn't take turns; hoards toys; won't share; overly possessive of his things

Friendship Skill Builder: Choosing Fairly

"But that Raggedy-Ann is mine!"
"No one touches my computer but me. It's off-limits."
"Sure he lost his textbook, but why should I let him have mine?"

WHAT'S WRONG?

"It's mine." "But I had it first." "I want a turn!" Sound familiar? All parents want their kids to "play nice" by sharing, taking turns, and cooperating with their friends. After all, it means that their child is learning how to socialize and get along. It also signifies a big moment in moral development and social

131

growth, because once a child can share it means he has transitioned from the "egocentric" stage (in which the world basically revolves around him and his needs). He can consider the needs and feelings of others, which is essential to making and keeping friends.

Learning to share, take turns, and cooperate doesn't always happen by chance. Some kids need a lot more reminders. But just telling kids to "play nice" doesn't change behavior; you need to show them how to share and help them understand why it's important that they do so. Sharing is one of the first social skills kids learn, so it's also one of the most important. If your child can't share and take turns, her friendship-making capabilities will be greatly jeopardized. After all, who wants to be with a kid who hoards the video games? And when will she learn those skills if not now? College or the workplace, in adult relationships and marriage will be too late. So start boosting this friendship builder right now.

WHY IS THIS HAPPENING?

Here are some things to consider as to why your child has difficulty sharing or taking turns. Check those that might apply to your child or family:

☐ Is your child young, so it's difficult for him to cooperate and think about the needs and feelings of others? 🛑 **Don't expect toddlers to be able to share and take turns without adult guidance: they're at the egocentric stage of development in which the world still revolves around them. By around two-and-a-half years of age, children are able to manage simple social interactions that contain the beginnings of turn taking and responding to others, but still will need frequent adult reminders.** 🛑

- [ ] Are you or another adult member of your family modeling taking turns and cooperating?
- [ ] Has your kid never been expected to share or consider the needs of her friends?
- [ ] Has he lacked social experiences with kids through which he would have learned how to take turns and consider the needs of others?
- [ ] Has he had previous bad experiences sharing with kids? For instance, might his generosity have been taken advantage of by kids? Were his shared items abused, broken, or stolen?
- [ ] Is he materialistic and selfish? Have you emphasized the importance of having things instead of respecting other people's feelings?
- [ ] Is the group he's hanging around with too aggressive or plain inconsiderate? Are other kids not sharing with him?
- [ ] Is she hesitant to share *all* her possessions or just *certain* possessions? If so, why? Do those items have special meaning or value to your child? Does your child *not* have many things, and thus covets those things she does have?
- [ ] Is this a power issue? Does she need to feel she's in control and to call the shots, including who plays with what?
- [ ] Is your kid angry or anxious, or does he have some other problem that makes it difficult for him to think of others?

What is your best guess as to why your child does not share or take turns? Write your idea.

_____

_____

_____

_____

_____

_____

FRIENDSHIP SKILL BUILDER

Choosing Fairly

There are a number of great gimmicks to help kids learn to share, take turns, and make things fair among friends. They're also handy for deciding who gets to go first, breaking ties, reducing conflicts, and making sure everyone gets to use a toy or object for the same amount of time. Here are a few strategies to teach your child; just make sure to practice them together before she tries them out in real life.

1. *Use "Grandma's Rule."* The rule is simple: If you cut the cake, the other person can decide which piece to take. The rule can apply to lots of things. For example: if you chose the game, the other person gets to go first; if you poured the lemonade, the other person gets to choose his glass first.

2. *Flip a coin.* This helps if you and your friend can't decide on rules, who gets to choose what to do, or who goes first. The friend who is to toss the coin asks the other to call heads or tails. If the caller correctly chooses the side that is face up, he wins the toss; if not, then the other kid wins and gets to choose.

3. *Use a timer.* First, agree on a set amount of time—usually only a few minutes—for using an item. Then set a timer (like an oven timer, a sand timer, or the minute hand on your watch). When the time is up, the item is passed to the next kid for her turn.

4. *Rock, paper, scissors.* At the count of three (sometimes counted out with the words "ro," "sham,"

"bo"), each kid simultaneously thrusts out a hand forming rock (fist), paper (flat), or scissors (two fingers). Rock breaks scissors; paper covers rock; scissors cut paper. Whoever survives the round is the winner.

5. ***Pick a number.*** One player chooses a number between 1 and 20 (or any specified number) and writes it on a slip of paper without telling the others. Each remaining player gets one chance to guess the number. The person whose guess is closest to the number gets to decide the game or goes first.

6. ***Eenie, meenie, meinie, moe.*** Say the old rhyme by pointing your finger to the other person and yourself with every other word: "Eenie, meenie, meinie, moe. Catch a tiger by the toe. If he hollers make him pay fifty dollars every day. My mother told me to choose the very best one, and you are not 'it.' " The person who is pointed at last is not "it," and the remaining person gets to go first or pick the activity.

WHAT SHOULD I SAY?

- ***Expect your child to share.*** Explicitly state to your child that you expect him to share and take turns. And right before a friend arrives is the best time to remind him, "Karen will be here shortly, so let's set out the toys you'd like to share and that you think she would enjoy." "Remember, sharing is not an option. I expect you to share." "Johnny's coming in a few minutes, so remember our house rule about being considerate of your friends."
- ***Remind your child about your sharing rules.*** It's a good idea to emphasize that your child may share only items that belong to her; otherwise, permission must be granted from

the owner. You might rehearse with your child things to say in those sometimes tricky situations with friends. "I'm sorry, we can't play with that. It belongs to my brother, so it's not something I can share." "That's my dad's. We have to ask him before we can use it."

- *Stress the value of sharing.* Pointing out the impact sharing has on the other child boosts the likelihood that your child will repeat the behavior. "Did you see Kali's smile when you shared your toys? You made her happy." "Joshua really enjoyed coming over because you were such a nice host and shared the equipment."

- *Point out the negative effect on others when your kid doesn't share.* Your child needs to understand *why* not sharing is not appreciated and turns kids off. "Not letting Stella play with your dolls wasn't kind. You need to share your toys, or your friends won't be happy and won't want to play with you." "Why do you think your friends wanted to go home early today? Yes, never letting kids have a turn isn't fun. Kids won't want to come over if they know they're just going to sit and watch you play." "Would you want to be in a study group with a kid who never lets you have a turn on the computer?"

- *Rehearse the right way.* "Instead of grabbing the toy, tell your brother that you'd like a turn. Now you try." "Pretend I'm you're friend. Ask me what I'd like to do." "Let's try that again so you give your friend a chance to play with the bubble blower."

- *Use role reversal.* When your child doesn't share, ask her to put herself in the other child's place. "How would you feel if John treated you that way and took more toys to play with?" "Josh left looking pretty unhappy. Put yourself in your friend's shoes. What do you think he'd like to say to you about the time he spent watching you on the computer all afternoon?" Doing this is one way to help your child shift from thinking about herself to considering how her friends feel.

- *Praise sharing efforts.* "I noticed how you divided the toys so you both had the same amount. Kevin really enjoyed playing with you this time." "Did you see Kelly's smile when you asked her what she wanted to do? You made her happy." "Thanks for giving your MTV video to your brother. I know you don't listen to rap anymore, but he just loves it." 🛑 Research finds that encouraging kids to report the sharing, kind deeds of their peers increases their cooperative actions as well as decreases their aggressive behaviors. 🛑

- *Provide opportunities to share.* "There are kids who don't have any toys, and you have so many. Why not choose a few you don't use so we can take them to the Salvation Army?" "Mrs. Jones next door is all by herself. Let's share some of the cookies we baked with her. She'd be so appreciative."

WHAT SHOULD I DO?

- *Teach by example.* The best way kids learn isn't by our lectures but by showing them. Let your child see you sharing and taking turns so she has a model to copy. Make a point of giving her the biggest portion of dessert, offer to share your favorite slippers or the funny hat she loves to put on, take an evening to share your time—the most precious commodity you have as far as she's concerned—with her.

- *Show how to share.* Instead of telling your kids to share, show them how to take turns. Get on the floor with your little one—and gently roll a rubber ball back and forth between you. As you do, say "My turn. Now it's your turn. Roll it back to Mommy." Your child will begin to get the idea that sharing means taking turns. For older kids, dust off those old board games, such as Monopoly, Clue, Chutes and Ladders, and checkers, then graduate to playing catch, Frisbee, or video games, and, ultimately, to doing work projects in the home, yard, or community. In each case you'll be teaching your child those essential friendship skills—sharing, turn taking, deciding who goes first, and cooperating.

- *Teach your child not to expect anything in return.* Emphasize that just because your kid should share, she should not anticipate getting something back. The reason to share is that it's "nice to be nice."

- *Tell her to store valuable equipment.* 🛑 Instructing your child to put away any toys he does not want to share before his guest arrives actually promotes sharing, especially in five- to nine-year-olds. 🛑 There are certain possessions that are very special to your child, so putting those items away before a guest arrives minimizes potential conflicts. Then say, "Anything you leave out are things you have to share."

- *Rotate family roles.* One way to help kids understand the value of sharing is to find opportunities to rotate different family roles and privileges so each family member gets a turn. Possibilities might include rotating chores; choosing the nightly television show, movie, video rental, family outing, or dessert; or even getting to sit in the coveted "hot seat" (front passenger seat of the car). If you hold family meetings, consider rotating roles, such as chairperson, parliamentarian, meeting planner, and secretary.

- *Turn TV viewing into a moral lesson.* 🛑 Research finds that kids who watch shows like *Mr. Rogers, SpongeBob SquarePants,* and *Sesame Street* (for younger kids) or *Seventh Heaven* and *Gilmore Girls* (for teens) are more likely to imitate the cooperative, sharing behaviors of the actors *if an adult discusses the positive behaviors with the child.* 🛑 So check out the TV listings and look for prosocial shows to watch with your child. Just be sure to discuss the considerate behaviors you see and their value: "Did you notice how Joanie shared with her brother? Did you see how much Kevin appreciated it?"

FRIENDSHIP TIP

Sharing and Character
Learning to share is not only necessary for making and
keeping friends but also essential to developing solid
character. Dr. T. Berry Brazelton, professor emeritus of
pediatrics at Harvard Medical School, strongly urges us
to help our kids learn to share as soon as possible, at least
by age two or three. The bottom line: toddlers are *not*
too young for us to start emphasizing this core friendship skill.

- *Model the value of sharing equipment.* Computers, tools,
  technological expertise—all have a role in working together and getting things done these days. Take a moment to
  tell a story to show your kids directly how even in this age
  of technology there are so many great ways to cooperate:
  sharing e-mail lists, creating website links, sharing computer
  files, creating cell phone networks, and making websites for
  family and friends are just a few. Then find ways to show
  your older child how to work out the shared use of your
  family's technology so that everyone's interests and goals
  are met in a timely manner. "Let's work together to make a
  computer schedule that's fair for all of us, so everyone gets
  what he or she needs."
- *Set a consequence.* If despite all your efforts your kid still
  continues to hoard and refuses to share, it's time to set a
  natural consequence. Some teachers set a classroom rule
  that works wonders: "If you don't share, you don't play."
  The rule can work for any age. Another idea: if your child
  refuses to share an item, the toy is given a "time-out" for a
  specified time. When the time-out is up, the friend who

had been denied the toy gets first option on it. For older kids, try this great teacher rule: "If you don't share, the other person takes two turns in a row."

21-DAY FRIENDSHIP FOLLOW-UP

Over the next 21 days, here's what I will do to help my child learn Friendship Skill Builder: Choosing Fairly:

_____

_____

_____

 FRIENDSHIP SKILL BUILDER BOOKS

For Parents and Teachers

Learning to Play, Playing to Learn: Games and Activities to Teach Sharing, Caring, and Compromise, by Charlie Steffens and Spencer Gorin (Los Angeles: Lowell House, 1997). Over sixty unique and entertaining activities that foster cooperation, nurture positive conduct, and help kids learn to get along.

For Kids

Cooperation (Values to Live By), by Janet Rieherck (Chicago: Child's World, 1990). A simple book that describes why cooperation is so important. Ages 5 to 8.

Harriet's Halloween Candy, by Nancy L. Carlson (Minneapolis, Minn.: Lerner, 2003). Harriet learns the hard way that sharing her Halloween candy makes her feel much better than eating it all herself. Ages 4 to 8.

I Am Sharing, by Mercer Mayer (New York: Random House, 1998). The cooperative Little Critter shows how he shares his toys, his crayons, and even his ice cream with his little sister. He even shares the TV—except when it's time for his favorite show! Ages 4 to 8.

It's Mine! by Leo Lionni (New York: Knopf, 1985). A little frog always bickers and fights about what's his until he finally learns about "ours." Ages 4 to 8.

Me First, by Helen Lester (Boston: Houghton Mifflin, 1995). Pinkerton Pig is pushy and greedy but overcomes his selfishness when he learns that being first isn't always the best. Ages 3 to 5.

Not Like That, Like This! by Tony Bradman and Joanna Burroughs (New York: Oxford University Press, 1988). Dad and Thomas go for a walk and find themselves in a most peculiar situation: both their heads are stuck through the iron railings of a fence. Everyone has to cooperate to get Dad unstuck. Ages 3 to 6.

The Kids Can Help Book, by Suzanne Logan (New York: Perigee Books, 1992). A wonderful compilation of ways that kids can volunteer and make a difference in the world by sharing. Ages 10 to 13.

Whipping Boy, by Sid Fleischman (Orlando: Harcourt, 1993). Young, self-centered Prince Brat runs away with his whipping boy in this briskly told tale of high adventure. A Newbery Medal winner. Ages 10 to 13.

10

Fights

Everyday Behaviors: Physically aggressive; pushes, pokes, bites, hits, and hurts others

Friendship Skill Builder: Expressing Your Feelings and Needs Without Violence

"I had to hit him. He wouldn't do what I wanted."
"I can't help it, Mom. She said the meanest thing."
"What do you mean I'm too rough? How else am I going to get a turn?"

WHAT'S WRONG?

Fighting. Hitting. Biting. Pushing. Inflicting pain. Hurting other kids. Sound familiar? They are typical behaviors aggressive kids use to make their needs known and to get their way. Aside from being signs of poor self-control, they are absolutely deadly to your child's friendship quotient. If you don't help him temper his physical aggression, you'll find that he will not only have problems keeping friends (believe me, no parent wants a fighter to spend the night, let alone spend time with her kid) but also earn a bad reputation. Fighting can be deadly to popularity and cause your child to be excluded from play dates, birthday parties, and sleepovers. And watch out: if you don't do something about this now, fighting can become entrenched as a behavior. So it's essential that you stop this friendship buster ASAP.

WHY IS THIS HAPPENING?

Before we jump the gun and go straight to squelching your kid's fighting, we need to figure out the mystery behind this behavior. *Hint:* Most "fights" actually are initiated by verbal barbs, insults, and put-downs. If this is true for your child, see Teased, Insensitive, or Bossy. You already have the evidence, so let's play Columbo and see if we can find some clues and causes. Check ones that may apply to your child. (See also Hot Tempered.)

- ☐ Could he be copying someone's behavior?
- ☐ Does he know how to calm down? Does he lack the ability to regulate his emotions?
- ☐ Is there a change in your family that might be causing undue stress?
- ☐ Is there anything going on at school that might be creating extra pressure?
- ☐ Is he aggressive toward *all* kids or just *some* kids? If it is just *some* kids, who are they? Or are the other kids aggressive toward him?
- ☐ Is he overscheduled, needing attention, or physically tired?
- ☐ Does he feel he isn't being listened to? Does he feel he isn't getting his needs met?

☐ Could she be defending herself? Has she now or in the past been bullied? Teased? Harassed? Threatened?

☐ What about what he watches: is he consumed by violent media images?

☐ If your child is older, have you ever smelled alcohol on his breath?

☐ Is there any trouble with relationships, romantic and otherwise? One of the biggest reasons teens fight is over romantic relationships. Could this be an issue?

What is your best guess as to why your child is fighting?

_____

_____

_____

_____

WHAT SHOULD I SAY?

- *Set zero tolerance for fighting.* Convey your expectation that flaunting aggressions will no longer be permitted. Not ever. "Fighting is never acceptable. There are no excuses for it, and you must stop now."

- *Be clear about consequences.* "Any time you hit, you will be grounded." For younger kids: "If you hit, you will go to time-out every time."

- *Be available before the hurt explodes.* If you see your kid is in a conflict with a friend and his feelings are starting to boil over, talk. He needs a sounding board and a way to defuse. "I notice how upset you are. Let's see if there's a way we can work this through so you and your friend don't come to blows."

- *Be sure to talk after a fight about "next time" possibilities.* "You hit your friend when you were angry. You are not al-

FRIENDSHIP
SKILL BUILDER

**Expressing Your Feelings
and Needs Without Violence**
To help your child stop fighting, make
friends, and solve conflicts peacefully,
one of the best things you can do right away is teach him
the following steps.

1. *Notice what's happening.* The instant you find
    yourself just a bit irritated, tune into your body.
    What is your body doing? Are you taking shorter
    breaths, is your heart beating faster, is your voice
    getting louder? Are you getting hot under the col-
    lar, clenching your fists, grinding your teeth? Once
    you've identified your anger body signs, you can
    watch out for them. They're your warning signal
    that you need to take control of yourself.

2. *Calm down.* Take a deep breath (getting extra oxy-
    gen into your brain is one of the fastest ways to re-
    lax), count to ten, take a step back, go get a drink of
    water, or leave. You could also tell yourself a simple
    message like "Stop! Calm down," "Stay in control,"
    or "Chill out." You need to get your body to relax
    so your brain can work. Find out what works for
    you and then do the same thing every time you
    start getting irritated to help you gain control again.

3. *Think about what's really bugging you.* Try to re-
    play in your mind what's been happening between
    you and your friend for the past few minutes. Is
    there something your friend did or said that ticked
    you off? What was it? Focus on what you saw or
    heard and not on who he is.

4. **Figure out how your friend's actions make you feel.** Do you feel hurt? Frustrated? Mad? Sad? Embarrassed? Name the feeling.

5. **Use the "BIG I" (message) to tell your friend.** No yelling, name-calling, or put-downs are allowed. Just tell your friend in a calm voice what's going on with you. Start with the word "I" and then go on to "don't like it when you . . . It makes me feel . . . I want you to . . .""I don't like it when you call me pea-brain. It makes me really mad. I want you to never say that again.""I don't like it when you take my CDs without asking. It makes me upset. Next time I want you to ask my permission." A shorter version is to say, "I don't like it when . . . I want you to . . ." It's always nice to add a sincere "please."

6. **Listen to your friend's response.** Don't interrupt. Consider what he says. Respect his point of view. Be willing to work through your conflict for as long as it takes.

Learning any new skill takes time. So be prepared for an occasional slip, and practice, practice, practice.

lowed to hit. So let's think about things you can do instead.""You could walk away or talk to a teacher. What else could you do?"

- **Talk about why fighting is wrong.** Ask your child why he thinks you don't approve of violence. Correct any misconceptions and give your own reasons. "It will ruin your friendship. You could get hurt. Your friend could be hurt. It will ruin your reputation. Parents don't like their kids to be around kids who fight. You could get in trouble. You will be suspended. Violence is something our family doesn't believe in. It is morally wrong."

- *Acknowledge efforts to control fighting.* Any time you notice that your kid is expressing his feelings to a friend without hitting, biting, or shoving, let him know you appreciate his efforts: "I noticed you were really mad, but you walked away to control your temper. That's really a good sign." "You used your words this time to tell Jenny how upset you were. Good for you!"

WHAT SHOULD I DO?

- *Heed warnings.* If other adults or kids tell you your child is fighting, pay close attention. (Many parents don't.) Your child may not be telling you everything you need to know.
- *Get to the source.* What did you write in the Why Is This Happening? section? Did you discover anything that might be triggering your child to fight? Is there one thing you might do to help him temper his aggression? Make a plan that will help him alter his behavior.
- *Be vigilant.* Keep a closer eye when your child is around friends. Especially with younger children, first watch to see what may be provoking the hitting; then, don't be shy: step right in and intervene.
- *Do damage control.* If you discover that your child has hit or injured another kid, insist that your child personally apologize and make amends. Then, if appropriate, you may need to make a phone call yourself to either the injured friend or his parents.
- *Use preventive measures.* Watch your kid's behaviors and interactions with friends. Figure out what sets her off: too long a period of play or social contact, too many friends at once, friends who are too aggressive, certain toys or activities that provoke fighting. You might need to have shorter play periods, fewer friends, calmer friends, less aggressive toys or activities.
- *Monitor media consumption.* Research shows that aggressive kids who also watch violent video games and movies

are more likely to fight with friends. So consider more careful supervision of your kid's media input. And if your child has a friend over, no aggressive video games and movies, please. 🛑 **The American Academy of Pediatrics and five other prominent medical groups conclude that the viewing of entertainment violence can increase kids' aggressive attitudes, values, and behavior. The American Psychological Association estimates that televised violence *by itself* contributes to as much as 15 percent of kids' aggressive behaviors.** 🛑

- *Sympathize with the injured.* When a child is hit or hurt, be sure to focus on her feelings and injuries. This helps show the fighter how to be empathic and to consider the results of his actions.

- *Get help.* If you're not seeing any change in your child's behavior despite everything you have done, seek the help of a trained counselor, social worker, child psychologist, clergyperson, or other professional.

 ## 21-DAY FRIENDSHIP FOLLOW-UP

Over the next 21 days, here's what I will do to help my child learn Friendship Skill Builder: Expressing Your Feelings and Needs Without Violence:

_____

_____

_____

_____

_____

_____

FRIENDSHIP TIP

The Hitting Epidemic
A national survey conducted in 1998 by the Josephson Institute of Ethics found that almost one in every four middle school and high school males said he had hit a person in the past twelve months "because he was angry."

 FRIENDSHIP SKILL BUILDER BOOKS

For Parents and Teachers

Angry Kids: Understanding and Managing the Emotions That Control Them, by Richard L. Berry (New York: Revell, 2001). Discusses the root causes of anger in kids and explains ways that parents can help kids learn techniques for expressing and defusing that anger.

Healthy Anger: How to Help Children and Teens Manage Their Anger, by Bernard Golden (New York: Oxford University Press, 2003). Plain, easy steps to help our kids guide and control their anger.

The Angry Child: Regaining Control When Your Child Is out of Control, by Dr. Tim Murphy and Loriann Hoff Oberlin (New York: Potter, 2001). Easy-to-follow strategies that help angry kids manage anger and help parents recognize signs of serious problems.

Tired of Yelling: Teaching Our Children to Resolve Conflict, by Lyndon D. Waugh (Athens, Ga.: Longstreet Press, 1999). A psychiatrist offers parenting solutions for defusing family tension and helping toddlers through teens learn skills of peacemaking.

When Anger Hurts Your Kids: A Parent's Guide, by Patrick McKay (New York: Fine Communications, 1996). A superb guide explaining how parents' anger affects kids and offering ways to regain control.

For Kids

Anger Management Workbook for Kids and Teens, by Anita Bohensky (New York: Growth Publications, 2001). Teaches effective coping behaviors to help stop the escalation of anger and resolve conflicts.

Harriet, You'll Drive Me Wild! by Mem Fox (Orlando: Harcourt, 2000). Harriet doesn't mean to be troublesome. She's always very sorry for her behavior afterward. Her mother doesn't like to yell and usually gently reprimands her. But as Harriet's shenanigans escalate, so does her mom's blood pressure. When mom's limit is finally reached, she yells and yells. Ages 4 to 8 years.

Hot Stuff to Help Kids Chill Out: The Anger Management Book, by Jerry Wilde (Kansas City, Mo.: Landmark Productions, 1997). A book that speaks directly to kids and adolescents and provides clear guidelines to help them handle hot tempers more constructively.

The Mad Family Gets Their Mads Out: Fifty Things Your Family Can Say and Do to Express Anger Constructively, by Lynne Namka (Charleston, Ill.: Talk, Trust and Feel Therapeutics, 1995). Useful ways to help kids who are struggling to express anger constructively, and to help families learn how to deal with anger in nonviolent ways and relate to each member positively.

When Sophie Gets Angry—Really, Really Angry . . . , by Molly Bang (New York: Scholastic, 1999). A little girl who has trouble managing her anger learns how to take time to cool off and regain her composure. Ages 3 to 7.

11

Gossips

Everyday Behaviors: Spreads rumors; talks about other kids behind their backs; loses friends through backstabbing

Friendship Skill Builder: Taking Responsibility and Making Amends

"You won't believe what I found out about her."
"So what if it's not true? She said bad stuff about me."
"I never said that. So why is Laura so ticked?"

WHAT'S WRONG?

Let's face it: we all gossip. Talking about other people is a normal and expected part of human life, especially for kids, who are learning to relate to one another in friendships. There's a problem when it gets mean, nasty, inaccurate, and malicious. Or when kids deny they've gossiped or don't take responsibility for hurting someone's feelings or reputation. Gossip can spread like wildfire, and recent cyberspace technology has accelerated rumors up a notch: e-mail, text messages, and cell phones are the latest ways to spread those nasty rumors quickly. "She's a cheater." "He's gay." "She drinks." "He sleeps around." Make no mistake: gossip may be here to stay with any group of friends, but we've got to help our kids understand how vicious and painful it can be, and we've got to help our kids take responsibility for any lies or exaggerations they've spread and any hurt they've caused. There's no question that gossip can prevent or destroy your child's friendships. After all, nobody likes a backstabber.

WHY IS THIS HAPPENING?

There are a number of possible reasons why your child is gossiping. Check the reasons why she is spreading rumors, backstabbing, and not caring who gets hurt.

- ☐ Needs prestige, status, approval of peers.
- ☐ Is getting revenge or retaliating against a friend who hurt her.
- ☐ Is jealous. Gossiping is a way to compete with a more "fortunate" peer or someone your child perceives as "having it all."
- ☐ Wants to be "in" or accepted in a group. Lacks friends and is trying to make friends or be included by putting others down or spreading tales that interest other kids.
- ☐ Is dealing with hurt.
- ☐ Is dealing with a rival or competitor. Spreading rumors is a way to take this kid down a notch in the eyes of the coach, teacher, other peers, or teammates.
- ☐ Lacks empathy or sensitivity to someone's feelings.
- ☐ Feels no remorse. "What's the big deal?" Doesn't understand why it's wrong or how much pain he has inflicted.

☐   Is part of clique culture. The group relishes picking on "out-group" kids.

☐   Is a copy cat. You're doing it, so why shouldn't your kid?

What is your best guess as to why this is happening? Write it here.

_____

_____

_____

FRIENDSHIP SKILL BUILDER

Taking Responsibility and Making Amends
If your child has hurt a friend and perhaps damaged the friend's reputation, she needs to admit her role and apologize for her actions. Doing so may or may not salvage their friendship, but it's the right thing to do. Here are the steps you need to help her take. It will take courage for her to take these steps, so encourage her efforts.

1. *Understand what you did that was wrong.* Be honest about the exact words you used and everyone you said them to. "This is what I really said. This is who I really told it to. This is how they really reacted."
2. *Find a private time to talk to the friend you hurt.*
3. *Admit what you did and say why it was wrong.* Stick to the facts. Look at the person straight in the eye. Use a sincere voice. "I told the kids the secret

about your mom." She may or may not accept your apology, so be prepared for either reaction. You can also try any or all of the next four steps.

4. **Apologize sincerely.** "I'm sorry I hurt you." "I made a big mistake. It won't happen again."

5. **Express empathy.** "I know you must feel really sad." "I know this embarrassed you."

6. **Try to make amends.** "I will make sure all the kids know it isn't true." "Is there anything I can do to make you feel better?"

7. **Express hope for your friendship.** "I hope we can still be friends. I really will try to be a better friend from now on."

WHAT SHOULD I SAY?

- *Report what you've heard.* "Mrs. White says you're saying things about her daughter, Sara, that aren't true. What's going on?" "I read your e-mail blast about Kevin's problems with his dad. How could you spread such a rumor?" It's important to confront your child about the inaccuracy or painful impact of their gossip. 🛑 **Around fourth or fifth grade, you can expect "who said what to whom" to become part of your child's normal conversation with her friends. Being "in the know" becomes essential to popularity.** 🛑

- *Explain how this kind of gossip hurts.* "Do you have any idea what it feels like to be called 'loose'? How would you like to have people say that about you when you can't defend yourself or your reputation? And it's not even true." "Did you know Ellen was in tears over what you said to the other kids about her?"

- *Discuss why it's wrong.* "Tell me at least five reasons why you shouldn't spread malicious gossip or rumors." Ideas might include: "It can give the person a bad reputation. I can get in trouble with the school. It's not fair. The other kids in the clique may not trust me anymore. It will hurt the person's feelings."
- *Talk about being the best kind of friend.* "What kind of friend would you like to have: someone you can trust or someone who is mean to you behind your back?" Kids need to practice treating others the way they want to be treated. "Amy told you her biggest secret, and you swore that you'd never tell. How do you think she feels about you as a friend when half the schoolyard has heard about it?"

WHAT SHOULD I DO?

- *Bite your tongue.* Check yourself. Could your child be learning this behavior from you? Be objective! Are you quick to pick up the phone and spread a rumor? Do you seem to relish juicy tidbits? If so, put a lid on it.
- *Put a moratorium on vicious gossip.* Vicious gossip is not the same as talking about who is wearing what, who got invited, and who is going out with whom. Vicious gossip is the spreading of false and malicious rumors without checking the facts. And even if the information is true, it can hurt others if it spreads. Be clear that there is zero tolerance in your family for this kind of gossip.
- *Start gossip police.* Your kid may have been gossiping for so long that you're trying to reform an entrenched habit. Therefore, begin by choosing some phrase like "Rumor Alert" or "Check that" and encourage all family members to say it whenever anyone sounds off with some nasty factoid.
- *Do damage control.* If your child spread something that wasn't true or caused severe pain or damage to someone

by gossiping, you need to be sure she makes amends. Although doing so may not erase the hurt, it can at least let your child know that if she causes someone distress, she needs to correct it.

- **Boost empathy.** Vicious gossipers rarely stop to think about the feelings of their victims. Stretch your kid's sensitivity so that she considers the impact gossip may have on the friend. Have her play the "How would you feel?" game so she can walk in someone else's shoes. Remind her how it felt when she heard that someone told a lie about her.

- **Help your child face reality.** Your child may have realized the damage he's caused and apologized to his friend. But the damage may be irreversible, the trust destroyed, and the friendship over. Help your child understand how to learn from this mistake and never make it again.

21-DAY FRIENDSHIP FOLLOW-UP

Over the next 21 days, here's what I will do to help my child learn Friendship Skill Builder: Taking Responsibility and Making Amends:

_____

_____

_____

FRIENDSHIP SKILL BUILDER BOOKS

For Parents and Teachers

Yes, these are primarily for parents of teenage daughters, but they offer such a poignant perspective of what it's really like growing up during these years that at least one of these should

FRIENDSHIP TIP

What's All That Gossip About?

Rosalind Wiseman, author of the best-seller *Queen Bees and Wannabes* and cofounder of the Empower program, has spoken to hundreds of preadolescent and teenage girls. One question that is always on her list is "What kinds of things do you gossip about?" *Hint:* If you're a parent of a younger child, be prepared. There's guaranteed excitement up ahead. Here are the most common gossip issues among girls:

Sixth grade: friendships, friend conflicts, rivalries in and between cliques, crushes on boys

Ninth grade: who's trying to become friends with seniors; who's popular, who's "in"; parties; who's drinking, doing drugs, having sex

Eleventh grade: which freshman girls are throwing themselves at seniors, who had sex at the last party, who got drunk and did drugs, who's getting used, who got together at the last party

be on *every* parent's "must read" list—especially if your daughter is young. Get ready!

Girl Wars: 12 Strategies That Will End Female Bullying, by Cheryl Dellasega and Charisse Nixon (New York: Simon & Schuster, 2003). Gossip, teasing, forming cliques, and other cruel behaviors are the basis of bullying. Here are twelve practical solutions to help girls stop hurting each other with words and actions.

Queen Bees and Wannabes: Helping Your Daughter Survive Cliques, Gossip, Boyfriends, and Other Realities of Adolescence, by Rosalind

Wiseman (New York: Three Rivers Press, 2002). Useful guide with tools to help your daughter handle the all-too-common cruelties of growing up.

Reviving Ophelia: Saving the Selves of Adolescent Girls, by Mary Pipher (New York: Ballantine, 1992). This now-classic should be on every parent's nightstand. Written by a gloriously empathic psychologist who chronicles many of her young female clients' tumultuous teenage years and gives us all a wake-up call.

Surviving Ophelia: Mothers Share Their Wisdom of the Tumultuous Teenage Years, by Cheryl Dellasega (New York: Ballantine, 2002). Stories from mothers of teenage girls offer readers advice on how to deal with (and survive!) tough issues.

For Kids

These movies were chosen because they can be great catalysts for discussions about the hurtfulness of gossip. All are more appropriate for preadolescents to young teens, but do check the rating for each to determine whether it is suitable for your child.

Emma (Miramax Home Entertainment, 2003). A lighter version of Jane Austen's novel, featuring a young woman engaged in milder gossip. Rated PG.

Heathers (Anchor Bay Entertainment, 2001). The three teenage girls who lead the popularity pack wield power by spreading vicious gossip and ruining reputations. Although they are influential, no one really likes or trusts them. Rated R.

Mean Girls (Paramount Home Video, 2004). A formerly home-schooled girl "makes it" in the sneaky, vicious world of the Plastics—three adolescent girls who dominate their public high school's social hierarchy. Rated PG-13.

Mystic Pizza (MGM/UA Studios, 2001). A comedy starring a younger Julia Roberts about the ties among three blue-collar sisters who work in a pizzeria. Wonderful example of girls supporting girls. Rated R.

She's All That (Miramax Home Entertainment, 2003). An unpopular girl constantly belittled and gossiped about by the popular girl clique gets invited to the prom by a popular boy. Although he takes her out as part of a bet with his buddies, he learns that his actions have consequences. He learns to see beyond the stereotypes placed on her by the cliques, and she learns to deal gracefully with the cruelty of peers. Rated PG-13.

12

Hot Tempered

Everyday Behaviors: Loses control; shouts and screams at friends; gets ticked off by the littlest things; his angry outbursts cause kids to be annoyed, resentful, or even fearful

Friendship Skill Builder: Tuning in to Body Temper Alarms

"I tried to stay calm, but it was too late!"
"I wish I could tell when I'm about to explode."
"Don't keep telling me I'm going to lose all my friends because of my temper. I just can't help it."

WHAT'S WRONG?

Your child and his best friend are having a great time (at least you think so). But your happy scene of peaceful harmony takes a sudden nosedive when *your* little darling's voice goes up a notch. His face turns beet red, his fists clench, he's breathing a mile a minute, and he looks like he's about to explode. Once again your child's hot temper has ruined another friendship. And once again your child is left alone.

Your child may be more excitable or passionate by nature, but sometimes this emotional temperament can get out of control and interfere with his friendships. You can't change your kid's basic personality, but you can teach him some strategies and skills to help him get along.

Hot tempers can cause serious damage in friendships and also ruin your kid's reputation. Unless kids learn ways to recognize their own unique danger signs and control their anger, problems are inevitable. After all, hot-tempered kids are no fun to be around. You've got plenty of reasons to work on this friendship problem ASAP.

WHY IS THIS HAPPENING?

There are a number of reasons why your child might have a hot temper. Check ones that apply to your kid.

☐ Has your kid always had a quick temper? For instance, even as a toddler did he resort to tantrums, biting, or hitting, and have a tough time calming himself down? (See also Fights.)

☐ Is he associating with a more aggressive group of kids and perhaps copying their behavior? Or might he be mimicking someone with a quick temper in your family?

☐ Is there trouble lately with a particular friend or group of kids? (See also Tiffs and Breakups.)

☐ Is your kid trying to be one of the group and nobody listens to him? Is he just trying to "hold his own"? (See also Left Out.)

☐ Is he being picked on, teased, or bullied? (See also Teased or Bullied and Harassed.)

☐   Has he learned somewhere that a quick temper is acceptable and been allowed to get away with using it? Has he learned that flaunting his temper is effective in getting his needs met?

☐   Is there a change in your family that might be causing undue stress and a quick temper? A divorce? Family friction? An illness? A recent move? (See also New Kid.)

☐   Does he not know more acceptable ways to calm down and express his needs?

What is your best guess as to why your kid has a quick temper? Write it here.

_____

_____

_____

WHAT SHOULD I SAY?

- *Explain body temper alarms.* Go over the way you see your child act when she's starting to get mad. "You always make that little hissing noise and grind your teeth. Sometimes you stamp your feet. Those are your danger signs that big trouble might be on the way." *Hint:* Each child (as well as you) has her own physiological signs. They materialize whenever we're under stress and have a fight–or–flight response. The trick is to help your child identify her unique signs *before* she loses her temper. Don't expect instant recognition: it may take a week or two before she can identify her signs.

- *Dig deep.* Talk to your child about what's causing her temper to flare so quickly. "You don't seem like the same kid lately. Anything you want to talk about?" "You seem so

FRIENDSHIP SKILL BUILDER

Tuning in to Body Temper Alarms
It may be a great revelation when you tell your child that her body actually sends out warning signs when a temper attack is approaching. Tell her how it happens to you: "My face gets flushed. My hearts starts beating faster. It's harder for me to breathe. My voice gets louder, and I can't think straight. Body temper alarms like these happen to everyone when she gets angry and begins to lose her temper. But good news! You can stop yourself before the volcano erupts." Then teach your child these steps:

1. **_Hear the bells going off._ Listen.** Whenever you're with a friend and things are getting rough, pay very close attention to changes in your body. Everyone is different, but usually alarms go off in your body that warn you when you're starting to lose control. So be on the alert for any familiar body signs that you might be losing your temper.

2. **_Hit the snooze control._ Stop.** Even a few seconds to pause are enough to stop your temper from exploding or causing you to do something you may regret later on. Find what works for you. Some kids imagine a big stop sign in front of their eyes or yell "Stop!" inside their heads. Doing something like this will help you put the brakes on your temper. Some kids say to themselves, "Chill out" or "I can keep my cool" or "Relax."

3. **_Turn down the volume._ Breathe.** Once you've told yourself to keep under control, you have to take a

> slow, deep breath. You can slow down your heart
> rate and get yourself back in control by taking
> slow, deep breaths.
>
> 4.   *Get back in tune.* **Separate.** Back off from what-
>   ever is about to blow up in your face. You could
>   count to 10 (or to 100), hum a few bars of the *Star
>   Spangled Banner,* think of a pepperoni pizza, gaze
>   up in the sky, or do whatever it takes to regain
>   your sense of calm.

tense and quick tempered with your friends. What's going on?" "I know the move was really tough. Do you think that's at the bottom of your bad temper lately?"

- *Point out bad effects.* On a piece of paper, print the word *ANGER* in large bold letters. Then write a large *D* so it now spells *DANGER*. Then say, "Anger can really hurt you. You could lose a friend, get a bad reputation, lose a job, get suspended from school, get hurt. If you don't control your temper, you could be headed for danger and lose your friends."

- *Stress the importance of remaining calm.* Use a balloon to help your child understand the importance of staying calm. "We all get angry with friends sometimes, especially when things aren't going the way we plan." Hold up the balloon and slowly blow it up halfway, then pinch the tip to keep the air in. "When we're upset, anger inside us can blow up very quickly. Watch what happens." Continue blowing the balloon to full size, then pinch the balloon to hold the air. "When there's so much anger in you, it's hard to think. Your heart is pounding, and you are breathing faster. This is when you can make poor choices and say things to friends you may regret later." Quickly let go of the balloon so that it flies around the room. "See how it spins out of control all over? That's what happens when you don't stay calm."

- **Brainstorm temper triggers.** Help your child recognize the things that bug him the most so he can handle the situation better when he's with his friends. "I noticed that you hit the roof whenever George starts exaggerating." "Have you noticed that whenever Lori criticizes your hair you clench your fists?" Help your kid identify the things that make his blood boil—that certain look, unfairness, not sharing, interrupting, telling secrets behind his back, put-downs—so he can avoid setting off his temper.

- **Refuse to engage.** If your child starts to lose his temper with you, say "I understand you're upset, but I won't listen until you get in control." Then walk away and go about your business until your child is calm. Be consistent so that your child understands she needs to control her temper if she wants your attention.

- **Be realistic.** "I know it's hard to change, but you've been using your quick temper for a long time. You will be able to control your temper, but it usually takes at least three weeks of practice before you see change. Hang in there and keep trying." If your child is younger, give her a piece of yarn about a yard long. Say this: "I know this is hard, but you will improve if you keep practicing. It will take about twenty-one days. So every time you remember to practice your temper-calming strategy, tie a knot in the yarn. When there are about twenty-one knots in your yarn, you will feel change."

WHAT SHOULD I DO?

- **Model control.** How do you act in front of your kids after a hard, stressful day? When you're driving with your kids and another car cuts in front of you? When the bank calls to say you're overdrawn? Your kids are watching, so make sure your behavior is what you want your kids to learn.

- **Set a rule: "Calm talk or no play."** Your kid needs to know you are serious about helping him alter his quick temper. So set a clear rule that if his anger gets out of control, there is a consequence. An appropriate consequence for older kids might be losing a *desired* privilege such as use of the telephone or television for a set length of time (an hour or the evening—depending on the circumstances). Use the same consequence every time.
- **Teach "back off" skills.** One of the best ways to handle a bad temper is to "disengage" from the situation. Kids can move quickly down the "temper chain": bad look, put-down, shout, shove, punch, fight. The key is to cut the links so things don't get out of control. Offer your kid a few of the following ideas to help him "postpone" a conflict for just a second so that he can get himself back in check.
  - **Admit you're ticked.** Tell your friend you need a breather. "I'm getting really upset. Let's stop a minute."
  - **Get a drink of water.**
  - **Ask for a postponement.** "Can we talk about this in a minute? Let's wait until we're both calm."
  - **Use self-talk.** Say a simple, positive message to yourself to control your temper: "Stop and calm down," "Stay in control," "Chill out," "I can handle this." Pick the most comfortable phrase, then rehearse it a few times each day.
  - **Imagine a calm place.** The beach, your bed, Grandpa's backyard, a tree house—whatever works for you. Right before your temper starts to flare and you feel those body warning signs kick in, close your eyes and imagine the spot, while breathing slowly.
  - **Leave.** Sometimes the best strategy is to exit the scene. If it doesn't feel safe, walk away.
- **Limit aggressive media consumption.** Kids learn attitudes

not only from watching parents, teachers, and peers but also from observing characters in books, movies, and television. And what they are watching is troubling. 🛑 **The typical preschooler who watches about two hours of cartoons daily will be exposed to 10,000 violent incidents per year. By the end of elementary school, the average child will have witnessed 8,000 murders; by age eighteen, he will have seen 200,000 other vivid acts of violence on the TV screen.** 🛑 If your kid's media diet is saturated with violence, monitor what he watches and set clear watching limits.

- *Seek help if angry outbursts continue.* If you've tried all these techniques and your child's anger persists, then it's time to seek help. Talk to your pediatrician, a psychologist, a school counselor, or an outside therapist to help your child work through what's beneath all the anger.

 FRIENDSHIP TIP

Hot-Tempered Parents
Studies by sociologist Murray Straus reveal that 90 percent of parents admit they've threatened their kids or yelled, screamed, or cursed at them. One quarter of all parents reported engaging in more than thirty-three acts of psychological aggression in the last year. The actual prevalence of verbal aggression is probably higher than the numbers indicate because people tend to underreport. So tune into your tone: could you be teaching your child to yell? If so, put a lid on it.

21-DAY FRIENDSHIP FOLLOW-UP

Over the next 21 days, here's what I will do to help my child learn Friendship Skill Builder: Tuning in to Body Temper Alarms:

_____

_____

_____

 FRIENDSHIP SKILL BUILDER BOOKS

For Parents and Teachers

Angry Kids: Understanding and Managing the Emotions That Control Them, by Richard L. Berry (New York: Revell, 2001). Discusses the root causes of anger in kids and explains ways parents can help them learn techniques for expressing and defusing that anger.

Healthy Anger: How to Help Children and Teens Manage Their Anger, by Bernard Golden (New York: Oxford University Press, 2003). Plain, easy steps to help our kids guide and control their anger.

The Angry Child: Regaining Control When Your Child Is out of Control, by Dr. Tim Murphy and Loriann Hoff Oberlin (New York: Potter, 2001). Easy-to-follow strategies that help angry kids manage anger and help parents recognize signs of serious problems.

Tired of Yelling: Teaching Our Children to Resolve Conflict, by Lyndon D. Waugh (Athens, Ga.: Longstreet Press, 1999). A psychiatrist offers parenting solutions for defusing family tension and helping toddlers through teens learn skills of peacemaking.

When Anger Hurts Your Kids: A Parent's Guide, by Patrick McKay (New York: Fine Communications, 1996). A superb guide explaining how parents' anger affects kids and offering ways to regain control.

For Kids

Anger Management Workbook for Kids and Teens, by Anita Bohensky (New York: Growth Publications, 2001). Teaches effective coping behaviors to help stop the escalation of anger and resolve conflicts.

Harriet, You'll Drive Me Wild! by Mem Fox (Orlando: Harcourt, 2000). Harriet doesn't mean to be troublesome. She's always very sorry for her behavior afterward. Her mother doesn't like to yell, and usually gently reprimands her. But as Harriet's shenanigans escalate, so does her mom's blood pressure. When her limit is finally reached, Harriet's mom yells and yells. Ages 4 to 8 years.

Hot Stuff to Help Kids Chill Out: The Anger Management Book, by Jerry Wilde (Kansas City, Mo.: Landmark Productions, 1997). A book that speaks directly to kids and adolescents and provides clear guidelines to help them handle hot tempers more constructively. Ages 8 to 13.

How to Take the Grrrr out of Anger, by Elizabeth Verdict and Marjorie Lisovskis (Minneapolis, Minn.: Free Spirit, 2003). Filled with good advice to help kids understand anger and how to handle it in healthy, positive ways. Ages 9 to 12.

The Mad Family Gets Their Mads Out: Fifty Things Your Family Can Say and Do to Express Anger Constructively, by Lynne Namka (Charleston, Ill.: Talk, Trust and Feel Therapeutics, 1995). Useful ways to help kids who are struggling to express anger constructively, and to help families learn how to deal with anger in nonviolent ways and relate to each member positively.

Understanding the Human Volcano: What Teens Can Do About Violence, by Earl Hipp (Center City, Minn.: Hazelden, 2000). Frank and helpful advice on how to help teens cope with an increasingly violent world. Ages 13 and older.

When Sophie Gets Angry—Really, Really Angry . . . , by Molly Bang (New York: Scholastic, 1999). A little girl who has trouble managing her anger learns how to take time to cool off and regain her composure. Ages 3 to 7.

13

Insensitive

Everyday Behaviors: Doesn't consider a friend's feelings; doesn't listen; doesn't see things from the friend's point of view; lacks empathy; is sometimes mean or cruel

Friendship Skill Builder: Showing You Care by Listening

"Why was Kevin crying? He's such a baby."
"So what if he's the only kid I didn't invite? He's not any fun and gives lousy presents."
"Come on, Mom, get real. I was just teasing. Jenny should learn to take it."

WHAT'S WRONG?

Research clearly shows that children are born with the natural and miraculous power to be sensitive to the feelings and needs of others. But your kids' sensitivity must be nurtured, and here's the real clincher: unless parents stretch their kids'

171

"feeling" capacities, those kids will be greatly handicapped in the social arena. And one thing is for sure: insensitive kids are no joy to have as friends. Admit it: would you choose to be around someone who is unsympathetic to your feelings and doesn't care about you? Real friendship is two sided: that means *both* kids in a relationship have to feel as though their needs are met. And because insensitive kids rarely stop to consider other kids' feelings or needs, it's no wonder they have problems getting along. 🛑 **A great deal of research shows that sensitivity and niceness do matter when it comes to rating peers' popularity and likability. Even preadolescents and teens, who are very tuned in to status, appreciate niceness and decency in peers.** 🛑 Yes, helping your child become more sensitive to others' feelings is hard work, but doing so is critical to enhancing his likability as well as his reputation as a human being. Besides, if you don't boost this friendship skill, you just may discover that the other kids—as well as their parents—won't appreciate your child's company. So get moving!

WHY IS THIS HAPPENING?

There are many reasons why your child may be insensitive. Do some serious reflecting, talk to others who know him well to hear their perceptions, and keep a watchful eye on your child's behavior for any possible clues. 🛑 **Kids are most self-conscious about their friends' reactions in fourth and fifth grade, and frequently compare their appearance and their athletic and intellectual abilities to those of the other kids. Their severe unease about themselves (and how they measure up to the other kids) can exacerbate insensitivity. Might this be your kid?** 🛑 To get you started, check the issues that you think apply to your child.

☐ Have friends or other kids been insensitive to him?
☐ Is he chastised or made fun of for showing his feelings?

- [ ] Does she lack self-esteem or feel "unworthy," so she brings her friends down?
- [ ] Has he been treated unkindly? Is he mimicking the same unkind, insensitive behaviors? (If so, also see Teased.)
- [ ] Is he not expected to be sensitive or kind? No one is telling him that insensitivity is not allowed.
- [ ] Is he disciplined too punitively, or is corporal punishment used? Beware! Research finds that overly harsh punishment will diminish kids' empathy.
- [ ] Does he have difficulty identifying other people's feelings? Does he fail to use the correct words to label feelings or lack an emotional vocabulary? (If so, also see Clueless.)
- [ ] Are feelings not acknowledged in your home, making it hard for him to talk about feelings to his friends?
- [ ] Has he been angry, depressed, or stressed lately? Could he be insensitive toward others because he's trying to deal with his own unhappiness or stress? (If so, also see Hot Tempered.)
- [ ] Are other kids bullying or teasing him? Is he appearing to be "insensitive" as a way of covering up his real feelings? Is this about wanting to "get back" because he has been picked on? (If so, also see Bullied and Harassed.)
- [ ] Is she anesthetized from stress? If so, from what? Could she be reacting to a crisis in her own world—divorce, death, illness? Has she witnessed or experienced trauma? Is she anxious about world events?

What is your best guess as to why your child is insensitive? Write it down so you'll remember your thoughts.

_____

_____

_____

_____

FRIENDSHIP SKILL BUILDER

Showing You Care by Listening
One of the best ways your child can let a friend know he's concerned about her needs and feelings is by listening. In fact, it's also one of the most important skills not only for boosting sensitivity but also for acquiring social competence. Share with your child these steps to learning to listen.

1. ***Make frequent eye contact and look at the speaker.*** It shows you're interested. Keep a pleasant face: no rolling eyes or negative facial expressions.

2. ***Lean in slightly.*** Not too much or it looks rude. Nod every now and then.

3. ***Pay attention.*** Stand or sit still and focus on the speaker. Don't look around, fidget, interrupt, or change the subject. Try to think about what he's saying. Make a comment to show you care: "You're kidding!" "Really?" "That's great!"

4. ***Show that you understand.*** "Okay," "Got it," "Right," "Thanks," "I see." Ask the person to explain if you don't understand: "Do you mean . . . ?" "What happened then?" "Did you want that to happen?"

5. ***End positively.*** Wait until your friend is finished, then say something so he knows you care. "Thanks for telling me," "I hope you feel better," "Do you want to talk more later?" or "I have to get to practice, but call me." Be sure not to leave hastily or before your friend is really through speaking. He should be able to tell that you heard properly and responded with kindness and sincerity.

WHAT SHOULD I SAY?

- *Set clear behavior expectations.* A major step in squelching kids' insensitivity is simply not to tolerate it. 🛑 **Research shows that parents who express their views about hurtful, insensitive behaviors and then explain why they feel that way tend to have kids who are more sensitive and who adopt those views.** 🛑 Start by clearly laying down your expectations:"In this house you are always to be considerate of others." "Kelly has been a good friend for a long time. She's going through a rough time at home right now, so be sensitive to how she's feeling and stick up for her." "Robby will be here in a few minutes. I expect you to respect his feelings." Then stand firm and be consistent.

- *Ask often, "How does your friend feel?"* Ask questions that help your kid think about other people's feelings, needs, and concerns. "Tim's dog just died. I imagine that's why he didn't want to play. How do you think he feels?" "Look at the devastation the tornado brought to that town: the people lost everything! How would you feel if you were one of them?" "That little girl was making fun of Dora. Did you see her face? How do you think she felt?" Pose the question often, using situations as they arise in books, the news, TV shows, cartoons, and movies as well as in real life. The more you encourage your child to tune in to others' feelings, the greater the chance his sensitivity will increase.

- *Point out emotions.* Studies of over one thousand youngsters found that those capable of reading nonverbal feelings were not only the most popular in school but also more emotionally secure. Pointing out the facial expressions, voice tone, posture, and mannerisms of people in different emotional states sensitizes your child to their feelings. "Did you see Joshua's face when you were talking today? I thought he looked mad because he had a frown and his hands were so clenched." "Did you see Molly's posture? Her shoulders were slumped, so I thought she might be worried about something." Share the clues that helped you make your evaluation so your kid can learn to use those same clues. "At practice today, remember to watch the faces of your teammates to see if you are playing too rough."

- *Focus on the friend's distress.* Each and every time your child is insensitive, call her on it ASAP. Tell her exactly what she did that was insensitive and explain the impact of her behavior. "That was insensitive. You didn't stop to think about your friend's feelings when you just left him there. Did you see how upset he was?" "Look how sad you made Kara feel when you teased her about her new glasses. That was insensitive."

- *Reinforce sensitive actions.* Acknowledge your child whenever she does display sensitivity. Just make sure you explain exactly what she did to deserve recognition so she'll be more likely to repeat the action: "Nancy, I loved how you hugged your friend when she was upset. That showed her you cared about her feelings." "Laura, that was so considerate of you to tell Peter you missed him." "Francesca, did you see the smile on Amber's face when you told her you'd call her when she moved? You made her feel so much better about moving."

- *Set a consequence if insensitivity continues.* If your child continues to be insensitive, it's time for consequences. Don't confront your child in front of his friends; that would do more harm than good. Instead, wait until you're alone and then describe the specific insensitive behavior, explain why it was wrong, and then give the consequence. "If you can't treat your friends nicely, you won't be able to have them over." "That was mean. Your friends will have to go home now. They can come back when you decide to treat them nicely." "You hurt your friend's feelings. You need to apologize." "You treated your brother meanly. You'll need to do his chores today as well as yours to make up for your behavior." Do not get drawn into an argument about your decision: be firm, stay calm, and don't give in.

WHAT CAN I DO?

- *Help your child develop an emotional vocabulary.* After all, in order for kids to tune in to their friends' feelings, they need to be able to read the feelings. One simple way to expand your kid's emotional vocabulary is to identify a few new words each week and then deliberately use them in your daily conversations with your child. Any age-appropriate feeling words will do: *frustrated, upset, stressed, angry, shocked, silly, afraid, sympathetic, grouchy, nervous, happy.* The trick is to say the words often enough that your child begins to use them on his own.

- *Encourage your child to understand the friend's perspective.* If you can help your child get inside someone else's shoes and feel things from the other person's perspective, it would be a huge step to boosting her sensitivity. The next time your child says or does anything insensitive, stop, get her attention, and ask her to "switch places" and pretend she is the recipient of her insensitivity. For younger kids you can literally have her get into Daddy's shoes, slip on her brother's jacket, or even put a picture of her friend in front of her face. Then you ask her: "How do you feel that someone said that about you?" 🛑 **Kids whose dads were positively involved in their care when they were age five were found thirty years later to be more empathic, sensitive adults than those whose fathers were absent. Involved dads can make a major contribution to raising sensitive kids, so get those males involved.** 🛑

- *Imagine your friend's feelings.* Help your kid imagine how the other person feels about a special situation. "Imagine you're a new student, and you're walking into a brand-new school and don't know anyone. How do you feel?" Asking often, "How would you feel?" helps kids understand the feelings and needs of other people. In preadolescence the connotation of a "good friend" is one who displays concern and tact, talks about feelings, and actively listens and tries to understand his chum. In short, good friends develop a real sensitivity to what matters to another person. The groundwork for learning that critical friendship component of empathy takes place with your guidance.

- *Demand amends.* Your child caused another child to be hurt. That action shouldn't be taken lightly, nor should your child be allowed to get away with it. Expect him to apologize. Ask, "Was what you did helpful or hurtful? . . . You're right. It was hurtful. And your friend's feelings are hurt. So what will you do to make up for what you did?" He could make an apology, call and express he's sorry, offer to do something to try to make up for the cruel act, or even think of something to do himself, without asking. Whatever your child does, the apology must be delivered sincerely, and he must recognize that his actions caused pain. (See also the Friendship Skill Builder titled Taking Responsibility and Making Amends.)

- *Help your child experience kindness.* The best way to help kids recognize the power of sensitivity is not by talking or reading about it but by actually experiencing it. Consider doing community service as a family. There are dozens of ways to get involved, lend a hand, volunteer, or show you care. Contributing to food drives, picking up trash in the park, painting battered women's shelters, serving meals at homeless shelters, delivering meals to sick and elderly folks who are housebound, and tutoring are just a few ways to help your child develop sensitivity and feel the joy of caring.

- *Be vigilant.* If you suspect your child of treating others insensitively (or if you have witnessed it), then monitor her closely. Supervise her with other kids when you're around or check on her actions outside your home. Have a conference with her teacher or coach and state your concerns. Your child needs to know that you neither support nor tolerate this kind of behavior. If she is picking on a particular

⊞ FRIENDSHIP TIP

**Nine Factors That Increase the Likelihood of Kids'
Being Sensitive**
Suzanne Denham, author of *Emotional Development in
Young Children,* identified nine factors that researchers
say generally increase the chances that a child will display more empathy and sensitivity to others' feelings (although there are certainly no guarantees):

1. *Age.* The ability to take the perspective of others increases with age, so older children are generally more
   empathic than younger kids.
2. *Gender.* Younger children are more likely to empathize with a peer of the same sex because they feel
   a greater sense of commonality.
3. *Intelligence.* Smarter kids are more likely to comfort others because they are better able to discern
   other people's needs and devise ways to assist them.
4. *Emotional understanding.* Children who freely express their emotions are usually more empathic because they are more capable of correctly identifying
   other people's feelings.
5. *Empathic parents.* Kids whose parents are empathic are likely to become empathic themselves because
   the parents model those behaviors, which in turn are
   copied by their children.
6. *Emotional security.* More assertive and well adjust-
   ed kids are more likely to assist others.
7. *Temperament.* Kids who are by nature happier and
   more social are more likely to empathize with a distressed child.

8. Similarity. Kids are more likely to have empathy for those who they feel are similar to them in some way or with whom they have shared a similar experience.

9. Attachment. Kids are more likely to empathize with their friends than with those to whom they feel less closely attached.

child, set an "off-limits" policy: your child is not to be within twenty-five feet of her. (For a younger child, use a visual reference such as the length of room.) No excuses allowed. If you don't stop your child's insensitivity now, chances are it will go up a notch into crueler behavior and bullying.

 ## 21-DAY FRIENDSHIP FOLLOW-UP

Over the next 21 days, here's what I will do to help my child learn Friendship Skill Builder: Showing You Care by Listening:

_____

_____

_____

 FRIENDSHIP SKILL BUILDER BOOKS

For Parents

Raising Compassionate, Courageous Children in a Violent World, by Janice Cohn (Athens, Ga.: Longstreet Press, 1996). Practical ways to help children learn the qualities of kindness, courage, and decency.

The Caring Child, by Nancy Eisenberg (Cambridge, Mass.: Harvard University Press, 1992). One of the most thorough guides to understanding how sensitivity develops in children.

The Moral Intelligence of Children, by Robert Coles (New York: Random House, 1997).Thorough, research-based ideas on how to raise a moral, compassionate kid.

For Kids

A Special Trade, by Sally Wittman (New York: HarperCollins, 1978).When the little girl was young, her grandfather pushed her in the stroller. Now she is five, and Grandfather has a stroke. The girl pushes Grandfather as he once pushed her. Plain glorious for kids ages 3 to 7.

Indian in the Cupboard, by Lynne Reid Banks (New York: Avon, 1980).An Indian toy given to a young boy comes to life, and through it the boy learns the value of sensitivity.Ages 8 to 12.

Lord of the Flies, by William Golding (New York: Perigee Books, 1959).A group of English schoolboys becomes stranded on a desert island. Gradually throughout the ordeal, their character transforms from "civilized" and "proper" to insensitive and cruel.Ages 12 and older.

Please Stop Laughing at Me! One Woman's Inspirational Story, by Jodie Blanco (Avon, Mass.: Adams Media, 2003). An inspirational memoir about how one child was shunned by her classmates from elementary to high school.A gripping account of the toxicity of insensitivity. For young teens.

Stone Fox, by John Reynolds Gardiner (New York: Harper-Collins, 1980). Sensitive ten-year-old Willy enters a dogsled race so that his grandfather's farm might be saved.Ages 7 to 11.

Wilfrid Gordon McDonald Partridge, by Mem Fox (New York: Kane/Miller, 1985). A young boy learns that his friend from the old people's home is losing her memory. He sets out to help her find it, and in doing so learns the power of sensitivity. Wonderful for kids 4 to 8.

14

Jealous and Resentful

Everyday Behaviors: Never satisfied with who she is or what she has; always feels that she can't keep up with the other kids; judges her worth based only on her friends

Friendship Skill Builder: Appreciating Your Personal Best

"Of course, all my so-called friends want to go to his house—it's the only one with a pool."
"But Mooommm, I've got to get an iPod just like his."
"I just hate Kelly—she's so skinny."

WHAT'S WRONG?

Jealous kids wish they could have the success, good fortune, possessions, or qualities of one, some, or all of the other kids. Never satisfied with who they are or what they have, they

183

compare themselves to their peers: "She's smarter." "He's richer." "She's skinnier." "He's got more cool stuff." And each of these longings to be "more like her" (or "him" or "them") strips away a little more satisfaction with what they do have, replacing it instead with resentment. This really isn't about the friendship—it's about "the other kid." It's about feeling inadequate, materialistic, not up to speed, and unconfident, and always wanting to be as good (smart, cute, well-dressed, popular) as another child. A good friendship is one in which *both* kids bring something to the relationship. And the only way that can happen is for both kids to recognize and be satisfied with their individual talents, skills, possessions, or strengths.

Jealousy is a normal feeling that we've all felt at one time or another, but harboring envy toward another can be toxic not only to the friendship but also to our emotional health. The key to this friendship-building skill is to help your child feel satisfied with himself. Only then will he be able to be comfortable in his own skin as well as in a relationship.

WHY IS THIS HAPPENING?

Start your diagnosis by identifying who or what your kid is most jealous of: a friend, a new gadget, something to wear, a sibling? Then think about what might be fueling that resentment. Here are a few possibilities. Check those that apply to your child:

☐   Do you or your family emphasize status, prestige, and materialism? Your child might merely be copying your example. Does your family feel that "what you have" is more important than "who you are"?

☐   Has she been pitted against the kid in competition? Are you (or a coach, teacher, another adult, or other peers) constantly comparing her to that particular object of jealousy? (If so, also see Too Competitive.)

- [ ] Do you live in a neighborhood that has a "country club mentality," where if your kid doesn't keep up material-ly, he really is out?
- [ ] Is competition (for grades, scores, popularity, status) em-phasized in your home? Might your kid feel she can never "win" in your eyes?
- [ ] Does she lack self-confidence or fail to recognize her own unique talents, strengths, or skills? Is she jealous of another child's abilities, appearance, or qualities because she feels she isn't good enough at anything?
- [ ] Has something happened at home (a divorce, an illness, a financial setback) that causes embarrassment among friends? Has she had a setback (an illness, an experience of failure) that might cause her to undermine her worth?
- [ ] Has she recently moved? Is she "new," so she feels that her "place" with this kid or group is shaky? (If so, also see New Kid.)
- [ ] Is she part of a group or clique that really stresses status? Do the other kids (or their parents) emphasize achieve-ment, looks, popularity, abilities? (If so, also see Cliques.)
- [ ] Is your child in an unequal or unbalanced relationship in which she might be "over her head"? Does she feel that she can't keep up or compete with this kid because the status of the other child (or family) is so high? Might she be correct?

What is your best guess as to why your child is jealous of this friend (or others)?

_____

_____

_____

_____

_____

_____

FRIENDSHIP SKILL BUILDER

Appreciating Your Personal Best
We've all experienced feelings of jealousy and bitterness about not being
unable to keep up. But harboring those
feelings against a friend can be disastrous. That's why it's
crucial to build your child's confidence to be content with
who she is, what she can do, what she has, and where she
is going. Here are a few things you can suggest your child
do to deal with her resentment and even to mend a torn
relationship.

1. *Take an honest look at yourself.* Stop comparing
    yourself to your friends. What are *your* strong
    points? Do you have a sunny smile? A quick wit?
    A kind heart? A good voice? Can you solve a math
    problem quickly? Everyone excels at something,
    and so do you.

2. *Rate your support system.* Can you count on your
    mom or dad? Is there a special aunt, uncle, or
    grandparent who really thinks you're the tops?
    What about your teachers, a coach, an old friend?
    Most of us have one or more people who really
    cheer us on. Who's in your fan club?

3. *Take stock of your past successes.* Has anyone ever
    said how much he appreciates you? Did you
    ever win a contest, first prize, blue ribbon, or tro-
    phy? Have you ever achieved a personal goal you set
    for yourself? Have you ever scored higher than any-
    one else? Don't forget any victories, large or small.

4. *Make a "personal best" log.* It could be a success
    scrapbook, victory box, collage, recording, DVD,

or journal. Whatever your preference, create a way to "check in" with your strong points whenever you may feel jealousy or resentment toward a good friend. Keep adding to it as good things keep happening to you.

Remember, there will always be others who have more than you, but there are also lots who have less. The trick is to learn to accept who you are so that your longing doesn't eat away at your friendship.

WHAT SHOULD I SAY?

- *Identify the trigger.* Your aim is to figure out what is really behind the jealousy. It could be a number of things, so don't dismiss your child's complaints or sympathize too quickly. Instead try to uncover what's really going on: "Do you always want to wear the same clothes he does?" "Have you noticed how critical you are of Jenna lately? Could it be because you're jealous that she was chosen team captain?" You can tell from your kid's reaction if you're on the right track, and if not, he'll usually quickly straighten you out. At least you'll have a clue as to what's causing the resentment. And that's your goal. 🛑 **Experts warn that kids low in friendship-making skills are more likely to be possessive because they fear rejection or lack confidence that they can make new friends. Their jealousy can make them want to keep the friend all to themselves and sometimes feel threatened if the friend seeks another child's company.** 🛑
- *Help her separate wants from needs.* If your kid is always buying stuff to keep up (or to "one-up" a friend), help her recognize that her buying frenzy may be based on wanting

her friend's approval rather than on real need. Ask: "What about those pricey sneakers you had to have last week because Jenna had them? How often do you wear them? Are you still glad you bought them?" Of course, your child may say yes, but you just might have caused her to question the "worth it" factor.

- **Get beneath the surface.** Sometimes all that's needed to get kids to open up and talk about what's really triggering their jealousy is to clarify their feelings. So try it. "You're hurt because you think Jeremy is being treated more fairly than you are." "You're upset because Josh isn't asking you over as much as he used to, and you're worried he doesn't think you're good enough."

- **Encourage empathy.** Kids often get so caught up in jealousy that they don't stop to think how their friend might be feeling. Nor do they stop and think about how their resentful words or behavior might hurt their friendship. So ask, "See it from her side now. How do you think your friend feels that you shunned her because she was invited and you weren't?" "If your friend treated you like that, do you think she'd want to continue to be your friend?" 🛑 **Jealousy generally declines as peer groups become more relaxed during adolescence. Teens begin to realize it's okay to grant friends the freedom to have relationships with others.** 🛑 (See also Insensitive.)

- **Contest the opinion.** If your child says, "All the kids like Josh better. They always choose him for their team," challenge his opinion: "Why do you think the kids choose him more than you? Could it be that Josh is a better hitter? Is that something you want to be? If so, then you might want to do something to improve your hitting." If your child says, "I've got to get a pair of those retro sneakers. The kids won't think I'm cool if I don't have them," contest it: "Do shoes make such a difference? John doesn't have a pair, and everyone wants to hang out with him." The key is to help your child realize that it's not so much what he has but who he is that improves his friendship chances.

- **Stress previous achievements.** If your child's resentment is aimed at another friend's success, point out your child's past accomplishments. "Sara did win the debate, but you won last time." "Yes, Matt did beat you, but remember you can't win all the time. Besides, you won the game last week." "You're right, Meghan is good at tennis. But you're the one who is great at golf."

WHAT SHOULD I DO?

- **Check your own role in creating jealousy.** Do some serious soul searching. Your own attitude could easily be one of the biggest reasons for your child's jealousy. Do you ever express envy or jealousy toward another family member, a friend, or a rival at work? For instance, do you complain about a coworker who has received what you perceive to be an unjustified praise or promotion? Could your child be feeling as though you are measuring her against her friends? When your child shows you her graded work, do you ask the grades of her friends? Do you ask whose house her friends are going to over the weekend or what invitations they received? Or which camp, sports, and music lessons her friends are attending? If so, curb those comparisons!
- **Help him recognize the poison of jealousy.** Your child may be so caught up in jealousy that he may not recognize how poisonous it can be to a friendship. If he continues, his jealousy can cause big-time problems with his friend. The fact is, he may just lose the friendship altogether. So how do you stop the deadly spiral? You might use an example from your past and tell your child how jealousy ruined one of your relationships. The Bible story of Cain and Abel, *Cinderella,* the

Greek myth of Venus and her jealousy of Helen of Troy—all are examples that might help your child recognize jealousy's destructiveness. ⏹ **When middle school–age females are asked why girls are often so mean and shunning toward one another (or use relationships rather than fists to hurt each other), jealousy is generally the top reason given.** ⏹ (See also Cliques or Gossip.)

- *Make an action plan.* Suggest a few ways your child can overcome feelings of jealousy or the need to keep up. Here are a few possibilities:

  - *Write a letter.* She might write a letter (a younger child can draw one) to the friend expressing all her pent-up concerns, then rip it up. Or make a list of all the reasons she is so resentful. Rereading the list sometimes helps her recognize how irrational her worries are.

  - *Talk about it.* Encourage her to talk with her friend about her jealousy. It will take courage to do so, but getting those feelings off her chest may help ease the strain in the relationship.

  - *Consult the "personal best" log.* Encourage your child to take a regular look at his scrapbook or victory box that chronicles his past successes. (See step 4 of the Friendship Skill Builder.) There's nothing like a little dose of self-confidence to overcome jealousy.

- *Enlist your kid's friends' support.* If you feel that kid parties and events are turning into extravaganzas (and your kid is getting sucked into the need to "keep up"), it may be time to talk to other parents. Can you find even just one parent who feels the same way and can support you in taking the spending down a notch? For example, a group of Seattle moms became so concerned about excessive spending on birthday presents that they agreed to make charitable donations in their children's names instead.

- *Help her develop a talent.* Each child needs to have her place in the sun, so find an area in which your child can excel—and ideally choose one that is different from the friend she is envious of. If your younger child is graceful, enroll her in ballet; if she is musically inclined, give her music lessons. If your teen has a flare for fashion, find a modeling class for her to join. Cultivate your child's talent so she can improve that special quality and boost her self-confidence.

 FRIENDSHIP TIP

Help Kids Link Jealousy to Low Self-Confidence
Cheryl Dellasega and Charisse Nixon, authors of *Girl Wars,* have interviewed hundreds of young girls and see an upsurge in relational aggression (bullying). They discovered that jealousy was almost always the cause. The authors recommend that parents help their daughters think about what's really behind the jealous feelings and help her link low self-esteem with mistrusting others. The authors say that your goal should be to help your child "see the connection between feeling threatened and insecure and behavior that manipulates and aggresses against others to build a sense of power."

 21-DAY FRIENDSHIP FOLLOW-UP

Over the next 21 days, here's what I will do to help my child learn Friendship Skill Builder: Appreciating Your Personal Best:

_____

_____

_____

📖 FRIENDSHIP SKILL BUILDER BOOKS 📖

For Parents and Teachers

Envy: The Enemy Within, by Bob Sorge (Ventura, Calif.: Regal Books, 2003). A book to help adults explore the basis of their own green-eyed ways.

Girl Wars: 12 Strategies That Will End Female Bullying, by Cheryl Dellasega and Charisse Nixon (New York: Simon & Schuster, 2003). Practical and effective solutions for preventing relational aggression—the shunning, gossiping, teasing, clique-forming, and other cruel behaviors that are often caused by jealousy.

Overcoming Jealousy, by Wendy Dryden (London: SPCK and Triangle, 1999). A simple book for adults that cuts right to the meat of the issue: Why are you jealous, and what can you do about it?

Raising Confident Boys: 100 Tips for Parents and Teachers, by Elizabeth Hartley-Brewer (Cambridge, Mass.: Fisher Books, 2001). A wealth of practical ideas to help boys recognize their talents and boost their self-esteem.

Raising Confident Girls: 100 Tips for Parents and Teachers, by Elizabeth Hartley-Brewer (Cambridge, Mass.: Fisher Books, 2000). Straightforward confidence boosters to help girls recognize their talents and trust and love themselves.

For Kids

Behind My Back: Girls Write About Bullies, Cliques, Popularity, and Jealousy, by Rachel Simmons (New York: Harvest Books, 2004). Best-selling author of *Odd Girl Out* writes a powerful book for preteen and teen girls.

Losers, Inc., by Claudia Mills (New York: Scholastic, 1997). Always comparing his abilities to others', the boy considers himself a loser—that is, until he finally learns to find worth in himself. Ages 8 to 12.

7 x 9 = Trouble, by Claudia Mills (New York: Farrar, Straus & Giroux, 2002). A third-grade boy struggles learning his multiplication facts. If only he were as smart as Laura or as quick as his brother. Wilson learns he doesn't have to be jealous: if he keeps on trying, he'll succeed at his own speed. Ages 7 to 10.

15

Left Out

Everyday Behaviors: Put down, ostracized, not chosen, excluded

Friendship Skill Builder: Bouncing Back Gracefully

"Mo-oommm, Sammy told me to get lost."
"I try to talk to Tiffany and Kimmy, but they just walk away."
"No, I didn't get invited. And I'm never asking them over again."

WHAT'S WRONG?

If your kid is nixed from the invite list, turned down by the girl he has a crush on, or has a new haircut that everybody makes fun of, it can be painful, but it's a normal part of growing up. Believe me, your kid will live. But if your child is continually and consistently excluded by his peers, then the problem can be more serious. In fact it can be emotionally debilitating and can greatly diminish your child's self-esteem. What's more, of all the friendship issues, rejection is highly correlated with depression and mental health problems further down the road.

WHY IS THIS HAPPENING?

Are the kids who are rejecting your child a bunch of mean-spirited, vicious bullies or kids she shouldn't be hanging around with anyway? If they do seem like pretty good kids, might there be a weakness in your child's friendship-building skills? Here are some things to consider:

- ☐ Is your daughter too bossy and domineering? Does she turn other kids off? (If so, also see Bossy.)
- ☐ Is she manipulative, whiny, or aggressive? (If so, also see Hot Tempered or Fights.)
- ☐ Does your kid dress, look, or act different from the other kids? (If so, also see Different.)
- ☐ Are you encouraging your child to be too snooty or competitive? (If so, also see Too Competitive.)
- ☐ Have you been overly critical of your kid's friends so that you're creating a barrier between them?
- ☐ Is he insensitive, selfish, or unwilling to share? (If so, also see Insensitive or Doesn't Share.)
- ☐ Are you pushing your kid to be friends with peers he doesn't like or has nothing in common with?
- ☐ Has your kid resorted to backstabbing or gossip to try to be included and is now excluded by other kids? (If so, also see Gossips or Tattletale.)
- ☐ Does your kid lack the skills the other kids in a particular group possess?
- ☐ Is she new to the neighborhood, class, or team and doesn't know anyone? (If so, also see New Kid.)

☐ Does he have difficulty reading the emotions of other kids? (If so, also see Clueless.)

☐ Is she trying to break into an established group that is exclusive? (If so, also see Cliques.)

What is your best guess as to why your kid is being rejected? Write it here.

_____

_____

_____

WHAT SHOULD I SAY?

- *Don't brush it off.* This is painful stuff, so do show some empathy and acknowledge your child's distress. "I'm so sorry Jenny hung up on you again. I know how hurtful that can be."
- *Ask for specifics.* Sometimes a reality check helps us understand the difference between everyday slights and cruel rejection. "What did you say to her before she hung up? Is this the same problem you told me about before?"
- *Share your experiences.* "I remember when kids in my fifth-grade class wouldn't let me on the basketball team. I begged my mom to let me stay home." It might help your kid appreciate that this kind of rejection by a friend has happened before, and even to you. 🛑 **Research has shown that even the most popular kids experience some form of rejection on a regular basis. So point out to your child that he's not the only one suffering from friends' rebuffs.** 🛑
- *Be optimistic.* "Don't worry. It may take a while, but we're going to work this out." Reassure your child that it may take time to learn a few new skills, but that you're confident she'll eventually bounce back and try again.

FRIENDSHIP SKILL BUILDER

Bouncing Back Gracefully

All kids are rejected, all kids are criti-
cized, and all kids are teased. But well-
liked kids know how to shrug off the
stings and slams. They're remembered not for their scenes
or tears but for how they move on. So teach these steps
to help your child learn how to deal with rejection gracefully and to move on.

1. ***Stay poised.*** Poised means keeping your composure and staying under control. Look at the person
   who told you no. Try not to make a face, glare, or
   grimace.

2. ***Stay calm.*** Keep your cool. Having a meltdown
   isn't a good way to make or keep friends. In fact,
   it turns kids off. So when you're rejected, try to
   relax. Take a deep breath, count to five inside your
   head, or think of something else if you start to get
   upset.

3. ***Say "Okay" and accept the answer.*** Using as firm
   and strong a voice as you can, reply, "Okay, maybe
   next time." Don't argue or beg. It doesn't work. If
   you disagree, bring it up at another time. Don't
   ask, "Why not?" every time, or the kids will see
   you as a moaner.

4. ***Move on.*** Hold your head high and walk away.
   Don't complain to another kid about the kid who
   just told you no. Instead try to learn from the experience.

5. ***Look at the big picture.*** Bouncing back means you
   have to think long term and understand that life

> goes on; you'll have another chance. If you make
> a big scene, that's all the kids will remember. If
> these kids keep rejecting you, then maybe you're
> trying for the wrong group.

- *Be frank.* The only way you can help your child improve
  the situation is to be kind but candid about what is going
  on. If you can point out one thing at a time that needs fix-
  ing, your child won't feel too overwhelmed and will be
  more encouraged to start tuning up. "I noticed you always
  whine if you can't go first. Did you see the looks the other
  kids were giving you? Your voice really turned them off."

WHAT SHOULD I DO?

- *Teach your child how to deal with rejection.* If your child
  whines, cries, or pleads to be included, chances are she'll
  turn the group off. So suggest she try to maintain her dignity despite her pain.
- *Figure out the cause.* Watch how your kid interacts with others. Talk to your child's teachers, counselors, and coaches.
  Find out what's really going on and heed their suggestions.
- *Watch for serious trouble.* Rejection can be the cause of serious emotional trauma and unhealthy reactions. 🛑 **Children who are repeatedly rejected by peers are also more
  likely to suffer from depression and other mental health
  problems. So be on the alert for behaviors that indicate
  that your child is really suffering, and seek help.** 🛑
- *Teach a new skill.* If your younger kid is hoarding toys,
  show him how to make friends by sharing. If the kids are
  playing baseball and your ten-year-old can't hit, take some
  time for batting practice. If your teen's gossip and backstabbing are turning off classmates, it's time for a serious

talk about how kids' disloyalty leads to rejection. (Also see Cliques, Tattletale, or Gossips.)

- *Provide opportunities for practice.* Let your kid try out the new skill on you or someone younger than her; she'll feel more comfortable rehearsing in a situation with less stress.
- *Find new friends.* You might cultivate other adults who have kids the same age. Or introduce your child to a hobby, sport, or interest he can share with other kids.
- *Help her fit in.* Take a good look at how the other kids dress and act. Watch what their interests are. If every other kid has a skateboard and your kid doesn't, get one. If all the other kids wear baggy jeans, then it's time to bite the bullet. Your kid needs to fit in more. (Also see Different.)
- *Teach resilience.* It's crucial for your child not to feel thoroughly defeated and give up on having friends because she has been experiencing rejection. 🛑 **Resilience has been found to be one of the most important factors in dealing with inevitable hard knocks and obstacles. Not only that, it's teachable. So be sure you take time to teach your child the importance and skills of bouncing back.** 🛑
- *Teach your child how to join a new group.* Some kids push too quickly and try too hard when they ask to join a group. And they are often rejected. If this is your child, help her learn how to join a group the right way. Here are the steps to teach your child:
  - *Watch the group from a few feet back for clues.* Do they appear closed or receptive? Is their game just starting or almost over? Do you know the game rules? Do you have the skills to play? Stand close enough so they can acknowledge you, but far enough back so you're not "in" the group.
  - *Walk toward the kid or group.* Hold your head high and shoulders back so you look confident.
  - *Look at one of the kids in the group.* Does the child look friendly? Does he acknowledge you? Does he smile? If

the answer is no to any of those questions, walk on. Chances are the kid doesn't want you to join. If yes, go to the next step.

- **Say hello or give a compliment.** Try "Hello," "Nice shot," or "Looks like fun."
- **Try to establish eye contact with one member and smile.** If the group appears interested (a good indicator is whether anybody looks at you and smiles back), ask to join. "Can I play?" "Need another player?" "Okay if I join?"
- **Walk on if they say no.** Don't beg, plead, or cry. Just walk on and try another group.

21-DAY FRIENDSHIP FOLLOW-UP

Over the next 21 days, here's what I will do to help my child learn Friendship Skill Builder: Bouncing Back Gracefully:

_____

_____

_____

FRIENDSHIP SKILL BUILDER BOOKS

For Parents and Teachers

Nurturing Resilience in Our Children: Answers to the Most Important Parenting Questions, by Robert Brooks and Sam Goldstein (New York: Contemporary Books, 2002). In this book based on real queries, the authors explain how parents can best help their children cope with specific adversities and bounce back from frustrations and challenges.

Playground Politics: Understanding the Emotional Life of Your School-Age Child, by Stanley I. Greenspan (Reading, Mass.: Addison-Wesley, 1993). An imminent child psychiatrist describes

FRIENDSHIP TIP

Rejection Really Hurts

Don't be too quick to shrug off your kid's complaints about how much his friends' rejections hurt. Psychology professors at Macquarie University in Sydney, Australia, recently set up brain-imaging tests on volunteers. They created tasks in which the volunteers were socially snubbed. When they were teased or rejected, their brain images lit up almost exactly the same way as the images of people experiencing physical pain. Those snubs really do hurt our kids.

---

the normal stages of emotional development in children from the ages of five to twelve. Chapters are also devoted to kid rejection and offer parents advice on ways to handle it.

What to Do . . . When Kids Are Mean to Your Child, by Elin McCoy (Pleasantville, N.Y.: Reader's Digest, 1997). A wonderful compilation of strategies for parents to help kids handle peer meanness, rejection, and teasing.

You Can't Say You Can't Play, by Vivian Gussen Paley (Cambridge, Mass.: Harvard University Press, 1993). Explores how to keep students from being ignored by their classmates. The author describes what happened when she asked students ranging from kindergarten to fifth grade to debate the proposition "You can't say you can't play." Woven throughout Paley's lessons is a parable about loneliness and rejection, which enables readers to share a child's view of the world.

For Kids

How to Lose All Your Friends, by Nancy Carlson (New York: Viking Penguin, 1994). Colorful pictures and simple text help kids learn a few of the most basic premises of what *will* turn kids off. Ages 5 to 10.

Joshua T. Bates Takes Charge, by Susan Shreve (New York: Knopf, 1993). Fifth-grader Joshua Bates's biggest worry is being left out. But being "in" depends on whether you're labeled as a nerd. Ages 8 to 11.

Reluctantly Alice, by Phyllis R. Naylor (New York: Atheneum, 1991). A mean girl and her pals reject another seventh-grade girl, making fun of her, throwing food, and tripping her in the hall. She handles it by choosing to interview the bully for a class project, and the incidents stop. Ages 9 to 12.

Stand Tall, Molly Lou Mellon, by Patty Lovell (New York: Putnam, 2001). A joyous story of a young girl starting a new school and how she manages to stand tall and overcome peer rejection by staying true to herself. Ages 5 to 8.

The Brand New Kid, by Katie Couric (New York: Doubleday, 2000). Two little girls show true compassion when a not-so-ordinary boy joins their classroom. A great springboard for discussing being left out and the importance of acceptance.

16

New Kid

Everyday Behaviors: Doesn't know anyone in the class, on the team, in the neighborhood; has difficulty breaking into a new social scene

Friendship Skill Builder: Making New Friends

"They only want to play with their old friends."
"Why did we have to move?"
"You ruined my life—everybody hates me here."

WHAT'S WRONG?

Any new social scene can be really tough. Having all new class-mates, joining an unfamiliar team, going away to camp alone, and especially moving aren't easy. And oh, how kids can pour on the guilt to remind us they're not happy campers: "You're ruining my life!" "Why are you sending me to that dumb old camp?" "Why can't we move back to our old neighborhood?"

"Do you have any idea how unhappy you've made me?" Knowing that our kids are lonely, feeling left out, and desperately missing their old group is tough. As much as we'd love to, we can't instantly wipe away their pain because they've left behind their best friends and can't fit in with the new crowd. But we can ease their discomfort by making the transition a bit smoother. We can help them find ways to make new friends. We can even teach them new friendship-making skills that actually may be ones they can use in other social arenas. So think positively and stay focused on what you can do to boost your child's friendship quotient and get her through this tough time.

WHY IS THIS HAPPENING?

You'd probably say that the obvious answer to the "Why is this happening?" question is "Because we moved!" or "My kid is in a new class." Your kid, of course, might have a slightly different response: "It's because you made me leave my real friends who like me." But let's pose the question a bit differently: Just why is your child having problems meeting and making new friends? Here are some things to consider:

☐ What about your neighborhood: Do any kids live there? Have you checked out all possibilities of where your child could meet new kids, such as park and recreation programs, organized sports, local parks, after-school programs, Boys and Girls Clubs, scouting, music programs?

☐ Are you making an effort to meet parents of children your kid's age? (*Hint:* If not, do.)

☐ Is your kid doing something very specific that turns the other kids off? Try looking at your kid through the eyes of would-be friends. If you see potential problems, target one and then make a specific plan for teaching a new friendship skill to replace it. (See the Contents for a list of friendship issues in this book.)

- [ ] Does your child fit in with how the other kids dress and act? Have you really taken a close look at the attire, speech, culture, and even haircuts of the other kids? (Also see Different.)
- [ ] Does your child know how to greet others, introduce herself to someone new, start up a conversation, and keep a conversation going? Is it hard for your child to meet kids because she is overanxious or too shy? (Also see Shy.)
- [ ] Is your child attempting to break into a clique of kids who have known each other a while and are exclusive? (Also see Cliques.)
- [ ] Is your child experiencing more than typical "changing pangs"? Are you seeing such behavior as loss of appetite, sleeping problems, nightmares, outbursts of anger, tears, reluctance to leave the house or you, difficult concentrating? If so, seek outside help.

What's your best shot at why your child is having such a hard time being the "new kid"? Write it here.

_____

_____

_____

FRIENDSHIP SKILL BUILDER

Making New Friends
Being the new kid with any group of kids may be a little scary at first, but there are a few tips to help your child learn how to make new friends. Here are some steps to teach your child to get started.

1. ***Choose someone you want to meet.*** Pick a kid who seems friendly and is not too busy with something or someone. It sometimes helps to look for someone who is doing something that you do too, like playing soccer or the guitar, or drawing. Walk up to the kid.

2. ***Look the person in the eye.*** Hold your head high. Smile! If the person doesn't look at you, it probably means he isn't interested in meeting you. Walk on.

3. ***Say hello and introduce yourself with a firm, friendly voice.*** "Hi, my name is John." You might even offer your hand and shake hands firmly.

4. ***Wait for the person to respond.*** If the kid doesn't give his name back, ask "What's your name?" or "And your name is?" Be sure to remember the name.

5. ***Say something friendly or ask a friendly question.*** "Glad to meet you." "You're great at soccer." "Do you go to school here?" "Do you live around here?" "Do you skate here often?" You can also tell the person something about yourself. "I just moved from Minnesota." "I live in the yellow house." "I like skateboarding, too."

6. ***Keep at it.*** If it doesn't work out the first or second time, try again. If you and the kid seem to hit it off, arrange to meet again or do something. You may want to write down her phone number or e-mail address.

WHAT SHOULD I SAY?

- *Acknowledge feelings.* If your child doesn't share her feelings, you can help her recognize how she feels: "You must be feeling lonely and miss your old group." "I can see you're worried." It's tough to join a new team when you don't know any of the kids. Let her know such feelings are normal.

- **Be reassuring.** "It may take time to meet new kids and make new friends. Many of these kids have been friends with one another for quite a while, and may not be too receptive to a new person joining in." "Remember way back when you didn't know anybody, even Kevin, and then you became great friends? It will take time, but you'll make new friends just like you did at our other home."

- **Keep communication open.** Even if your kid won't talk to you, keep talking. "Is there anything I can do to make you feel more comfortable?" "Do the kids wear or have anything different from the kids back home? Do you need anything?" "Would you like me to talk to your teacher?"

- **Identify strengths.** One way kids learn to cope in a new situation is by relying on their strengths. So remind your child of his talents. "It will be hard at first because we don't know anyone, but I know you'll make friends. Once the kids get to know you, they'll like you. You're fun to be around." "You made friends back home whenever you played soccer. The kids saw how good you were and wanted to be on the team with you."

- **Support old friendships.** "I bought a prepaid phone card for you to use any time you want to call your friends back home." "Would you like to invite your friend to come and stay for the weekend? I can talk to his mom about the possibility if you'd like."

WHAT SHOULD I DO?

- **Become acquainted with other parents.** Be a room parent, offer to carpool, sign up to coach, be the team mom, meet other camper parents, and attend PTA meetings and other school functions. Getting to know parents of your child's potential friends is often a great way to invite the families over, giving your child the opportunity to have a new playmate. Also introduce yourself to the neighbors; sometimes our kid's best friends can be literally next door. Find out who among your work colleagues has children; it's a way not only to learn about available kid activities but also to arrange play dates for younger children (or find a babysitter!).

- *Tour the new surroundings.* Take your child to visit his new school and neighborhood, ideally before the move. Schedule times to meet the principal and his teachers. Ask the camp to send photos and phone numbers or e-mail addresses of other kids who have attended before to get an idea of what it's really like. If possible, watch a team practice and talk to the coach or to former members to find out what it's like to be on this team.

- *Talk to the teacher or coach.* Ask for a list of phone numbers of the other students or teammates. Also ask your child's teacher or coach for the names of other children who might have common interests or temperaments to your kid and could possibly become friends.

- *Find outlets for your kid that attract peers.* Look for opportunities for your child to meet kids anywhere or elsewhere—for example, scouting, park and recreation programs, Boys and Girls Clubs, the YMCA, 4-H, teen clubs, church groups, sports teams, library programs, afterschool programs, or other youth groups. Pediatricians' offices and libraries often are a good place for picking up schedules of upcoming kid events. Your goal is to help your kid find ways to meet new kids. Making friends is her job—helping her find potential friendship possibilities is your role.

- *Seek activities that match your child's interests.* If your child enjoys tennis, make sure she's on the courts. If he likes music, sign him up for classes. If he loves to swim, enroll him in the YMCA. Find out if there's a particular sport or hobby that seems to be hot in town with the kids your child's age: soccer, skateboarding, rollerblading, dirt biking, jazz, band, chess. The trick is to match the activity with *your child's* strengths and interests. Then provide lessons and help him practice so his confidence grows and, you hope, he can use the new skill to meet new kids. Meeting kids with the same interests raises the chances of going from acquaintance to friend. That's because kids who share the same interests are more likely to want to be together.

- *Help your kid blend in.* Clothes, haircuts, shoe styles, and accessories really do matter in helping kids gain peer approval, and communities do have their own culture. So visit your kid's school (if possible even before the move) and study the appearance of the more popular kids. Does your kid dress like them? If not, help him find the styles that let him blend in.

- *Provide a telephone book.* Provide your child with a small book (or at least a note card) to keep in his pocket or backpack. If he does meet someone new, suggest that he write the kid's name, phone number, and even e-mail address on the card.

- *Teach new social skills.* Learning any new skill takes practice. So role-play with your child this chapter's Friendship Skill Builder (see page 205) as often as it takes for him to be comfortable using it on his own. Begin by introducing yourself to your child so he can see what it looks like. Try to find opportunities for your child to see you using the skill in the real world: deliberately introduce yourself to as many new people as you can (in the grocery line, at school, at the park). Kids really learn new skills best by first watching, then trying. So give him plenty of opportunities to see this skill in action.

FRIENDSHIP TIP

Like a Rolling Stone
Data show that one-fifth of all Americans move every year. In fact, over a five-year period, almost half of Americans move at least once. Your kids may be giving you a heavy dose of guilt about your "making him move," but keep the perspective that hundreds of other families are facing the same pains as yours. The real statistic you should be aware of is this: 23 percent of children who moved frequently repeated a grade compared with 12 percent of children who never or infrequently moved. The lesson here is this: stay in close contact with your child's teacher—even if your kid tells you "Everything's fine, Mom."

 21-DAY FRIENDSHIP FOLLOW-UP

Over the next 21 days, here's what I will do to help my child learn Friendship Skill Builder: Making New Friends:

_____

_____

_____

 FRIENDSHIP SKILL BUILDER BOOKS

For Kids
Alexander, Who's Not (Do You Hear Me? I Mean It!) Going to Move, by Judith Viorst (New York: Aladdin, 1998). Alexander's

family is moving a thousand miles away, and he does not want to go. His adamant voice is one kids will identify with. Ages 5 to 8.

Goodbye House (Moonbear Books), by Frank Asch (New York: Aladdin, 1989). Baby Bear and his family are moving; just as the van is about to leave, Bear says good-bye to each room in the now empty house. He learns the importance of saying good-bye and that he'll carry his memories forever. Ages 4 to 8.

How to Start a Conversation and Make Friends, by Don Garbor (New York: Fireside, 2001). This book is written for adults, but because there are so many great tips, it might be just the resource a parent or teacher needs to help an adolescent make new friends. For older children and teens.

I Like Where I Am, by Jessica Harper (New York: Putnam, 2004). A six-year-old expresses his doubts about heading off to Little Rock and can barely utter the word *move,* preferring to call it *trouble.* After the move takes place, he discovers that he likes his new home after all but will always keep fond memories of his old home. Ages 3 to 8.

I'm Not Moving, Mama, by Nancy White Carlstrom (New York: Aladdin, 1999). Little Mouse refuses to leave his room on moving day. But Mama tells him about all the good new things they'll share in their new home. Little Mouse realizes that what's most important is being together. Ages 4 to 8.

Who Will Be My Friends? (Easy I Can Read Series), by Syd Hoff (New York: HarperTrophy, 1985). Freddy likes his new room and new street. The policeman and mailman are very nice. But what Freddy *really* wants are friends—and he looks everywhere until he finds them! Ages 4 to 8.

17

Peer Pressure

Everyday Behaviors: Submissive; follows the crowd; doesn't stand up to peers; loses confidence and status as equal

Friendship Skill Builder: Standing Up for Yourself

"I knew you'd be mad—but I wanted the girls to like me."
"I tried to say no, but Jake wouldn't listen."
"It's hard to tell the kids what I want to do, Mom. I really do try."

WHAT'S WRONG?

"What were you thinking?" "But didn't you tell the kids it wasn't right?" "You did what?!" Are you concerned that your kid always seems to go along with the crowd? Does she have a tough time speaking up and letting her opinions be known? Have you noticed that your child can be easily swayed to do what the other kids want? Some kids may call him a wimp or a scaredy-cat; your terms may be more along the lines of *submissive, follower,* or even *pushover.* This may not seem such a big deal now, but peer pressure gets nothing but tougher as kids get older. After all, if he has a hard time saying no to the tamer challenges of younger kids, fast-forward your concerns to the kinds of wilder, scarier issues he may face later. And there is cause for some concern. 🛑 **A survey of 991 kids ages nine to fourteen revealed that 36 percent feel pressure from peers to smoke marijuana, 40 percent feel pressure to have sex, 36 percent feel pressure to shoplift, and 40 percent feel pressure to drink.** 🛑

Here's the good news, though: assertiveness skills can be taught to kids. Though it is never too late, the sooner you start boosting this Friendship Skill Builder, the greater your child's confidence will be in social settings and the easier you'll sleep.

WHY IS THIS HAPPENING?

There are many reasons why kids are submissive or easily swayed by peers. Here are some things to consider:

- [ ] Has your child always been more hesitant to speak up, or is this a new trait? If it is new, what might be triggering it? For instance: a new self-consciousness due to approaching adolescence? An acne flare-up? New braces? Glasses?
- [ ] Has he been humiliated for his ideas? Has a traumatic public experience left him a bit leery of speaking up?
- [ ] Is he unsure of his social status? Does he go along with the kids because he wants to be "one of the guys"? Is he afraid if he doesn't do what the kids want he'll be ostracized?
- [ ] Is your child the youngest in the family? Or does he hang around with older children? Is he less mature than the other kids?

☐ Does he just plain lack confidence in his ideas? Has he been told that his opinions don't matter or are "stupid"?

☐ Does he have a speech impediment of any kind? Does he have a lisp, stutter, delayed speech, or limited vocabulary, or is he hearing impaired? Was his speech delayed when he was young? Did he rely on someone (such as you, a sibling, or a friend) to speak for him?

☐ Has he been overprotected by adults? Does he always rely on someone else to speak up for him?

☐ Was your child reinforced for his assertiveness or told to "stay quiet"? Are you a family that follows the "children should be seen and not heard" philosophy? Is assertiveness seen as an undesirable trait? Is it part of your culture for children to be quiet?

☐ Is your child's temperament shy or more sensitive? Is it just harder for him to speak up? (If so, also see Shy or Too Sensitive.)

☐ Might she be hanging around a faster or tougher crowd of kids? Or has she been bullied or harassed by peers? Might she actually be fearful or intimidated by a peer or peers? (If so, also see Teased or Bullied and Harassed.)

☐ Does your child have a strong moral compass? Does he know what is right and wrong? Does he know your views? Have you had frequent talks on what kind of behavior you expect? Simply, does your child know what he stands for so he can share those beliefs with peers?

What do you think is the primary reason your child is so easily influenced by peers and goes along with the crowd? Write it down.

_____

_____

_____

_____

FRIENDSHIP SKILL BUILDER

Standing Up for Yourself

It's not always easy to buck the crowd. Everyone wants to be liked. But for your child's own self-confidence, independence, and future success in life, it's important she learn to stand up to a friend. Here are some tips to help your child learn to assert herself and do what she knows is right.

1. ***Check your moral compass.*** What is your friend telling you to do? Is it something against your family rules or that your gut tells you is just wrong? If you don't feel comfortable doing it or think it's not wise or safe, then get ready to assert yourself.

2. ***Use confident body posture.*** Hold your head high. Look the person right in the eye.

3. ***Speak in a strong tone of voice.*** No yelling or whispering. Be friendly but determined.

4. ***Tell the friend where you stand.*** A simple no or "No, I don't want to" is fine. You could give reasons: "Nope, I don't want to smoke. My luck, I'll get cancer like Grandpa" or "No, I studied too hard to give you the answers." It's not your job to change your friend's mind, but to stay true to *your* beliefs.

It will help your child to see what confident body posture looks like so she can use it herself. So role-play with your child the "confident look" and the "hesitant look." Then encourage your child to be on the lookout for confident or hesitant posture in other people. Look everywhere: at the mall, on the playground, even at television and movie actors. Soon your child will be able to spot confident posture instantly and to copy and use it himself. (Also see the Friendship Skill Builders in Teased and Bullied and Harassed.)

WHAT SHOULD I SAY?

- **Bring the issue into the open.** If your kid is suffering from a lack of assertiveness skills, it may be very hard for him to talk about this problem, so take the lead. "I noticed during playgroup today that Johnny told you to throw sand in the sink, and you did it. You know better. So let's talk about why you went along." "You know Renee's house is off-limits, but you went along with the group anyway. You have to learn to stand up to your friends and do what you know is right."

- **Share your beliefs.** Parents who raise assertive kids who can stand up for their beliefs don't do so by accident. They make sure their children know what they stand for. "In our family we don't watch violent movies. Plain and simple. So tell your friends you can't go." "I don't care if all your friends use four-letter words, for you that's forbidden." "The next time a friend dares you to smoke a cigarette, just stand up and walk out. You need to stick up for what you know is right. I know how much you hate smoking."

- **Refrain from labeling.** Be careful *not* to apply or let others apply nicknames or derogatory terms—"What a wimp!" "You're such a follower," "She's shy," "He's a scaredy-cat"— to your child. Labels can become self-fulfilling and are often tough to shake.

- **Teach your child how to say no.** Ask your child to choose phrases he is most comfortable using. "No" can be said alone: "NO!" It can also be followed by a reason: "No, it's just not my style." "No thanks. My parents would kill me."

"No, I don't feel like doing that." "No, I don't want to." "No. I have to get home, and I'm already late." Your child can suggest an alternative: "No. Let's think of something else." "Nope. How 'bout we go to the skate park instead?" *Hint:* Tell your child to repeat the reason a few times using a firm voice. This "broken record" technique helps many kids stand up to peers because they gain confidence just from hearing their own reason over and over. 🛑 **Pushover kids usually stand with heads down, shoulders slumped, arms and knees quivering, and eyes downcast. Even if he says no to his friends, his body sends a far different message, and his words will have little credibility. So it's crucial to teach your child assertive body posture: to hold his head high with shoulders slightly back, look his friend in the eye, and use a confident, firm tone of voice.** 🛑

WHAT SHOULD I DO?

- *Do a reality check.* Is your child being overly submissive or just resisting the influence of a bad crowd? Maybe he should try a different group. (Also see Bad Friends.)
- *Stop rescuing.* If your role has been apologizing, explaining, or basically "doing" for your child, then stop. You child will never learn how to stand up for himself. Instead he'll be forever relying on you.
- *Model assertiveness.* If you want your child to be confident and assertive and to stand up for his beliefs, make sure you display those behaviors. Kids mimic what they see.
- *Point out strong, confident models.* Share examples of courageous historical figures who stood up for their beliefs and didn't follow the crowd: Abe Lincoln, Gandhi, Rosa Parks, and FBI whistle-blowers are a few. Also look for examples in your community or on the nightly news.
- *Reinforce assertiveness.* If you want to raise a child who can stand up for her beliefs, then reinforce any and all efforts

your child makes to be assertive. "I know that was tough telling your friends you had to leave early to make your curfew. I'm proud you were able to stand up to them and not just go along."

- **Hold family debates.** The best way for kids to learn to express themselves is right at home, so why not start "Family Debates," or if you prefer a gentler-sounding approach, "Family Meetings"? Start by setting these five rules: (1) everyone is listened to; (2) no put-downs are allowed; (3) you may disagree, but do so respectfully; (4) talk calmly; and (5) everyone gets a turn. Topics can be the hot-button issues in the world, in school, or right in your home. Here are just a few discussion possibilities: house rules, sibling conflicts, allowances, chores, curfews, parent-set movie restrictions. Real world issues for older kids could include reparations, the Iraq war, the draft, lowering the voting age, legalizing drugs, or stem cell research. Whatever the topic, encourage your hesitant child to speak up and be heard.

- **Don't tolerate excuses.** If you've been working on these skills but your child is still agreeing to do things she knows are wrong so as to go along with the group, such as sneaking into an R-rated movie or using bad words, be sure to take clear action to reestablish your rules and your child's need to stand up to peer pressure.

 **21-DAY FRIENDSHIP FOLLOW-UP**

Over the next 21 days, here's what I will do to help my child learn Friendship Skill Builder: Standing Up for Yourself:

_____

_____

_____

FRIENDSHIP TIP

Don't Hover

Parents who encourage their children's social endeavors at a distance are more successful in raising confident and assertive kids. In fact, those parents who tend to intervene and interfere in their kids' social lives actually hinder their children's relationships with friends. Better to stand back and supervise your child informally whenever he's with friends.

 FRIENDSHIP SKILL BUILDER BOOKS

For Parents and Teachers

A Teacher's Guide to Stick Up for Yourself! A 10-Part Course in Self-Esteem and Assertiveness for Kids, by Gershen Kaufman and Lev Raphael (Minneapolis, Minn.: Free Spirit, 1999). A helpful guide for caregivers.

Queen Bees and Wannabes: Helping Your Daughter Survive Cliques, Gossip, Boyfriends, and Other Realities of Adolescence, by Rosalind Wiseman (New York: Three Rivers Press, 2002). Valuable ideas for parents who want to help their daughters survive the friendship jungle.

For Kids

Coping with Peer Pressure, by Leslie Kaplan (New York: Rosen, 1987). Ideas for helping kids learn to stand up for themselves. For young teens.

Liking Myself, by Pat Palmer (San Luis Obispo, Calif.: Impact, 1977). A great source of ideas for helping kids learn assertiveness skills. Ages 5 to 9.

Stick Up for Yourself! Every Kid's Guide to Personal Power and Positive Self-Esteem, by Gershen Kaufman and Lev Raphael (Minneapolis, Minn.: Free Spirit, 1990). Tips and advice to help kids learn how to use "personal power" responsibly in their relationships. Ages 9 to 13.

The Mouse, the Monster and Me! by Pat Palmer (San Luis Obispo, Calif.: Impact, 1977). Assertiveness concepts taught in a simplified way for kids. Ages 8 to 12.

18

Shy

Everyday Behaviors: Avoids other kids; clingy and dependent; uncomfortable or nervous in most social situations; anxious away from home

Friendship Skill Builder: Making Eye Contact

"Can't I just stay with you?"
"Do I have to go to the party, Mom? I'll just end up sitting by myself again."
"I tried to talk to those kids, but I can't get the words out."

WHAT'S WRONG?

Watching a shy, timid, or hesitant child can be painful. They hang back, look uncomfortable or tense, cry or cling to their parents. As a result they lose out on having fun and experiencing life at its fullest. Being unable to join a group and make

221

new friends will haunt them the rest of their lives if you don't help them do something about it.

If your child is shy, chances are he was born with a more introverted, sensitive personality. This is not about trying to turn him into an extrovert. After all, you can't change your child's personality and natural temperament. But you can help your child learn the skills he needs (and deserves) to feel more comfortable and confident with other kids. And that *is* doable: *shyness doesn't have to be debilitating.* So let's focus on what you can do to enhance your kid's friendship aptitude. 🛑 **Studies have shown that about 90 percent of all anxious kids can be greatly helped by learning coping skills.** 🛑

WHY IS THIS HAPPENING?

Yes, your child may have been born with a shy disposition, but there can be other factors contributing to her reluctance to be with other kids and make new friends. Do any of these factors apply to your child?

☐ If shyness just materialized, what might have triggered it: a divorce, a move, an embarrassing incident in your family?

☐ Does she lack skills for making friends?

☐ Has your child been isolated for one reason or another so that she's had no or limited experience on the social scene?

☐ Is she "with it"? Is she up with the latest music, fashions, dances, movies? Though she may not feel comfortable participating, can she "talk the culture"? Are the other kids dressing or acting in ways she's plain not comfortable participating in?

☐ Is she hanging around with a group of friends who are at the same level? Or is this bunch too advanced, too mature, too "smart" for her?

The Top 25 Friendship Problems

- [ ] Is she the "new kid" to the neighborhood, class, school, club, or team? (Also see New Kid.)
- [ ] Is there a sudden physical change he might feel uncomfortable about: puberty, acne, or weight gain?
- [ ] Does she look and act similarly to other kids? Or is she "different" in some way (be it in intellectual ability, appearance, or physical ability; economic status; or cultural, racial, or religious background)? (Also see Different.)

What is your best guess as to why your child is hesitant or even reluctant to be around kids his age? Write it here.

_____

_____

_____

FRIENDSHIP SKILL BUILDER

Making Eye Contact

Researchers have discovered that one of the most important skills for shy kids to learn is using eye-to-eye contact. Think about it: we like being with people who look at us while we're talking. So here are a few ways to help your child tune in to his friends and appear more at ease.

1. *Stop what you're doing.* When you're with your friend, pay attention. If he starts to talk, focus on what he's saying. Hold your head up and face him.

2. *Look into your friend's eyes.* You don't want to stare—that will make her uncomfortable. So

glance away for a second or two from time to time, but stay focused on her. You might feel uncomfortable at first, so here's a trick: just look at the spot in the middle of the person's eyes on the bridge of her nose. She won't know the difference, and it might make you feel more comfortable.

3. *Listen to the speaker.* Wait until the other person finishes talking; don't interrupt. Try to think about what the person is saying.

4. *Look interested.* Nod your head or say yes. Lean in a bit. And smile if you are enjoying what your friend is saying. You might say "Oh," "I see," "I understand," "Thanks," or "That was interesting." If you don't understand what she has said, you could ask a question: "What do you mean?" "Could you say that again, please?" or "I don't quite understand."

WHAT SHOULD I SAY?

- *Acknowledge anxiety.* Tell your child you can see the problems she's having feeling comfortable with other kids. "I saw you biting your nails a lot yesterday at Jim's house. I also get a little anxious when I'm with people I don't know." "You didn't say anything in carpool today. What would it take to make you feel more comfortable?"

- *Model eye contact.* 🛑 One of the most common traits of well-liked kids is that they use eye contact. In fact, in conversation the average person spends 30 to 60 percent of the time looking at the other person's face. 🛑 As you're talking with your child, say "Look at me" or "Put your eyes on my eyes" or "I want to see your eyes." If your kid is uncomfortable about using eye contact, tell her, "Look at the bridge of my nose."

- *Praise prior success.* It's natural for a shy child to focus on past failures. So help her recall previous experiences when things went really well. "Remember last year's swimming lessons? You begged not to go, but did and met a new friend." "Before you went to Sara's birthday party last month you wanted to stay home. But when you agreed to stay at least half an hour, you ended up one of the last ones to leave."
- *Reinforce smiling!* 🛑 **One of the most common characteristics of confident, well-liked kids is that they smile and smile.** 🛑 So whenever your child displays a smile, reinforce it: "What a great smile!" or "That smile of yours always wins people over." Also point out how your child's smile affects others: "Do you see how kids smile back when you smile?" "That little boy saw your smile and came over to play. Your smile let him know you were friendly."
- *Debrief a stressful event.* If your kid has had a really embarrassing attack of shyness, find a time to discuss what happened and how she could handle it better next time. "Let's think of one thing we can do in the future so you won't be so uncomfortable at Jerry's house." "It sounds like you really didn't like being with so many kids. What if you invite only one friend at a time?" "So what really bugged you was asking Kevin face-to-face. Why not ask him on the phone next time?"
- *Reinforce any social efforts.* Any and every effort your child makes to be even a tad more social deserves a pat on the back: "I saw how you walked up to that new boy today. Good for you!" "I noticed that you really made an effort to say hello to Sheila's mom. She looked so pleased!"
- *Don't ever label.* Experts agree that one of the biggest reasons kids act shy is because they are labeled shy. *Never* let anyone—teacher, friend, relative, sibling, stranger, you—call your child *shy.* "He's not shy. He just likes watching first and sizing things up." "You just take time to warm up. That's fine. Lots of people do the same thing." 🛑 **Research shows**

that although our children may be born with the tendency toward shyness, whether or not they *become* shy is largely due to whether or not we *label* them shy. 🛑

WHAT SHOULD I DO?

- *Check your expectations.* Be sure you're not pushing your child to do things that are difficult or beyond his comfort zone. Here are kinds of adult behaviors that can exacerbate shyness. Do any apply to you or your parenting partner?

  ☐ Do you ever force your kid to perform in public?
  ☐ Do you push her too quickly to join into a group and not allow "warm-up" time?
  ☐ Do you push him to do things that might be important to you but not to him?
  ☐ Do you compare her performance and personality to those of her siblings?
  ☐ Do you label your child "shy" or reinforce this trait?
  ☐ Does your child depend on you to initiate his conversations, set his social schedule, or take care of him in social settings?
  ☐ Is your child now relying on you to help him cope?

- *Schedule warm-up time.* Some kids take longer to warm up in a social setting, so give your child time to settle in. Be patient and don't push too quickly. 🛑 **Researchers found that parents who tend to gently encourage and loosely supervise their kids' social activities are more successful in boosting their kids' friendship skills than parents who micromanage and supervise too closely.** 🛑 Let her watch a bit, figure out what's up, and set her own time frame for joining in.

- *Help him fit in.* All kids need to feel as comfortable as possible when they're with their friends. So make sure your son or daughter has a cool haircut and the "in" sneakers, backpack, jacket, or jeans. These can make a big difference in boosting a kid's comfort level.

- *Make time to know the parents.* Your child will feel more supported if you know his classmates' parents. It will also open up more social opportunities and invitations. So get acquainted and become involved. Doing so will also help your child feel more comfortable in social settings.

- *Practice skills with younger peers.* ⛔ **Research finds that pairing older kids with younger children for brief periods is an excellent way to help the older child try out new social skills that he may feel uncomfortable using with friends his own age.** ⛔ Create opportunities for your kid to play with one other child who is younger: a younger sibling, cousin, or neighbor, or one of your friend's younger kids. For teens, try baby-sitting: it's a great way for a shy kid to earn money as well as practice social skills—such as starting a conversation and using eye contact—that she may be reticent about trying with kids her age.

- *Build on strengths.* Identify a hobby, interest, sport, or talent that your kid enjoys and can excel at. Then help develop the skill so her self-esteem grows. This will increase both her social assets and the likelihood of her being invited by another child with a similar interest to do the activity together.

- *Rehearse social situations.* Prepare your kid for an upcoming social event by describing the setting, expectations, and other kids who will be there. Then help him practice meeting others, using good table manners, making small talk, and even saying good-bye. Practicing conversation skills on the telephone with a supportive listener on the other end is always less threatening for shyer kids than doing so face-to-face. This will decrease some of the anxiety he's bound to have from being in a new setting.

- *Make one-on-one play dates.* ⛔ **Dr. Fred Frankel, a psychologist and developer of the world-famous UCLA Social Skills Training Program, suggests one-on-one** play dates as one of the best ways for kids to build social confidence. Many kids can be overwhelmed in groups, so limit the number of friends to one at a time. Then gradually increase the number as your child gains confidence.

 FRIENDSHIP TIP

Forty Percent Shy
Your child is not alone. Philip Zimbardo and Shirley Radl, authors of *The Shy Child,* tell us that two out of every five people consider themselves shy. So reassure your child and yourself that shyness is a universal, widespread feeling that millions of people cope with every day.

 21-DAY FRIENDSHIP FOLLOW-UP

Over the next 21 days, here's what I will do to help my child learn Friendship Skill Builder: Making Eye Contact:

_____

_____

_____

 FRIENDSHIP SKILL BUILDER BOOKS

For Parents and Teachers
The Shy Child: A Parent's Guide to Preventing and Overcoming Shyness from Infancy to Adulthood (2nd ed.), by Philip G. Zim-

bardo and Shirley Radl (New York: Doubleday, 1999). A must-read for parents of shyer kids of any age. Invaluable!

The Shy Child: Helping Children Triumph over Shyness, by Ward Kent Swallow with Laurie Halse Anderson (New York: Time Warner, 2000). This parenting manual offers pragmatic step-by-step solutions to help shy kids lead more confident lives.

The Shyness Breakthrough: A No-Stress Plan to Help Your Shy Child Warm Up, Open Up, and Join the Fun, by Bernardo J. Carducci (Emmaus, Pa.: Rodale, 2003). Written by one of the world's leading authorities on shy behavior, this one is a must. Packed with ideas that help you understand your child's unique shyness profile, the book also includes an easy-to-follow plan to help your child successfully face the challenges that shyness poses for her.

For Kids

I Don't Know Why . . . I Guess I'm Shy: A Story About Taming Imaginary Fears, by Barbara S. Cain (Washington, D.C.: American Psychological Association, 1999). Shows children that shy feelings don't have to get in the way of having fun and making friends. Ages 5 to 8.

Little Miss Shy, by Roger Hargreaves (New York: Putnam Publishing Group, 1998). Part of the delightful Mr. Men and Little Miss series. The simple text and illustrations are perfect for younger kids. Ages 3 to 7.

Painfully Shy: How to Overcome Social Anxiety and Reclaim Your Life, by Barbara G. Markway and Gregory P. Markway (New York: St. Martin's Press, 2001). Written by two clinical psychologists for adults, the book offers techniques to help shy individuals master social anxiety. A parent could offer several of these ideas to an anxious teen.

Shy Charles, by Rosemary Wells (New York: Penguin Putnam Books for Young Readers, 2001). Preschooler Charles is as quiet as a mouse—and it doesn't bother him one bit. Charles resists all of his parents' efforts to make him become more outgoing. Ages 4 to 7.

19

Siblings

Everyday Behaviors: Friction, arguments, tears, and hurt feelings; feeling of resentment or favoritism

Friendship Skill Builder: Solving the Problem Between You Without an Adult

"Mo-oommm, make Kara stop fighting with me!"
"Stay away from my friends. Can't you find your own?"
"I hate her! Can't you put her up for adoption?"

WHAT'S WRONG?

Sibling rivalry is among the most exasperating issues on the home front. After all, most parents would readily admit that they always envisioned their children not only getting along but considering each other to be their best and closest friends. So it's a rude awakening when your children's tears, battles, friction, and jealousies replace your image of a lifetime of love, friendship, and adoration. What comes out of these brothers' and sisters' mouths can make you wonder why you didn't go for the only child (or space them twenty years apart).

Sometimes there are serious issues among siblings over jealousy, rivalry, verbal or physical abuse, birth order privilege, and domination. But more often there are simply the continuous day-to-day conflicts that arise among people living together in the same house, such as who gets to use the computer, who has first crack at the shower, who's got the remote control, and who's using the phone. If you let this stuff slide and don't deal with the nitpicking and bickering, the situation at home can escalate into World War III.

So what can you do? Don't go crazy trying to make things equal—it's impossible! And don't have unrealistic expectations about continuous harmony, as battles are inevitable and sometimes unavoidable. But endless night-and-day blitzkrieg doesn't have to be the alternative. There are a few things you can do that will minimize jealousies, conflicts, and bickering and help your kids appreciate one another. Not only that, the same skills can work with their friends. Who knows? Your kids may just end up liking and supporting each other after all. Now that's a pleasant thought, isn't it?

WHY IS THIS HAPPENING?

Here are a few causes of sibling battles, resentment, and animosity. Check ones that apply:

- ☐ Do you expect more of your oldest child?
- ☐ Is one child getting more attention?
- ☐ Do you take sides?
- ☐ Is one sibling feeling she is not being listened to or is being taken advantage of?
- ☐ Do you pamper your youngest?
- ☐ Do you compare your kids in front of each other?

- [ ] Do you provide opportunities for each child to nurture her special talents?
- [ ] Do your eyes light up with the same intensity when you see each of your kids?
- [ ] Do you pay equal attention to each child's hobbies, friends, school, and interests?
- [ ] Do you set rules and expectations for each child that your other kids consider fair?
- [ ] Do you distribute chores, rewards, and opportunities fairly among your kids?
- [ ] Do you expect your kids to share their friends? Are they always together when their friends come over? Is it causing resentment because there's no "alone" time with friends?
- [ ] Are your kids really different in temperament, personality, abilities, priorities, and style?
- [ ] Do any of your kids have different parents? Are you a blended family?
- [ ] Do you think you just don't have enough time and energy and other resources for all your kids? Or do your kids have that perception?
- [ ] Are you fighting with your spouse? Are your kids imitating your behavior?
- [ ] Or might all this friction among siblings be because they simply don't know how to solve their own problems? Have they been depending on you to be their negotiator?

What is your best guess as to why your kids are battling away? Write it on the lines here.

_____

_____

_____

_____

FRIENDSHIP SKILL BUILDER

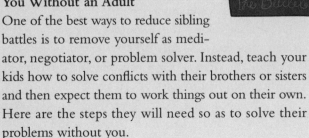

Solving the Problem Between You Without an Adult

One of the best ways to reduce sibling battles is to remove yourself as mediator, negotiator, or problem solver. Instead, teach your kids how to solve conflicts with their brothers or sisters and then expect them to work things out on their own. Here are the steps they will need so as to solve their problems without you.

1. ***Calm down.*** You'll never solve a problem when you're upset. So decide if you need to take a recess from each other. Walk away until you're calm or call a "time out" until you're both in control and can talk things through.

2. ***Figure out the real problem.*** Take turns saying what's bugging you. Don't interrupt.

3. ***Focus on the problem, not the sibling.*** It helps to first think what your brother or sister did that bothered you and stay away from making angry attacks on your sibling's personality and character. No blaming. No name-calling. No put-downs. Stick to the facts.

4. ***Use an "I message" to say what's bothering you.*** Don't get into "You did this, you did that" mode. Instead say, "I get really upset when you take my stuff. I want you to ask me for permission first." "I don't like to be teased. Please stop." "I'm not getting a turn playing Nintendo, and it's not fair. You need to take turns." "I have to find out my homework and need to use the phone."

5. ***Remain respectful and calm.*** Name-calling, insults, and sarcasm are not allowed. You must remain respectful, and you must also listen to the other side.

6. ***Agree to a fair solution without using a parent.*** Brainstorm solutions to your problem. Make a rule: no going to Mom or Dad unless someone is hurt or you've really tried to solve this on your own and it's too big a deal. Then agree on the solution that feels best to both of you and try it.

WHAT SHOULD I SAY?

- ***Talk to yourself about what's going on.*** Your role in conflicts between siblings is much more important than it is in conflicts your kids may be having with their friends. So take a moment and ask yourself, "Am I playing favorites? Do I really feel more comfortable and enjoy being with Joey more than with Alicia? Have I been unfair? Am I always rushing in to solve their problems so that now they expect me to rescue them every time?" You can also talk to your partner and other members of your family to get their take on what's going on and what needs to be done.

- ***Calm everyone down.*** If there is friction, intervene when emotions are high but *before* an argument escalates. Use whatever works best to calm everyone down: "Why don't you two run a quick lap outside?" "Do five jumping jacks," "Go watch TV," "Take three slow, deep breaths," "Lie down for a few minutes," or "Cuddle a teddy bear." If necessary, separate the two kids until they can be calm and work things through: "I see two angry kids who need to cool down. You go to your room and you to the other room until you can talk calmly."

- *Let each sibling tell the story.* After they've calmed down, have them come back in to you. Ask each kid to take turns explaining her view of what happened. Set rules: "Each of you will have a turn to speak. But as the person is speaking, you must really listen. No interrupting is allowed." If you don't understand, ask for clarification: "Could you explain that to me again?" When the sibling is finished, briefly restate her view to show that you do understand. "Now I want to hear your brother's side." *Hint:* Your goal is to gradually wean your kids from having to use you as their mediator. Help them learn the skills of negotiation and problem solving so they can resolve their own conflicts. It will greatly reduce feelings of sibling resentment and unfair treatment.
- *Identify feelings.* Sometimes all that is needed is for someone to acknowledge the hurt kid's feelings: "You're hurt because you think your sister is being treated more fairly than you are." "You're upset because you're not getting a turn at the computer."
- *See it from the other side.* Kids often get so caught up in feeling they're being treated unfairly that they don't stop to think how the other person might be feeling. So ask, "See it from the other side now. How does your sister feel?" 🛑 **Studies show that preschool- and kindergarten-age kids are just beginning to develop the ability to think about how other people feel; they'll need help and constant reminders to "think about how your sister might feel." So keep guiding your kids.** 🛑
- *No tattling.* Make one rule stick: "Unless you are telling me something that will keep your brother *out of trouble or from being hurt,* I don't want to hear it." Be consistent: "Is this something you can't work out yourself?" or "Is this helpful or unhelpful news?" The rule works wonders in curbing siblings' tattling, putting others down, and gossip.
- *Encourage cooperation.* The next time you observe your

children sharing or playing cooperatively, let them know you are proud of their behavior. If the children know you appreciate their efforts, they are more inclined to repeat them. "I really appreciate how you two worked things out calmly this time. Good for you." "I noticed how you both made an effort to help each other figure out how to put the DVDs away. Nice job." 🛑 **Kids learn cooperative behaviors—such as taking turns, sharing, and helping— best by copying others. They are much more likely to adopt the new behavior if the person modeling it is important to them. So if you really want your kids to cooperate, model the behavior yourself.** 🛑

WHAT SHOULD I DO?

- *Be honest.* No parent is perfect. Every parent occasionally plays favorites, is unfair, or puts too much pressure on one kid or another. Accept this about yourself and do your best to turn it around. 🛑 **Experts suggest that you write a list of what you like most and what you like least about each child. If your list is more slanted to one side or the other, it may signal you have a potential problem. So do some honest reflecting and make a commitment to change your behavior.** 🛑
- *Never compare.* Don't say "Why can't you bat like your brother?" A child may begin to think that she is inferior to her sibling in their parents' eyes. "When your sister was your age she always got all A's." These statements may also create anxiety for the praised child, who feels increased pressure.
- *Avoid labeling.* "Funny" family nicknames such as Klutz or Piggy may not be so funny to the child who is hearing them. These monikers may stick, even outside the family, and help foster feelings of inadequacy.

- *Encourage other friendships.* Some parents feel that brothers and sisters don't need other relationships outside the family or think that the siblings should share one set of friends between them. Actually, each kid needs his own group of friends and close relationships outside your family. In some cases you may want to be sure that if one child's friends are coming over, the sibling doesn't interfere with or annoy them.

- *Nurture unique strengths and differences.* For example, if you have a child who excels in art, supply her with colored pencils and sketch books and encourage her to take art classes. Acknowledging her special talent sets her apart from her siblings and may even boost her self-esteem.

- *Don't take sides.* During conflicts between friends or siblings, stay neutral and make suggestions only when your kids seem stuck. Taking sides builds resentments and feelings of favoritism. 🛑 **Children are often at their peak for potential sibling jealousy during the ages of five to eleven. Younger children may lack the maturity to understand the reasoning behind their parents' actions; therefore, exhibiting extra sensitivity around rivalry issues at this time may go a long way in keeping the peace.** 🛑

- *Find time alone for each child.* Depending on your schedule, set aside blocks of time when each of your children can have your exclusive attention. While the other siblings are gone or another adult watches them, take turns taking each of the children on a special outing, such as going shopping, seeing a movie, or getting ice cream.

- *Realize it's impossible to make things fair all the time.* Don't drive yourself too crazy trying to make everything equal and equitable. It's just not realistic. Besides, real life isn't always fair. The trick is to minimize conditions that break down sibling or peer relationships and cause long-lasting resentment.

FRIENDSHIP TIP

The Long-Term Value of Problem Solving
Have you taught your kids how to solve their own problems? Research shows that doing so will help minimize those sibling battles. Drs. George Spivack and Myrna Shure, Philadelphia-based psychologists who conducted over twenty-five years of research on the topic, found that children as young as three and four years old can be taught to think through their problems. They also discovered that children skilled in problem solving were less likely to be impulsive and aggressive when things didn't go their way, tended to be more caring and less insensitive, were better able to make friends, and tended to achieve more academically.

 21-DAY FRIENDSHIP FOLLOW-UP

Over the next 21 days, here's what I will do to help my children learn Friendship Skill Builder: Solving the Problem Between You Without an Adult:

_____

_____

_____

_____

_____

_____

📖 FRIENDSHIP SKILL BUILDER BOOKS 📖

For Parents and Teachers

Kids, Parents, and Power Struggles: Winning for a Lifetime, by Mary Sheedy Kurcinka (New York: HarperCollins, 2001). Creative techniques for using power struggles as pathways to better understanding within any family. Addresses the causes of power struggles rather than just the symptoms.

Loving Each One Best: A Caring and Practical Approach to Raising Siblings, by Nancy Samalin (New York: Bantam Books, 1997). A guide for parents that offers advice on how to deal with competing demands, sibling rivalry, stress, and feelings of guilt and inadequacy.

Positive Discipline A-Z: 1001 Solutions to Everyday Parenting Problems, by Jane Nelsen, Lynn Lott, and H. Stephen Glenn (Roseville, Calif.: Prima, 1999). An excellent parenting resource. Particularly helpful sections include "fighting friends," "sibling rivalry," and "fighting siblings."

Siblings Without Rivalry: How to Help Your Children Live Together So You Can Too, by Adele Faber and Elaine Mazlish (New York: Avon, 1998). An absolute "must" parenting book that covers sibling jealousies, fighting, and intense rivalries.

For Kids

Bang, Bang, You're Dead, by Louise Fitzhugh (New York: HarperCollins, 1969). Two kids battle for command of a hill, then work out their disagreement. Ages 5 to 8.

Katie Did It, by Becky Bring McDaniel (Danbury, Conn.: Children's Press, 1994). The youngest child always gets blamed for all her siblings' mishaps, until one day she takes credit by doing something wonderful all by herself. Ages 4 to 8.

Superfudge, by Judy Blume (New York: Bantam Books, 1994). A kids' favorite about an older brother who must deal with his very annoying younger brother. Ages 8 to 12.

The Berenstain Bears Get in a Fight, by Stan and Jan Berenstain (New York: Random House, 1995). Brother and Sister Bear get into a major sibling battle, and Mama Bear helps them work things out. Ages 4 to 8.

The Pain and the Great One, by Judy Blume (New York: Simon & Schuster, 1984). An eight-year-old sister and six-year-old brother tell all about each other and the contest to see whom Mom and Dad love most. Ages 5 to 10.

Sleepovers

Everyday Behaviors: Afraid to leave; wants to come home

Friendship Skill Builder: Being Away from Home with Confidence

"Don't make me go, Mom. Pleeeeease!"
"What if they serve that broccoli again?"
"Can I come back if I don't like it?"

WHAT'S WRONG?

Sleepovers are a great way to help a relationship gel. Here's a chance for two kids to be alone together for a whole night and really learn how to get along. Not only that, if your kid's the one who's spending the night, then you get some free time. Sounds like a joy, but to some of us it's just one big headache. For many kids the idea of spending the night away from you is really scary—especially the first few times. And it may put some doubts in your mind as well: Should I let her go? Is he old enough? Will he make it through the night? Why doesn't she want to go—should I insist? If your kid is older, there's a whole different set of worries: Will he be supervised? Will she get any sleep? Will there be any alcohol? Are he and his buddy *really* going to stay in the house all night? If you're not aware of the new trend of coed sleepovers for preadolescents and teens, you might as well add that to your worry list. Will members of the other sex be spending the night together? Ah, the joys of parenting!

WHY IS THIS HAPPENING?

If your child is anxious about spending the night, here are some things to help you figure out what's going on.

☐ Are you pushing your kid too soon, too fast?

☐ Is there a fear or worry triggering your child's reluctance to spend the night? For instance, is he afraid of the dark, the host's dog or cat, an older sibling or the parent, your unavailability in case something happens?

☐ Could she be embarrassed that she sucks her thumb at night, needs the light on, sleeps with a stuffed animal, snores, or wets the bed?

☐ Are the rules in the other kid's house different from yours, or are there no rules? Either case could be a big problem for your child.

☐ Is she afraid she might disappoint you if she can't spend the night? Might other friends or siblings tease her if she doesn't make it? Or did you set a rule that once you dropped her off, you won't pick her up until the next day?

☐ Do you really know what goes on in the other house? For instance, might your kid be reluctant because the parents are yelling, drinking, smoking, or watching late-night movies that your child knows are unacceptable? For your older kid: might there be drugs or alcohol, no curfew, or a "sneak-out plan" that the parent may not be aware of?

☐ Is your kid picking up on *your* worries? Maybe you're sending a mixed message: "Sure I want you to go, but underneath I'm not comfortable letting go of you." Has your child overheard you expressing some concern about whether this will work out, or have you heard rumors about things that went on the last time there was a sleep-over? Have you established that those rumors are true or fabricated? Is it something else that concerns you— not the kid's parents but the other kids who are invited? What can you do to alleviate your concerns?

☐ Is there a "bad group" of friends also spending the night? Or is there a group of kids or a certain child with whom your child seems to get in trouble whenever they're to-gether? What might you do to ease your fears? Can you get a pledge from your child that previous problems will not be repeated?

What do you think is the main reason your child doesn't want to leave you for the night? Write it here.

_____

_____

_____

WHAT SHOULD I SAY?

- *Inquire about any concerns.* "Is there anything you'd like me to find out, like what's on the dinner menu, whether any other kids are invited, or what's for breakfast?" "Should

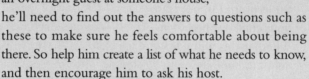

FRIENDSHIP SKILL BUILDER

Being Away from Home with Confidence

Whenever your child is invited to be an overnight guest at someone's house, he'll need to find out the answers to questions such as these to make sure he feels comfortable about being there. So help him create a list of what he needs to know, and then encourage him to ask his host.

1. *Time frame.* What time should I arrive, and when will I be leaving?
2. *Supplies.* What should I bring? Should I bring my own sleeping bag? Do I need any special clothing?
3. *Other kids.* Will there be other kids staying overnight? If so, who? What adults will be around?
4. *Activities.* What will we be doing? Is there a plan?
5. *Eating.* What will we do for food? Should I eat before I come over, or will there be dinner, snacks, breakfast? What food will be served?
6. *Special concerns.* Do you have any pets? Where does the dog sleep? Is anyone else a vegetarian? Is it okay if I don't take a shower? Do you keep a light on at night?

I tell Annie's mom to plug in your nightlight?" "Do you remember where the bathroom is?" *Hint:* You can encourage your child to ask these questions. But your first goal is to help your child feel comfortable staying away from home for one night.

- *Clarify your schedule.* "I'll be home all night." Or "I'll have my cell with me all night, so you can call me anytime."

- *Set a definite pickup time.* "I'll be at the door at ten o'clock sharp tomorrow morning to pick you up."
- *Downplay failure.* So what if your kid doesn't make it all through the night? If you want this to work in the long run, emphasize the positive accomplishment. "You stayed there two hours past your bedtime. That was much longer than last time." "It's not a big deal. You'll have lots of opportunities to spend the night at friends' houses again."
- *State behavior expectations.* "I expect you to tell Annie's mom if you want anything or anything's wrong." "Remember, it's their house rules you follow tonight, not ours."
- *Appreciate disclosures.* If there is a problem, be grateful that your child feels safe and close enough to tell you. "I'm glad you told me the dog scared you. I'll make sure their dog stays outside." "I appreciate your telling me about the boys planning to sneak out to drink at the park. Now I know why you didn't feel comfortable staying there."

WHAT CAN I DO?

- *Be sure your kid is ready.* Is your child sleeping in her own bed through the night, or is she climbing in with you at 2 A.M.? Does she have any problems separating from you when she goes to school, the baby-sitters, or day care? Does your child get along with this kid well enough to spend a whole night together? Does she feel comfortable with the child's parents? Has your child ever spent the night away from home without you, even with a relative? 🛑 **A survey conducted by *Sesame Street* found that most parents say children are old enough to spend the night at around the age of seven. Do keep in mind that the age is not set in stone: it all depends on the child, and *you* are the one who knows your child best.** 🛑
- *Do a practice.* For a reluctant child, have the first sleepover be at *your* home. It sometimes helps if your child uses the

same "security items" (see the next point) for a real sleep-over at your home first. Or try having your child spend the night with Grandma and Grandpa or a special cousin.

- **Pack a few "security items."** A few packed items can make even the most anxious kid more comfortable. The following are some possibilities: a flashlight if she fears the dark or staying in a strange house, a granola bar or sandwich (in case she "hates" the meal), her own pillow or blanket, or even a cell phone for reassurance that she can call you any-time if she really needs to. A sleeping bag with a rubber sheet tucked inside might help a bed wetter feel more com-fortable just in case she has an accident. Think of what might make your child feel more secure.

- **Meet the parents.** No matter how old your child is, do meet the parents face-to-face. You want to be sure they will be supervising the whole night and have your phone number handy. Clarify that you want to be called if there are any problems and specify any particular issues that could arise.

- **Have a positive send-off.** Be cheerful and optimistic as you pack and get read to go. Go to the door, meet the parents, and wait until your child looks settled. Give her a big hug and kiss. Then leave. Don't linger.

- **Establish a signal if needed.** If your child might change her mind at the last minute, establish a private signal between the two of you ahead of time, such as a wave or a tug on her ear. Your child can send it to you when you first arrive. Another option is to phone the house at an agreed-on time to talk to the parent (or to your child) and check how things are going.

- **Pick your child up if necessary.** If your child does call beg-ging to come home, keep calm and drive to the house. Talk to her privately to determine what she wants to do. You never know: she may have changed her mind. Whatever you do, don't make a big deal out of the "spoiled evening" or plead for her to stay. Instead, just reassure her (and your-self) that there will be other times.

FRIENDSHIP TIP

Backsliding
Okay, you've gone through all the steps, and your child has already had several successful sleepovers at his friend's house. You're home congratulating yourself and getting ready for a quiet evening curled up with a great book in front of the fire. Suddenly, "Riiiinnnnnggggg." It's the sleepover host. "Can you come and get Johnny please? He's really having a hard time." Don't get discouraged. Just go pick him up and remember this is perfectly normal. Backsliding is a regular and predictable part of learning new skills. So don't overreact, stay upbeat and supportive, and try again next time. Things will get better.

 21-DAY FRIENDSHIP FOLLOW-UP

Over the next 21 days, here's what I will do to help my child learn Friendship Skill Builder: Being Away from Home with Confidence:

_____

_____

_____

FRIENDSHIP SKILL BUILDER BOOKS

For Parents and Teachers
Slumber Parties: What Do I Do? by Wilhelminia Ripple, Kathryn Totten, Heather Anderson, and Dianne Lorang (Lit-

tleton, Colo.: Oakbrook, 2002). The whats, whys, and hows of slumber parties, with answers to almost every conceivable parental query, from handling bed-wetting accidents to ascertaining if a child is really ready for a sleepover. For parents of children ages 9 to 12.

For Kids

Ira Sleeps Over, by Bernard Waber (Boston: Houghton Mifflin/ Walter Lorraine Books, 1975). Ira is thrilled to spend the night at Reggie's, until his sister raises the question of whether he should take his teddy bear. A perfect book for talking about sleeping at your friend's house the very first time. Ages 4 to 7.

Slumber Parties, by Penny Warner (Minnetonka, Minn.: Meadowbrook, 2000). Twenty-five complete slumber party themes, including ideas for invitations, decorations, games, activities, food, favors, and videos. Ages 9 to 12.

Super Slumber Parties (American Girl Library), by Brooks Whitney and Nadine Bernard (Middleton, Wis.: Pleasant Company, 1997). How to make slumber parties even more fun: all kinds of themes, crafts, invitations, food, games, and more. Ages 9 to 12.

The Sleepover Book, by Margot Griffin and Jane Kurisu (Toronto: Kids Can Press, 2001). Everything necessary for slumber party success, from pre-party planning to breakfast the next morning. Ages 9 to 12.

Tattletale

Everyday Behaviors: Tells bad stuff about friends that gets them in trouble

Friendship Skill Builder: Knowing What and When to Tell

Mo-oommm, Sara spit again."
"Wait 'til I tell the teacher what you just said."
"You're gonna get in big trouble for doing that."

WHAT'S WRONG?

Who wants a friend who can hardly wait to snitch about the bad stuff about you to someone in authority? Kids may spread rumors about friends, but usually tattling is a child's telling a parent, teacher, or coach something. And almost always the goal is to get the other kid in trouble. Tattling is a learned behavior that usually starts when kids are preschoolers. It's really the first step on the road to that other annoying "any age" behavior called malicious gossiping. (Also see Gossip.) Tattling has no redeeming qualities—it only causes bad feelings between the tattletale and the accused and often leads to resentment and broken friendships. To the other kids a tattler is someone who can't be trusted or who wants to be a kiss-up Goody Two-Shoes. A tattler can also get a bad reputation among adults. Would you want a kid around who is constantly complaining or bothering you about trivial grievances?

WHY IS THIS HAPPENING?

Start by first asking yourself what might be provoking your child to tattle. Here are a few possibilities:

- [ ] Could he be craving your attention?
- [ ] Is he seeking control? Think about it: it's pretty powerful knowing you can get a sibling or friend in trouble.
- [ ] Is he trying to get back at a kid who hurt him? Could this be his way of retaliating? (If so, also see Tiffs and Breakups.)
- [ ] Is she stuck in a problem that she doesn't know how to solve and looking for the adult to step in and fix everything? (If so, also see Argues.)
- [ ] Does he not have enough time to be with you and uses tattling as his way of letting you know what's going on with his life?
- [ ] Does she have poor impulse control and can't keep those thoughts to herself? (If so, also see Hot Tempered.)
- [ ] Is he trying to align himself with the grown-up population because kids his age aren't letting him into their world?
- [ ] Does she have an overzealous conscience? An overly strong moral compass can lead to self-righteousness that puts friends off. 🛑 **Jean Piaget's comprehensive**

research on child development has shown that children between four and five years of age are especially sensitive to following adult rules and expectations; they see things in black and white, and often feel it's their duty to report on all perceived "bad stuff" they see going on. 🛑

☐ Does he lack assertiveness skills and can't stick up for himself? Is he resorting to tattling so you can translate his needs to the other kid? (If so, also see Peer Pressure.)

☐ Does she think she's being your "little helper"? Might you have reinforced this? "Thanks for telling me!" "Well, that isn't the kind of friend you should be hanging around." Might you be unintentionally encouraging her tattling by responding positively to her every little complaint?

What is your best guess as to why your kid is tattling? What is one little thing you might do to start changing his ways? Write it here.

_____

_____

_____

WHAT SHOULD I SAY?

- *State your new policy*. "From now on I will not listen when you tell me bad things about your friends. And I don't want you to tell other people either." The rule could be as simple as "Is this helpful or unhelpful news?"
- *Point out the damage done*. "I notice George hasn't spoken to you for over a week. Do you think it has anything to do with your telling on him to the teacher that he took an extra helping in the cafeteria?"

FRIENDSHIP SKILL BUILDER

Knowing What and When to Tell

Here are some important steps your child can go through to help him distinguish between tattling and acting responsibly. Explain the difference between tattling and reporting. Tattling is when you're telling on someone purposely to get them *in* trouble. Reporting is when you're telling on someone to keep them *out* of trouble.

1. ***Is there really a problem?*** Look around and ask yourself if this is really a problem that needs to be reported. Could someone be hurt? Could someone get in trouble? If so, then report it. If not, it's best to keep the issue to yourself.

2. ***If so, act responsibly.*** Who is the best person to report this to? Choose a person who can help you: a parent, teacher, coach, or older friend. If no one is around and this is an emergency, dial 911.

3. ***Be safe not sorry.*** You may worry that reporting something really wrong and that needs solving could embarrass or anger your friend. But if your gut tells you that someone could be hurt, you must report your concerns for everyone's sake and safety.

4. ***If there isn't a problem of safety, don't say anything.*** That's unnecessary and possibly hurtful tattling.

- *Moderate an overly conscientious child.* "I know that it really bothers you if other kids sharpen their pencils when they're not supposed to. But the teacher tells me you're disrupting the class and making your friends mad at you." "I admire how concerned you are about recycling, but if you tell the coach every time one of your teammates throws a can into the regular garbage, he just gets annoyed."
- *Explain your role.* Tell your kid that you're a guider, not the solver, and stick to your guns. Some kids tattle not to "tell on" another child but so you'll be the one to solve their problems. "I know you can solve this on your own. I have full faith that you can figure this out."

WHAT SHOULD I DO?

- *Ask around.* Talk to other adults who know your kid well. Does he exhibit the same tattling behavior around them that you may have observed at home? Tell them you're working on the problem and would appreciate feedback about your child's behavior in the future.
- *Enforce a no tattling rule.* Establish a clear policy about what's appropriate to report and what isn't. The best way to extinguish tattling is to lay down one law: tell your child that unless the report is intended to *keep the accused out of trouble or harm* you won't listen. The rule works not only in your home but also in the carpool, when other kids come over, and outside your house.
- *Explain the difference between tattling and acting responsibly.* Tell your child there are definite moments when you want her to tell you if someone is in danger or if a disaster might occur. 🛑 **Before they take their own lives or take the life of another, 75 percent of kids tell a friend their intentions. The friend is frequently reluctant to tell an adult for fear of getting the kid in trouble.** 🛑 "If any-

one you know ever threatens to hurt someone or himself, I want you to tell me right away."

- **Role-play.** It may be hard for your child to understand the difference between tattling and acting responsibly, so you might make up different scenarios and play different roles to make the situations more real.
- **Use the Golden Rule.** Ask your kid, "Is it the kind of thing you'd like somebody to say about you?" Help her understand why she doesn't need to tattle on a friend.
- **Be consistent.** The secret to eliminating snitching is to be consistent with your policy every time your kid tattles.
- **Build impulse control.** Is your kid blurting this out because he can't contain himself? If so, then the best way to stifle tattling is to make a Wait sign by putting your index finger in the air. That gives him a chance to pause, contain the thoughts, and, you hope, stop his urge to tattle.

 FRIENDSHIP TIP

To Tell or Not to Tell

A recent survey found that 81 percent of American teens said they are now more willing, following a wave of horrific shootings on high school campuses, to report students who might pose a threat to school safety. Make sure your kid understands that this is not tattling or malicious gossip. You want him to be one of the "willing" students. When it comes to school safety, kids may well be the best metal detectors: three-fourths of adolescents who commit homicide or suicide share their intentions with a peer. Impress on your kids the importance of telling an adult their legitimate concerns, with the guarantee that their report will be taken seriously.

21-DAY FRIENDSHIP FOLLOW-UP

Over the next 21 days, here's what I will do to help my child learn Friendship Skill Builder: Knowing What and When to Tell:

_____

_____

_____

FRIENDSHIP SKILL BUILDER BOOKS

For Parents and Teachers

Dealing with Tattling: The Conflict Resolution Library, by Don Middleton (New York: Rosen, 1999). Explains what tattling is, why people do it, and what the consequences might be, then suggests alternatives to this behavior and ways to resolve problems created by tale bearing.

For Kids

Armadillo Tattletale, by Helen Ketteman (New York: Scholastic, 2000). Minding your own business can be tough sometimes, especially if your oversize ears are just the right size for eavesdropping and telling distorted tales. The text conveys a great message: gossip can hurt, and it's important to respect the privacy of others. Ages 5 to 8.

Telling Isn't Tattling, by Kathryn M. Hammerseng (Seattle: Parenting Press, 1996). Many kids have trouble knowing the difference between telling and tattling. This book for young kids helps them learn when to tell an adult they need help and when to deal with problems themselves. Ages 4 to 7.

The Way It Happened, by Deborah Zemke (Boston: Houghton Mifflin, 1988). Here is the classic example of how rumors can grow so big they blow out of proportion. Ages 6 to 9.

22

Teased

Everyday Behaviors: Can't handle it when friends poke fun; feels picked on; overreacts to playful banter

Friendship Skill Builder: Delivering Comebacks

"She's not my friend anymore. All she does is make fun of me."
"He called me Four-Eyes, and now everyone's doing it. I hate him!"
"I did tell her to stop picking on me, but she just laughed!"

WHAT'S WRONG?

Teasing is one of those unpleasant aspects of growing up that almost all of us have experienced, but the plain truth is that some kids sure do seem to get more than their fair share. Of course we tell our children to just "shrug it off" and "not take it so seriously," but some kids just can't. Those verbal barbs sting!

How your child reacts to being teased can really affect his ability to make and keep friends. A reputation for over-reacting, taking things too seriously, or being unable to shake off playful banter can damage your kid's social ranking. Let's face it, kids don't want to be around someone who's always teased. It just ups the chances that they'll be picked on as well. And they especially don't want to be around someone who is always crying, whining, or threatening to "tell" when teasing is playfully delivered among friends.

Although we can't stop kids from saying nasty stuff to our children, we can do things to reduce the chances that our sons and daughters will be targeted. The best way is by teaching them how to respond in a way that discourages future teasing. When you think about the number of mean-spirited kids these days who seem to get a charge out of picking on their so-called friends, you can see that learning those come-back strategies is an essential part of every child's friendship aptitude arsenal.

WHY IS THIS HAPPENING?

Here are some questions to help you pinpoint why your child is having a problem with teasing. Check those that might apply to your child.

☐ Is she overly sensitive? Does her thin-skinned disposition make her take friendly teasing too seriously? (Also see Too Sensitive.)

☐ Is this the first time your child has ever been teased? Has your family always discouraged playful, friendly bantering at home?

☐ Is your child unable to tell the difference between friendly teasing and hostile attacks? Might the kids really just be "playing around"? (Also see Bullied and Harassed.)

☐ Is he an easy target because he reacts by crying, whining, or threatening to "tell"? (Also see Tattletale.)

☐ Does your kid tease other kids? Does he use humor to try to "win" friends? Can he "dish it out" but not "take it"? (Also see Too Sensitive.)

☐ Is he immature—either developmentally or by actual years—and does he therefore act a little younger than kids his own age?

☐ Is your kid "different" from the other kids for one reason or another? (Also see Different.)

☐ Is there a child or a clique doing most of the teasing and tormenting? Are other kids experiencing the same thing? (Also see Cliques.)

Review the list and jot down your thoughts. What are the main reasons you think your child is having trouble with this issue?

_____

_____

_____

WHAT SHOULD I SAY?

• **Bring it up.** Kids rarely come to parents and ask for help about teasing, so turn on your radar. "You look really mad. Did someone tease you?" "Sally told me that you and Kevin had a big blowup because he was making fun of you again. Let's talk about it." The amount of teasing and kid

FRIENDSHIP SKILL BUILDER

Delivering Comebacks

Your child is certain to be teased: it's a fact of life and a big part of growing up. Some kids handle it a whole lot better than others, and so can yours. Review the comeback strategies in the What Should I Do? section and then pick the idea your child likes best. Rehearse the comeback together again and again until she feels comfortable trying it on her own. Use the following steps.

1. **Decide if it's friendly or unfriendly teasing.** If it's friendly teasing (the person is having fun *with* you), shake it off. If it's unfriendly teasing (making fun *of* you), try not to get worked up.

2. **Decide if you want to confront your teaser.** If it looks like you could be hurt, get help.

3. **Look the teaser in the eye.** Don't look down. Hold your head high and stand tall.

4. **Stay calm.** You can't let the teaser think he's got your goat. So don't get worked up. Take a deep breath to stay calm, tell yourself to "chill out," or count to ten inside your head.

5. **Use a strong, firm voice and say your rehearsed comeback to your friend.** "Cut it out!" "Get real." "Thanks, but I've heard that one already." "You noticed; it's been a problem all my life." "So?"

6. **Walk away.** Do not insult or tease the teaser back. Just keep walking.

meanness in our society is steadily increasing; let your child know he's not alone, even if that won't relieve all the pain.

- *Gather facts.* You want to find out if this is friendly or hurtful teasing or if it could even be sexual harassment or bullying. (If it is, also see Bullied and Harassed.) "What happened? Has this happened before? Is it the same kid who always teases? What's he teasing you about? What did you say back? Did it work? Is there anything you might have done differently?" 🛑 **The top ten things eight- to thirteen-year-olds are teased about are (from most to least): appearance, abilities, identity (gender, race, religion, culture), behavior, family circumstances, possessions, opinions, names, feelings, and friends.** 🛑

- *Acknowledge feelings.* Teasing can hurt, so acknowledge your child's feelings, but don't overreact or tell him you'll take care of it. Don't underplay your kid's hurt if he is being repeatedly teased in an unfriendly manner. The latest research shows that our brains react the same way to teasing or rejection as they do to physical pain. Those verbal snubs really do hurt our kids. "You seem upset by what Scott said." "It sounds like Kelly really hurt your feelings." "You must be really mad. Those were some pretty hurtful things your friend said to you."

- *Distinguish the two kinds of teasing.* There are two very different types of teasing—friendly and unfriendly—and kids must learn to distinguish them. 🛑 **One study found that 80 percent of kids admit to unfriendly teasing, saying their intent was to make someone else miserable. Only 20 percent claimed to tease with a friendly intent.** 🛑 "It's unfriendly when your friend makes fun of your accent or weight or glasses. They're *making fun of* you as a person and don't care if they make you sad or make you cry. It's friendly teasing when kids are just being playful and your friend doesn't mean to hurt your feelings." Your child may need lots of talks to help him learn to distinguish the two teasing types, so plan to discuss the difference frequently. Preadolescence—and especially middle school age—is a prime time for teasing that deals with sexual language and behavior. Boys often focus on physical changes in girls' development. Not only is this inappropriate and emotionally damaging, but it is considered sexual harassment. Talk to your son.

- **Talk about why kids tease.** Here are some reasons elementary and middle schoolers often tease: "To get a laugh." "They don't feel good about who they are, so they put the other kid down." "They do it for attention." "They say it's just a joke, but it's really because they're mean inside." "They do it to get even." "The other kids in their clique do it, and they want to be 'in.'"

WHAT SHOULD I DO?

I've included the most effective comeback strategies that kids tell me have worked for them. Your job is to share the strategies with your child and then have her choose the one she feels most comfortable doing. What works for one child won't work for another. Use the steps in the Friendship Skill Builder: Delivering Comebacks to practice the technique again and again until your child feels comfortable delivering it in the real kid world. Suellen Fried and Paula Fried, the authors of *Bullies and Victims,* stress that most kids can learn to manage teasing incidents if they have a repertoire of strategies to counter the verbal abuse.

- **Question it.** "Why would you say that?" "Why would you want to tell me I'm dumb [or fat or whatever] and hurt my feelings?"
- **Send a strong "I want" message.** "I want you to leave me

alone" or "I want you to stop teasing me." The trick is to say the message firmly so that it doesn't sound wimpy.

- *Turn it into a compliment.* "Hey, thanks. I appreciate that!" "That was really nice of you to notice." "Thanks for the compliment."

- *Agree.* "You've got that right." "One hundred percent correct!" "Bingo, you win!" "People say that a lot about me."

- *Say "So?"* "So? . . . Whatever." "So? . . . Who cares?" "So? . . . And your point is?" If your child likes this strategy, be sure to read the book *The Meanest Thing to Say,* by Bill Cosby (New York: Scholastic, 1997).

- *Use manners.* "Thanks." "Thank you for that comment." "I appreciate that." Be sure to say it so that it sounds sincere and then turn and walk away.

- *Use sarcasm.* "Like I would care?" "Give me a break." "Oh, that's just great." The "look" has to match: rolling your eyes and walking away can do the trick. This usually works only on older kids who understand sarcasm.

- *Ignore it.* Walk away without even a look at the teaser, pretend the teaser is invisible, glance at something else and laugh, look completely uninterested, or pretend you don't hear it. This one works best if your child has a tougher time delivering verbal comebacks. It works best in places where your child can escape his teasers, such as on a park or playground. It *doesn't* work in close quarters, such on a school bus or at a cafeteria table. (Also see Too Sensitive.)

- *Be amazed.* "Really? I didn't know that." "Thanks for telling me." Sounding like you really mean it is the trick.

- *Express displeasure.* "It really makes me mad when you tease me like that." "I don't like it when you make fun of me in front of the other kids. You may think it's funny, but it isn't to me." "If you want us to continue being friends, stop teasing me." If this really is your kid's friend who is causing him such distress, then encourage your child to express his displeasure.

FRIENDSHIP TIP

The Teasing Epidemic
The National Education Association reports that every day, 160,000 children skip school because of fear of being harassed, teased, and bullied by other students. It's just further proof that your child needs to learn a repertoire of comeback strategies to use on both friendly and unfriendly teasers.

 21-DAY FRIENDSHIP FOLLOW-UP

Over the next 21 days, here's what I will do to help my child learn to use Friendship Skill Builder: Delivering Comebacks:

_____

_____

_____

 FRIENDSHIP SKILL BUILDER BOOKS

For Parents and Teachers
Easing the Teasing: Helping Your Child Cope with Name-Calling, Ridicule, and Verbal Bullying, by Judy S. Freedman (New York: McGraw-Hill, 2002). Filled with reassuring advice, real-life success stories, and ideas to help your child cope with taunts and teasing.

Good Friends Are Hard to Find: Helping Your Child Find, Make and Keep Friends, by Fred Frankel (Los Angeles: Perspective,

1996). Excellent suggestions for helping younger kids handle teasing.

Mom, They're Teasing Me: Helping Your Child Solve Social Problems, by Michael Thompson and Lawrence J. Cohen with Catherine O'Neill Grace (New York: Ballantine, 2002). Solid advice for helping parents help their kids deal with some of the more painful aspects of growing up.

Sticks and Stones: 7 Ways Your Child Can Deal with Teasing, Conflict, and Other Hard Times, by Scott Cooper (New York: Random House, 2000). A wealth of strategies, sample scripts, and easy-to-follow exercises to give kids the confidence to speak up for themselves and counter verbal barbs.

What to Do When Kids Are Mean to Your Child, by Elin McCoy (Pleasantville, N.Y.: Reader's Digest, 1997). A compilation of helpful strategies to help your child deal with teasing and bullying.

For Kids

Dealing with Teasing, by Lisa Adams (New York: Rosen, 1998). Part of the Conflict Resolution Library that provides a number of great selections on friendship issues for kids. This one describes the difference between playful teasing and hurtful teasing. Ages 6 to 9.

How to Handle Bullies, Teasers and Other Meanies: A Book That Takes the Nuisance out of Name Calling and Other Nonsense, by Kate Cohen-Posey (Highland City, Fla.: Rainbow Books, 1995). Useful tips on how to turn a teaser's slurs inside out. Ages 10 to 13.

Let's Talk About Teasing, by Joy Wilt Berry (Chicago: Children's Press, 1985). Good book for talking about teasing with younger children. Ages 4 to 8.

Marvin Redpost: Why Pick on Me? by Louis Sachar (New York: Random House, 1993). Unfairly accused of being a nose-picker by the class bully, Marvin Redpost is shunned by his classmates, until he can prove his innocence. Ages 8 to 11.

Simon's Hook: A Story About Teases and Put-Downs, by Karen Burnett (Roseville, Calif.: GR Publishing, 2000). A helpful resource filled with tips and comebacks to help kids handle teasing. Ages 6 to 11.

Stick Up for Yourself! Every Kid's Guide to Personal Power and Positive Self-Esteem, by Gershen Kaufman, Lev Raphael, and Pamela Espeland (Minneapolis, Minn.: Free Spirit, 1999). Ages 11 to 14.

The Berenstain Bears and Too Much Teasing, by Stan and Jan Berenstain (New York: Random House, 1993). Helps younger ones realize that everyone is teased. Ages 4 to 8.

The Meanest Thing to Say, by Bill Cosby (New York: Scholastic, 1997). I love this one! It's not only humorous but also practical. Read it together and then practice the comeback strategy Cosby suggests called "So." Ages 5 to 10.

Friendship Issue 23

Tiffs and Breakups

Everyday Behaviors: Always arguing with a close friend; overly possessive and can't "let go"; has lost a close pal

Friendship Skill Builder: Apologizing and Making Amends

"So what if she was my best friend? I'm never talking to her again as long as I live."
"Why does Jack hate me? I thought we were best friends."
"I don't want to find another friend. I want my old friend back."

WHAT'S WRONG?

Tiffs and breakups are some of the hardest lessons kids need to learn about getting along. But they should also be expected. After all, any kids who spend a great deal of time together will inevitably quarrel—just as married couples do. It's actu-

268

ally a rarity if they don't. But that doesn't diminish the anguish those quarrels can produce and most especially if they involve a best friend. 🛑 **The ending of a close friendship can be stressful even for very young children. Researchers find that parents often underestimate the impact or seriousness of best friend breakups, so don't take your child's anguish lightly.** 🛑 After all, a close friend is very special: this is the child with whom your son or daughter has spent a lot of close time, shared secrets, developed interests, giggled, and even cried. Although most "tiffs" are temporary, not all have happy endings. And when a parting involves an especially close friend, the loss can be devastating. Although you usually can't mend a friendship (nor should you), there are things you can say and do to help your child handle the rift. In fact, even though the disagreement or loss may be hard, the experience may help your child learn critical life lessons: how to handle disagreements and how to recognize when it's time to move on and find new friends.

WHY IS THIS HAPPENING?

Friendship tiffs and breakups are to be expected, but some kids have more than others and some have a harder time bouncing back. Here are a few issues that may indicate that you need to keep a closer eye on your child for possible friendship problems.

- ☐ Is the tiff causing your child to have difficulty sleeping or trouble concentrating? Is he withdrawing or appearing depressed?
- ☐ Does he not want to be with others, go to school, or be with other kids? Does he anger easily? Are his grades slipping? If any of these symptoms have continued for a few weeks, seek help.

- [ ] Is the friend the one who wants to "let go," and your child is unwilling to break off the friendship? Is she overly possessive?
- [ ] Is she "hanging on" to the old friendship because she fears she won't be able to find another friend? Does she lack friendship skills?
- [ ] Is she unforgiving or unable to let go? Is she unwilling to apologize or make amends? Does she know how to apologize? See the Friendship Skill Builder in this chapter, Apologizing and Making Amends.
- [ ] Are these two kids really suitable for one another? Do they share the same interests, temperament, values, or maturity level? Should the relationship continue?
- [ ] Does your child (or the other child) know how to solve conflicts or work through her problems?

What is your best guess as to why your child is having problems letting go of the friendship or continues to have tiffs with this friend? Write it here.

_____

_____

_____

FRIENDSHIP SKILL BUILDER

Apologizing and Making Amends
Admitting you were wrong and saying you're sorry are basic skills of not only making and keeping friends but also getting along in any relationship. In some situations it's all your child's fault, and he needs to take the lead. On other occasions, of course, there's fault on both sides, and

therefore both your child and his friend need to make amends. Here are the steps your child should take whenever he needs to apologize to a friend.

1. **Think about what you did that was wrong.** OK, your friend was mean and insensitive, but what did you do that caused the pain? Did you do something your friend thinks is equally annoying? Were you not thinking about how she felt? Did you say something that hurt her feelings? Did you say something behind her back? Do you need to apologize?

2. **Find the best time, place, and approach to apologize.** Find a good time to talk to or call your friend. If you really can't face her, you could write a letter.

3. **Say what you're sorry for.** Be sincere and honest. Tell your friend exactly what you did that you're sorry for. "I . . . [say what you did], and I'm sorry." And if you still think your friend was wrong, say "I'm really sorry for my part in this." Then briefly describe what happened. Your friend may see it differently, so it's a good idea to share your view of the problem.

4. **Tell how you are going to make it better.** Just saying "sorry" doesn't necessarily fix things. Let your friend know what you plan to do to make things better. Is it that you'll deal with your anger? Not gossip? Listen more? Take turns? Be a better sport?

5. **Give your friendship time to heal.** Remember, you can't make anybody do anything she doesn't want to, and that means you can't make your friend accept your apology. All you can do is admit you were wrong and try to make amends. After that, it's up to your friend.

WHAT SHOULD I SAY?

- *Don't dismiss the hurt.* Tiffs are painful, especially when they involve a close or long-term friend. 🛑 **Myron Brenton advises parents to help their child "realize that in time he'll find other friends but that he mustn't expect a new friend to 'replace' a former one."** 🛑 So acknowledge your child's pain and convey optimism that she will make up with her friend or find more friends.

- *Hold a "what-if" dialogue.* Disagreements, though painful, are a part of relationships, but if kids can learn from the tiff, they'll know what to do the next time so things might not have to go sour. Help your child think through his situation by asking such questions as "What went on between you two? How did it start? And what did you say? How did he respond? What did you do then? How did things end up? Is there anything you could have said or done differently? Is there anything you could do now to patch things up between you two?"

- *Keep things in perspective.* Tiffs and arguments are normal in any friendship, but sometimes kids blow things out of proportion. And in no time a little tiff can ruin a great friendship. So help your child weigh whether the tiff is such a big deal. Here are a few questions to ask: "Did she really mean to hurt you? Does she know how upset you are? Is this the first time she did this, or does she do this often? Will you really care about this tomorrow? Next week? Is this something that you really can't forgive? Are you willing to give up your friend if you can't work this out? Can you really live with not having her as your friend?"

- *Share friendship stories.* Tell your child your own friendship stories—struggles, losses, and makeups. Help your child understand that such tiffs are normal. You could also use books dealing with the theme of friendship loss. Refer to the Friendship Skill Builder Books section in this chapter.

- **Suggest an apology.** If you've surmised that your child was in any way responsible for the tiff, suggest that she apologize. "Do you think you can fix the misunderstanding?" "Do you think you should tell your friend you're sorry? I know it's something that you don't want to do, but think about it. It may be the only way to repair what happened." See the Friendship Skill Builder in this chapter, Apologizing and Making Amends.

WHAT SHOULD I DO?

- **Be optimistic.** Friendship tiffs and losses don't mean the end of the world. 🛑 **The renowned pediatrician Benjamin Spock said, "The very fact that friendships wax and wane is evidence that at each phase of growth children are apt to need something different from their friends and, therefore, have to find a new one from time to time."** 🛑 So expect your child to be upset for a while. But in most cases your child will bounce back.
- **Don't buy in to tattling.** Make one rule stick: unless your child is reporting a problem that could cause a friend injury, don't encourage whining or complaints. Once the rule is set, be consistent: "Is this something you and your friend can't work out yourselves?" or "Is this helpful or unhelpful news?" The rule works wonders in curbing tattling, gossip, and putting others down. It also makes your child recognize that it's her job to solve her problems with her friend—not yours.
- **Stay out of it!** Promising your child that you're going to solve this problem does him no good. In fact, studies confirm that friendship tiffs are quite common and to be expected. It's normal for schoolchildren to change best friends on a regular basis. School-age children tend to form small friendship groups. So don't overreact, get too worked up

about it, or try to take matters into your own hands. You (and your child) are better off if you let things calm down a bit. This is your child's problem—not yours—and he needs to learn how to deal with the bad as well as the good parts of friendships.

- *Urge your child to settle things.* Because kids usually don't know how to settle tiffs, on some occasions you may need to help. Until about ten or eleven years of age, kids have a lot to learn about how to handle disagreements. The friendship can become stronger after they successfully settle a tiff. Here are a few skills your child needs to learn in order to settle a disagreement.

  - *Don't let things fester.* If there has been a tiff, fix things between the two of you quickly—even if you don't want to remain friends. Everyone deserves a second chance.

  - *Cool off.* Don't talk to a friend when you're really upset. You might say something you regret. So calm down first.

  - *Don't leave before your dispute is settled.* Once you start trying to work things through, stay until you settle your disagreement.

  - *Be willing to listen.* Chances are your friend may have a different view of the situation. So listen to his side. See Friendship Skill Builder: Showing You Care by Listening. (See Insensitive.)

  - *Apologize if appropriate.* If you've done anything to cause hurt, say you're sorry. See the Friendship Skill Builder in this chapter, Apologizing and Making Amends.

  - *Forgive and move on.* Tiffs happen in every friendship. Once the tiff is over, try to let bygones be bygones.

- *Catch a rebuff early.* Friendships rarely stop overnight. Instead, they usually cool off gradually. These are some of the signs that a best friendship is cooling: the two kids are no longer interested in the same things; one child does most of the inviting; one kid frequently declines invitations, waits a few days to accept them, or refuses the invitations altogether. "Points of no return" in a relationship include one child's telling the other that he doesn't want be with him, or others' beginning to tease the "rejected" one for still trying to hang around or for "annoying" them. Watch for those signs; if the friend wants to cool the relationship with your child, slow down the contact and encourage your child to seek the company of other kids.

- *Accept the snub and move on.* If the other child makes a habit of neglecting your child, can't be trusted, or isn't being an "equal partner," it's time to suggest to your child that she move on. You might want to read the section "What Makes a Good Friend?" in Part One (page 11) with your child. Doing so can help your child recognize that the friendship may be one sided and realize it's time to let go. Or talk about your own experiences so he realizes that everyone "gets dumped" by a friend.

- *Fill up your child's schedule.* Not having an old friend around can be tough. Your child may have relied on their time together and may be at a loss as to what to do. So find positive ways to occupy your child's time for a while, such as a movie, a new hobby, or even a weekend getaway.

- *Seek help if the problem persists.* For most kids, friendship tiffs and breakups are a normal part of growing up. But if the distress continues and after a period of a few weeks your child can't bounce back, if he continually loses friends or rejects his companions, there may be deeper problems. Friendship losses and tiffs can cause stress, depression, sleep difficulties, behavior problems, and trouble with school. If this is the case with your child, and these problems continue, do seek professional help.

Friendship Tip

Traits of a Good Friend
Kenneth H. Rubin, director of the Center for Children, Relationships, and Culture at the University of Maryland and author of *The Friendship Factor,* surveyed over six hundred children and found three traits kids consider basic to a good friendship:

1. The relationship is mutual. Both kids have reasonably equal power.
2. It's voluntary. Both kids want to be part of the friendship.
3. It's positive. Both members genuinely like each other, enjoy spending time together, and trust each other enough to share secrets and personal information.

 21-DAY FRIENDSHIP FOLLOW-UP

Over the next 21 days, here's what I will do to help my child learn Friendship Skill Builder: Apologizing and Making Amends:

_____

_____

_____

_____

_____

FRIENDSHIP SKILL BUILDER BOOKS

For Parents and Teachers

Best Friends, Worst Enemies: Understanding the Social Lives of Children, by Michael Thompson and Catherine O'Neill Grace with Lawrence J. Cohen (New York: Ballantine, 2001). A wonderful guide to help caregivers understand the motives and meanings of children's social behavior.

The Friendship Factor: Helping Our Children Navigate Their Social World—and Why It Matters for Their Success and Happiness, by Kenneth H. Rubin (New York: Viking Penguin, 2002). An important book for enlightening us as to what makes some children well liked and accepted by peers while others are not.

For Kids

A Smart Girl's Guide to Friendship Troubles: Dealing with Fights, Being Left Out and the Whole Popularity Thing, by Patti Kelley Criswell (Middleton, Wis.: Pleasant Company, 2003). Great advice for helping girls get through the tough times with friends, including problem solving, practical tips, and quizzes to help them get to know their friends. Ages 10 to 15.

Can You Relate? Real-World Advice for Teens on Guys, Girls, Growing Up, and Getting Along, by Annie Fox (Minneapolis, Minn.: Free Spirit, 2000). The author shares advice on getting along and dealing with friendship problems. Ages 12 to 17.

I Hate My Best Friend, by Ruth Rosner (New York: Hyperion, 1997). The perfect book to help kids recognize that everyone has problems with friends. Ages 7 to 10.

Matthew and Tilly, by Rebecca C. Jones (New York: Puffin Books, 1995). Matthew and Tilly discover how to solve their problems after a disagreement. Ages 5 to 8.

The Cybil War, by Betsy Byars (New York: Viking Penguin, 1981). A tiff between two longtime friends arises from a misunderstanding. Ages 8 to 12.

The Hating Book, by Charlotte Zolotow (New York: Harper-Collins, 1989). A young girl never, ever wants to see her best friend again. Her mom urges her to talk to her friend, and when she finally does, she recognizes that their "tiff" was just a big misunderstanding. Ages 4 to 8.

Too Competitive

Everyday Behaviors: Winning is everything; constantly compares performance, achievement, appearance, abilities to other kids; overly frustrated when losing; judges herself not as good as others

Friendship Skill Builder: Respecting What's Great About Your Friends

"So what if it's just a game? I've got to beat him!"
"I don't want him on my team—he's not good enough, and we're just gonna lose."
"She's so much prettier than I am!"

WHAT'S WRONG?

There's nothing the matter with have a strong competitive spirit. And there certainly is nothing wrong with trying to do our best. In fact, competitive kids generally do excel, do achieve, do win, and do succeed in life. It's only human.

The danger comes when competitive kids push the envelope too far and don't know when to stop. Everything becomes a contest, and the only objective is to win, win, win. This kind of ruthless, "take no prisoners" mentality can seriously damage friendships and destroy relationships. Although it's true that your child may be quite talented or very gifted, unless you help her learn to temper that competitive spirit she won't win any popularity contests.

WHY IS THIS HAPPENING?

There are many possible reasons why your child is so competitive that he's ruining his relationships with other kids. Here are some questions to consider.

- ☐ Is your child trying to live up to your expectations, and are they realistic?
- ☐ Are you using your child to compensate for your own frustrated hopes and dreams?
- ☐ Is the emphasis in your family all about win-win-win? Is your kid modeling what he's been taught?
- ☐ Do you praise, reinforce, and reward victory and punish defeat?
- ☐ Is your child overly competitive because she can't handle failure? Does she have low self-esteem and need the "win" for validation?
- ☐ Is your child too dependent on peer status and approval?
- ☐ Does she lack friends or not know how to go about making them? Is she acting this way to try to impress others?
- ☐ Is winning the only way to gain your acceptance and approval?
- ☐ Is there a sibling or close friend whom your kid has to beat out to earn love and respect? (Also see Jealous and Resentful, and Siblings.)

- [ ] Is your child hanging around with a group of kids who are highly competitive, status-oriented, and keenly ambitious?
- [ ] Is your kid in a one-down position that makes him feel he has to be the best at something to get that scholarship and succeed in life?
- [ ] Does overcompetitiveness seem to be part of your child's natural temperament? Have you been aware of this tendency since he was quite young?

What is your best guess as to why your child is overly competitive with friends? Write it here.

_____

_____

_____

FRIENDSHIP SKILL BUILDER

Respecting What's Great About Your Friends

Ultimately you don't succeed in the long term by defeating and humiliating your opponents. It's important to learn cooperation, mutual regard, and teamwork to get along and build friendships. Instead of focusing only on the short-term goal of beating out somebody, teach your kid to honor and respect their friends as individuals with unique characters and abilities. Here are the steps to teach your kid.

1. ***Look for good things other kids have said or done.*** Whether you're in a competitive situation or not,

pick out someone you really admire, who deserves to be complimented. Find a particular aspect of her personality, talent, deed, appearance, or attitude you think is special. Think of the words you want to say.

2. *Tell the person exactly what you admire.* Look at the person and smile. Tell the friend what you admire. Say the compliment like you mean it. "Hey, nice haircut." "I like your writing." "Great job at second base." "Wow, your dancing was impressive." Don't overdo it: one simple statement is fine. It doesn't have to be long.

3. *Be sincere.* Make sure the statement is honest and true. Kids can tell whether the compliment is real or phony. It won't help to say something nice to someone unless it is deserved.

4. *Pause for a response.* If the person says "Thanks," you can say "You're welcome." If the person doesn't say anything, just leave things as is.

WHAT SHOULD I SAY?

- *Stop rewarding the killer mentality.* Don't succumb to the philosophy that winning is everything and your kid should do anything he can to accomplish it. So avoid saying, "If you win today, the whole family is going out to dinner." "You take after your old dad. I used to win everything when I was your age, too." "You keep up like this, and Harvard will be banging on the door." "You know you can do better; now get out there and push yourself harder." "You are so drop-dead gorgeous. All the other girls will have to go home and hide in the closet." "Nobody will remember you if you come in second." "You creamed that defensive end. I bet she won't be able to play in the next game."

- *Point out the impact on others.* Your child may not understand how his intense competitive drive turns other kids off, so look for real examples. "Sure, you won the match, but you lost your friend by fighting over every call." "Asking Lynn to copy her test answers sure didn't get you a better grade with her." "You may be a great violinist, but I can see you're alienating your friends by always telling them you're such a musical genius."

- *Praise camaraderie.* Yes, you can congratulate your child for winning and doing well, but also praise actions that show compassion, concern, teamwork, and encouragement toward the other kids. "Nice pass to Samantha." "I love how you always care about your classmates and keep things positive."

- *Stress effort.* "Hey, you were really flying down to third; you put everything you had into it." "Your recital wouldn't have been so wonderful if you hadn't put so much time into practicing." "Being first doesn't matter as much as knowing you've done your best."

- *Emphasize going for personal best.* Take the focus off always trying to outperform other kids and instead emphasize doing the very best you can. "How did you play?" "Did you do the best *you* could?" "What's the most important thing you learned today?" "Is there anything you wish you had done differently?" "What will you do differently next time?" "Don't worry about the other kids. You can't change their performance."

- *Use celebrity examples.* Famous people are great at being the best and the worst. "Just because he catches a perfect pass in the end zone doesn't mean he should make us watch his silly dance." "He may be as rich as King Midas, but I wouldn't want to spend three minutes with such an arrogant guy." "That contestant was so far ahead and still lost it all, but did you see how gracious he was and what a good sport?"

- *Boost sensitivity.* "How do you feel about going against your best friend?" "Put yourself in Josh's place. Did you say anything to him to make him feel better?"
- *Reaffirm what really matters.* Convey to your child through your actions as well as words that it's who she is that you love—not what she gets. The message your child must hear is: "Win or lose, you know we love you," "Just do your best—that's all we ask," and "It doesn't make a darn bit of difference if you come in first or last. We love you."

WHAT SHOULD I DO?

- *Get your priorities straight.* Kids have so much pressure these days just growing up. So watch yourself! If your kid is already a keen competitor, he doesn't need you to jump-start him anymore. What he does need is help in keeping things in perspective, lightening his load, emphasizing the enjoyment of life, and learning cooperation, collaboration, and mutual support. And do make sure there is time for fun with other kids.
- *Watch out for coaches.* Your influence on your kid is significant, but so too is that of teachers, coaches, and mentors. So if you're ever in a position to choose your kid's instructor, be picky. If you can't choose, talk to him about his competitive approach. The last thing an overly competitive kid needs is an overly competitive coach with a win-at-all-costs philosophy. 🛑 **Youth programs in a least 163 cities are so concerned about the trend of poor parent sportsmanship that they now require parents to sign a pledge of proper conduct to be allowed to attend their kids' games. How do adults display sportsmanship around your kid? What about you?** 🛑
- *Stress self-improvement.* Always trying to be smarter, faster, cuter, more successful, or more popular is guaranteed to be

self-defeating. After all, there will *always* be someone better than we are, whether it be in appearance, talent, or ability. So encourage your child to compete instead against *himself.* His goal should be to surpass his last performance and keep improving in whatever he's doing. By learning to set realistic personal goals, he'll begin to look for his own accomplishments instead of those of the other kids. That change of emphasis will not only boost your child's self-esteem but also improve his friendships.

- *Balance the load.* Overly competitive kids tend to put heavy loads on themselves. So make sure his friends aren't taking a real backseat to his drive. Find ways to manage this kid's practice schedule and workload so there is enough time just to be a kid.

- *Watch for stress.* Overly competitive kids can push themselves so much that they overdose on their own need to excel. Maintaining a frantic pace can lead to burnout, and friendships will take a toll. So watch for trouble sleeping, weight loss or gain, difficulty concentrating, negative attitude, and blaming others. At the first of those signs, insist that your kid cut back and make more time to focus on fun and friendships.

- *Channel natural leadership.* Usually kids with competitive drive also have leadership potential. But with all the emphasis on push-push-push and win-win-win, that positive trait may be squelched. So help nurture her leadership capabilities. Instead of concentrating on competition, help her find one way she can take charge of something she cares about and make a difference.

FRIENDSHIP TIP

Having Fun
The Athletic Footwear Association conducted a survey of over twenty thousand kids to find out the top ten reasons why kids participate in sports. Kids said their top reason was "to have fun." Their bottom reason: "to win." Let your child know that the majority of the kids he is "competing" against are really participating to have a good time.

 21-DAY FRIENDSHIP FOLLOW-UP

Over the next 21 days, here's what I will do to help my child learn Friendship Skill Builder: Respecting What's Great About Your Friends:

_____

_____

_____

 FRIENDSHIP SKILL BUILDER BOOKS

For Parents and Teachers
How to Talk to Teens About Really Important Things: Specific Questions and Answers and Useful Things to Say, by Charles E. Schaefer and Theresa Foy DiGeronimo (San Francisco: Jossey-Bass, 1999). This book is packed full of specific ways to talk to your kids about essential topics, including drugs, cults, gangs, vio-

lence, depression, and tattoos. The chapter on competition is especially recommended.

My Kid's an Honor Student, Your Kid's a Loser: The Pushy Parent's Guide to Raising a Perfect Child, by Ralph Schoenstein (New York: Perseus, 2003). Sharp observations spun out in a humorous style about today's parents' obsession with creating superkids.

Positive Pushing: How to Raise a Successful and Happy Child, by James Taylor and Jim Taylor (New York: Hyperion, 2002). The authors contrast parents who push their kids negatively, by focusing on grades and soccer scores, with parents who push their children positively, by inviting them to enjoy and celebrate their personal achievements.

The Cheers and the Tears: A Healthy Alternative to the Dark Side of Youth Sports, by Shane Murphy (San Francisco: Jossey-Bass, 1999). Offers parents and coaches sensible advice and healthy alternative approaches to the competitive and stressful world of youth sports.

Toilet Trained for Yale: Adventures in 21st Century Parenting, by Ralph Schoenstein (New York: Perseus, 2002). A humorous yet scathing look at parenting in overdrive and the effect it's having on our kids. Interesting reading!

For Kids

Be a Perfect Person in Just Three Days! by Stephen Manes (New York: Bantam-Skylark, 1991). Milo finds a book at the library on how to be the perfect person. He follows the directions carefully and finally learns the real message behind the instructions in the book: "Perfect is boring!" "You can . . . be as imperfect as you please and still be a good person." Ages 8 to 12.

I Made a Mistake, by Miriam Nerlove (New York: Atheneum, 1985). A young child recognizes that "It's okay to make a mistake." Ages 4 to 8.

Nobody Is Perfick, by Bernard Waber (Boston: Houghton Mifflin, 1971). A young boy finally realizes through much trial and error that nobody is "perfick," including him. Ages 4 to 8.

Friendship Issue 25

Too Sensitive

Everyday Behaviors: Cries easily; takes friendly teasing hard; has lots of highs and lows; extremely aware of everything going on around her; too worried about what friends think of her

Friendship Skill Builder: Accepting Criticism

"Jerald called me a crybaby again. I hate him!"
"It's not funny when Jenna makes jokes about my glasses."
"Did you notice how the new kids kept staring at me?"

WHAT'S WRONG?

Does watching a sad movie or reading a distressing book cause your kid anguish? Are you finding yourself thinking carefully before you speak to your kid because one wrong comment can cause an all-night tirade? Does your child appear "fine" one minute and then suddenly moody and irritable? Would you label your kid "high maintenance": fussy, picky, with a lot of highs and lows? If so, you have a sensitive critter on your hands.

Most parents would tell you that sensitive kids usually arrive that way. By nature these children seem more "touchy" from birth: they're more sensitive to sound and change, cry easily, and take criticism far too seriously. Although those traits can be highly desirable (after all, the world certainly needs more compassionate people), being overly sensitive can cause problems in the social jungle. And the biggest reason is that sensitive kids don't know how to respond to put-downs, teases, and critical comments. Instead of shrugging them off, they take the jabs with too much emotion and drama. And that turns the other kids off big-time, so oversensitivity is a frequent cause of friendship problems.

Sure, you can't change your sensitive child into a little thick-skinned toughie. And besides, you shouldn't: your child's sensitive nature is an asset, so you'll want to help him see it positively. Besides, your role isn't to change your child's natural personality but to help him cope more successfully and learn to control *how* he responds. Doing so can make a huge difference in boosting your tenderhearted child's friendship aptitude and helping him survive in a not-so-sensitive world.

🛑 **Approximately 15 to 20 percent of kids have been shown to be highly sensitive. They are also empathic, smart, intuitive, careful, and conscientious. The flip side is that they are also easily overstimulated and require informed parenting in order to prevent temper tantrums, stress-related illnesses, and the avoidance of pleasurable group activities.** 🛑

WHY IS THIS HAPPENING?

Here are some triggers that could cause kids to be overly sensitive. Check the ones that apply to your child.

- [ ] Has your child always been more sensitive, high-strung, moody, or temperamental?
- [ ] Does he lack self-esteem or self-confidence? If so, why?
- [ ] Is there anything about your home or your family that could be making her more sensitive lately? Have you recently moved? Is there family friction? A potential divorce? Military deployment? What about your family's reputation?
- [ ] Have you brought up your kid to be compassionate and empathic, and now he's having a tough time dealing with the cold, cruel world?
- [ ] Might she be overtired, physically ill, depressed, or under a lot of stress?
- [ ] Does he have a speech impediment or a physical or learning disability that has made him the butt of kids' jokes?
- [ ] Is there something about his appearance that's causing him to be more sensitive around his friends, such as new braces, glasses, freckles, large ears, acne, weight, height? Is his dress style causing him not to "fit in" with kids? Are the other kids making fun of the issue? (Also see Different.)
- [ ] Does she have trouble regulating her emotions? Is he prone to meltdowns and quick to anger? (Also see Hot Tempered.)
- [ ] Has he been babied or pampered? Does he still depend on you to stick up for him, so it's now hard for him to stick up for himself? (Also see Peer Pressure.)
- [ ] Is this preadolescence, and your kid's hormones are kicking in and causing mood swings?
- [ ] Is a clique rejecting her? Are there boyfriend problems? (Also see Cliques.)
- [ ] Has he had limited opportunities to be with kids his own age, so he's not used to normal teasing? Is he an only child? Does he live in a no-kid neighborhood? Is he so scheduled that there's no time to be around other kids?
- [ ] Is perhaps his sensitivity justified? For instance, is he with

a group of kids who are just crueler? Is this really not "friendly" teasing but verbal abuse, bullying, or sexual harassment? *Are you sure?* (Also see Teased, and Bullied and Harassed.)

Look over the list. Talk to others who know your child well. What is your best guess as to why your kid is so sensitive? Write your response.

_____

_____

_____

WHAT SHOULD I SAY?

- *Don't say "Toughen up."* Overly sensitive kids can't toughen up. They really don't want to get so teary-eyed and be so hypersensitive; it's usually part of their personality. So refrain from saying things like "Don't be such a baby," "Cut it out, the kids are going to call you a sissy," "Boys don't cry," or "You're too old to act like that." 🛑 **Kids are most self-conscious and sensitive to peer reactions in fourth and fifth grade. This is when kids are most apt to compare their appearance and athletic and intellectual abilities to those of their friends.** 🛑

- *Respect feelings.* Your sensitive kid is a feeling person, so acknowledge his feelings. Doing so often helps him open up and discuss his concerns. "You look so distressed." "I'm so sorry you're so upset. When you calm down a bit we can talk." "I know you're really mad that your friend made fun of you."

- *Emphasize his power.* Stress to your child that he has control of how he chooses to react to another child. "You can't control what another person says or does, but you *can* con-

FRIENDSHIP SKILL BUILDER

Accepting Criticism

Help your child understand that not all criticism is hostile or mean-spirited. In fact, some kinds of feedback are constructive. These steps will help your kid learn not to overreact to criticism but to handle it in a more useful way.

1. **Listen to the criticism.** Don't interrupt; stay quiet while the person is talking. Hear him out.
2. **Stay calm.** Take a deep breath if necessary. Count to five inside your head. If you feel like you're going to cry, try to hold your breath. Turn off your upset face.
3. **Pick out what really counts.** Ask yourself, "Is this true or false? Is he trying to help or hurt me? Could he be right? Is this really something I should get worked up over?"
4. **Show that you understand.** "Okay." "I understand." Use as friendly a voice as you can.
5. **Try to correct the problem.** If you are asked to do something different and it makes sense to you, do it.

trol how you respond." "You may not be able to stop that kid from being so mean, but if you practice, you can learn not to cry when he calls you names." "I don't want you ever to stop being such a caring person. That's one of your greatest gifts. But you can learn how to make your face not look so upset."

• **Point out the "wrong look."** Don't assume that your child knows what she does that turns kids off. She may have been using that grimace, pout, scowl, or whatever else for so long that's she unaware she's doing it. So casually bring it up when the two of you are alone: "I notice that when you're upset you make a certain face. Do you know what I mean?" (If not, show her.) "Do you think that face would make friends want to be with you or to leave you alone? What do kids do when you make that face? Let's think of other things you can do when you're upset that won't turn kids off."

- **Offer replacers.** If your child cries easily, he'll need to learn what to do instead of crying. Talk about possible alternatives and then have your child choose the one he likes best. "Think of a really fun place inside your head, and make your mind go there." "Walk away really quickly." "Clear your throat and bite your tongue." "Count to ten inside your head." "Hum a song (only inside your head)." "Take a long, slow breath." In order for the "crying replacement" to become a habit, he'll have to practice it again and again.

WHAT SHOULD I DO?

- **Teach "So what?"** The moment your child knows he might get upset is when he needs to look as if he couldn't care less. He needs to learn a "So what?" or "No big deal" kind of look. Try modeling it. Tell him not to even glance at the kid. Instead, he should shrug his shoulders, look off in the sunset, and walk away if possible. Even a subtle shaking of the head can help achieve a "So what, I couldn't care less" appearance. 🛑 **The most important thing you can do for an overly sensitive child is help her learn how to control her reactions to peers. Teach her coping skills so she can deal with any situation that may come her way.** 🛑
- **Teach how to use a firm voice.** Whimpering, crying, whining, yelling, whispering, and quivering voice tones are kid turnoffs. Tell your child to clear his throat and think solid and strong before he talks. He'll need to distinguish between voice tones, so role-play various tones and have him

practice different voices until he can speak with a confident voice.

- **Switch facial expressions.** Unless your child learns to "switch off" that upset or ticked-off look on his face, he'll never make the kids believe he's not upset. Try modeling or discovering together a different expression to substitute, such as smiling or looking surprised or puzzled, so it's harder for his friends to tell what he's feeling.

- **Teach how to deflect the barbs.** Find a way to help your kid brush off those critical or insensitive messages. Many kids say it helps if they pretend they're wearing a special armored vest that bounces taunts, teases, and critical comments off of them so they don't look afraid.

- **Watch out for labels.** Highly sensitive kids are often stereotyped as overly inhibited, fearful, or fussy, or as problem children. So don't let teachers, family, or friends label your child and don't do so yourself.

- **Keep a routine.** A sensitive kid has trouble with change and transition, so planning ahead, preparing him for what's going to happen, and keeping things on a regular schedule are often helpful.

- **Watch out for overstimulation.** Big groups, crowded carpools, noisy classrooms, and hyped-up parties can be a real nightmare for a sensitive kid. Watch out for too much, too many, too fast.

 FRIENDSHIP TIP

Losing Face
Surveys of kids six to eleven years of age in six countries showed that the number one concern to kids in *all six countries* (next to losing the security of their family) is losing face among friends. Humiliation and being laughed at cause big-time distress.

Too Sensitive

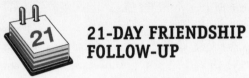

21-DAY FRIENDSHIP FOLLOW-UP

Over the next 21 days, here's what I will do to help my child learn Friendship Skill Builder: Accepting Criticism:

_____

_____

_____

📖 FRIENDSHIP SKILL BUILDER BOOKS 📖

For Parents and Teachers

Raising Your Spirited Child: A Guide for Parents Whose Child Is More Intense, Sensitive, Perceptive, Persistent, and Energetic, by Mary Sheedy Kurcinka (New York: HarperPerennial, 1998). A parent educator and parent of a spirited child provides strategies to help you work with your child. She also helps you understand your own temperament and the role it plays in how you deal with your child.

The Highly Sensitive Child: Helping Our Children Thrive When the World Overwhelms Them, by Elaine Aron (New York: Broadway, 2002). A psychotherapist and self-identified highly sensitive person provides a wealth of useful suggestions and case studies for parents of overly sensitive kids from infancy to adolescence.

The Out-of-Sync Child: Recognizing and Coping with Sensory Integration Dysfunction, by Carol Stock Kranowitz and Larry B. Silver (New York: Perigee Books, 1998). Do you know a child who plays too rough, is uncoordinated, hates being touched, or is ultrasensitive (or unusually insensitive) to noise or sensations of heat and cold? If so, you may find these suggestions not only helpful but comforting. Also see *The Out-of-Sync*

Child Has Fun: Activities for Kids with Sensory Integration Dysfunction, by the same authors.

Too Loud, Too Bright, Too Fast, Too Tight: What to Do If You Are Sensory Defensive in an Overstimulating World, by Sharon Heller (New York: HarperCollins, 2002). Could your child's oversensitivity be caused by sensory defensiveness? If your child displays such symptoms as flinching from touch, an overly acute sense of smell, fear of escalators, or irritation at certain lights, you may find this an interesting read.

Final Words:
An Invitation to the Party

Shakespeare was right: friends are more precious than gold, fame, and power. Without friends, nothing is meaningful or fun. With friends, even the worst hardships and losses are bearable.

I'm sure anyone reading this book would agree with these sentiments, yet something so obvious appears to be universally overlooked these days. We're living in a time when very few parents would put friends at the top of their daily priorities list for their children's lives. We're all so swept up in pushing them ahead, worrying about the right preschool, fearful that they won't learn to read at an early age, concerned about their math and science skills, sweating over their test preparation classes and scores, making sure their résumés include the politically correct mix of academic achievement, athletic competition, community service, creative expression, club memberships, leadership, and travel.

Meanwhile, we ourselves are so pressured and stressed that we don't always take time for a nightly family dinner.

We're so darn busy multitasking and putting out seven fires at once that we can't always give our kids the focused attention they need to learn cornerstone friendship-building skills, such as listening, being empathic, showing respect, and appreciating others. Even our discipline is so quick these days that we don't take the time to help our kids reason through what went wrong so they can to act differently with their friends. "Okay, that's a five-minute time-out. See you later!". . . may put a band-aid on the situation and make you feel that you've handled it like a good parent. But you've actually lost an opportunity for your child to understand how he could have calmed down, taken turns, asked nicely, been more sensitive to his friend, and avoided upsetting their relationship in the future.

Not only that, the moment we log on to the Internet, turn on the tube, or walk out the door clutching our Palm Pilot, cell phone, or Blackberry, we're slammed in the face by a society that's going a million miles an hour. Everything is going so fast, everyone is so preoccupied and worried. What's so much on everyone's mind these days is fear of an unknown, faraway terror that might strike at any time, fear of job loss and economic downfall, fear for personal safety and the security of our home and family. But shouldn't we really be thinking about the single most important thing for our kids' future? And isn't that really their ability to love and have committed relationships—like lifelong friendship and marriage—with other people?

Love, commitment, and friendship: what more could we hope for for our children? Think about it. What would you rather have on your gravestone:

HERE LIES A PARENT WHO HELPED
HER CHILDREN GET 800S ON THEIR SATS

or:

HERE LIES A PARENT WHO TAUGHT
HER CHILDREN TO LOVE AND CHERISH
OTHERS

So remember this. Please. And in the spirit of this mission—to love and cherish others—let's celebrate. Let's have a party—a big party. Ask your kid to invite all his friends. Invite a few of your own, too. Turn on the music if that's what you enjoy—or better yet, pull out those instruments and play, sing, and play some more.

I really hope the ultimate benefit of this book is that your child will have good friends and that they'll all come to your house and fill it with laughter, singing, the warmth of sharing, and the joys of camaraderie. What could be more important?

March 2005   Michele Borba
Palm Springs, California

References

PART ONE: WHY DO FRIENDS MATTER SO MUCH TO YOUR KID?

Survey (43 percent of children afraid to use school bathrooms) cited by A. Mulrine, "Once Bullied, Now Bullies—with Guns," *U.S. News & World Report,* May 3, 1999, p. 24.

Research (one in seven U.S. schoolchildren is either bully or victim) cited by C. Goodnow, "Bullying Is a Complex, Dangerous Game in Which Everyone's a Player," *Seattle Post-Intelligencer,* [http://www.seattle-pi.com/lifestyle/bull1at.shtml], Sept. 1, 1999.

Research by the National Education Association quoted by S. Fried and P. Fried, *Bullies and Victims: Helping Your Child Through the Schoolyard Battlefield* (New York: Evans, 1996), p. xii.

Two-thirds of school police officers say younger children are acting more aggressively: R. Carroll, "School Police: Youths Getting More Aggressive," *Desert Sun,* Aug. 20, 2003, p. A5.

Students hitting out of anger: Josephson Institute of Ethics and CHARACTER COUNTS! Coalition, "1998 Report Card on the Ethics of American Youth," [www.josephsoninstitute. org/98-Survey/violence/98survey.htm], Oct. 19, 1998.

Four out of five adolescents say sexual harassment is widespread: cited by C. C. Giannetti and M. Sagarese, *Cliques: 8 Steps to Help Your Child Survive the Social Jungle* (New York: Broadway Books, 2001), p. 3.

Survey of hate crimes of Massachusetts high schools: L. M. Everett-Haynes, "Hate Crimes Prompt Campus Campaign," *Arizona Daily Wildcat,* Jan. 13, 2000.

Survey of 991 kids about peer pressure cited by A. Goldstein, "Paging All Parents," *Time,* July 3, 2000, p. 47.

Cyberspace bullying as growing trend among middle schoolers: A. Harmon, "Internet Gives Teenage Bullies Weapons to Wound from Afar," *New York Times,* Aug. 26, 2004, p. A1.

FBI says the number of serious child kidnappings has not risen: S. Dunnewind, "Experts: Parents Going Overboard to Protect Kids," *Seattle Times,* Feb. 3, 2003, p. D3.

U.S. population mobile (over five-year period, 46 percent of Americans move at least once): cited by Dalton Conley, *The Pecking Order: Which Siblings Succeed and Why* (New York: Pantheon Books, 2004), p. 181.

Pairing an older "shy" child with a younger or less skilled child to learn new social skills: P. G. Zimbardo and S. Radl, *The Shy Child: A Parent's Guide to Preventing and Overcoming Shyness from Infancy to Adulthood,* 2nd ed. (New York: Doubleday, 1999), pp. 87–90, 204–209.

PART TWO: FRIENDSHIP BEGINS AT HOME

Reasons parents must make time for kids to be with friends: Z. Rubin, *Children's Friendships* (Cambridge, Mass.: Harvard University Press, 1980), pp. 3–6.

UCLA studies on play dates: F. Frankel, *Good Friends Are Hard to Find: Help Your Child Find, Make and Keep Friends* (Los Angeles: Perspective, 1996), p. 3.

Parent guidelines for arranging play dates: F. Frankel, *Good Friends Are Hard to Find: Help Your Child Find, Make and Keep Friends* (Los Angeles: Perspective, 1996), p. 80.

"Principle of Similarity": W. W. Hartup, "Peer Interaction and Social Organization," in Paul H. Mussen (ed.), *Carmichael's Manual of Child Psychology,* Vol. 2 (New York: Wiley, 1970).

Peer rejection continues in organized groups: L. E. Shapiro, *How to Raise a Child with a High EQ: A Parents' Guide to Emotional Intelligence* (New York: HarperCollins, 1997), p. 206.

Statistic from the Centers for Disease Control and Prevention on rate of overweight teens: K. O'Connor, "Active Kids: Children, Teens Work Out at Home to Stay Fit," *Desert Sun,* July 2, 2004, p. B1.

Ages and stages of children's group behaviors: Z. Rubin, *Children's Friendships* (Cambridge, Mass.: Harvard University Press, 1980), pp. 93–109.

Three things to do when children's friends are present: M. Thompson and C. O'Neill Grace, with L. J. Cohen, *Best Friends, Worst Enemies: Understanding the Social Lives of Children* (New York: Ballantine, 2001), p. 246.

Indirect supervision helps kids play together longer and more cooperatively: K. H. Rubin, *The Friendship Factor: Helping Our Children Navigate Their Social World—and Why It Matters for*

Their Success and Happiness (New York: Viking Penguin, 2002), pp. 89–90.

UCLA Social Skills Training Program on interactive toys encouraging cooperation: F. Frankel, *Good Friends Are Hard to Find: Help Your Child Find, Make and Keep Friends* (Los Angeles: Perspective, 1996), pp. 25–26.

Inductive discipline as a predictor of child's peer status: K. H. Rubin, *The Friendship Factor: Helping Our Children Navigate Their Social World—and Why It Matters for Their Success and Happiness* (New York: Viking Penguin, 2002), p. 90–91.

PART THREE: THE TOP 25 FRIENDSHIP PROBLEMS AND HOW TO SOLVE THEM

1—Argues

National survey (43 percent of middle school students have conflicts one or more times a day): Josephson Institute of Ethics and CHARACTER COUNTS! Coalition, "1998 Report Card on the Ethics of American Youth," [www. josephsoninstitute.org/98-Survey/violence/98survey.htm], Oct. 19, 1998.

Statistics (45 percent of middle school students have conflicts; 80 percent see arguments): N. Drew, *The Kids' Guide to Working Out Conflicts: How to Keep Cool, Stay Safe, and Get Along* (Minneapolis, Minn.: Free Spirit, 2004), p. 21.

Kids' top conflict starters: N. Drew, *The Kids' Guide to Working Out Conflicts: How to Keep Cool, Stay Safe, and Get Along* (Minneapolis, Minn.: Free Spirit, 2004), p. 7.

2—Bad Friends

Busy kids keep out of trouble: L. Gormley, "Study Finds Busy Teens Keep out of Trouble," *Desert Sun,* Jan. 31, 2004, p. B1. To read the full report go to [http://www.fightcrime.org].

3—Bad Reputation

Only 7 percent of messages are verbal: A. Mehrabian, *Silent Messages* (Belmont, Calif.: Wadsworth, 1987), p. 7, as cited in M. P. Duke, S. Nowicki, and E. Martin, *Teaching Your Child the Language of Social Success* (Atlanta: Peachtree, 1996), p. 7.

Image versus reputation: R. Wiseman, *Queen Bees and Wannabes: Helping Your Daughter Survive Cliques, Gossip, Boyfriends, and Other Realities of Adolescence* (New York: Three Rivers Press, 2002), p. 125.

4—Bossy

Altruistic, "kind" preadolescents are named as more popular: K. H. Rubin, *The Friendship Factor* (New York: Viking, 2002), pp. 192, 194; they are also seen as happier in peer relationships: P. Mussen, E. Rutherford, S. Harris, and C. Keasey, "Honesty and Altruism Among Preadolescents," *Developmental Psychology*, 1970, *3*, 169–194.

Kids need to understand the value of sharing and turn taking before they will partake: N. Eisenberg, *Altruistic Emotion, Cognition, and Behavior* (Mahwah, N.J.: Erlbaum, 1986).

5—Bullied and Harassed

Rates of sexual harassment among fifth through eighth graders reported by the Center for Children, *Steps to Respect Research Review,* [http://www.cfchildren.org/strres.html#6].

Research (one in seven schoolchildren is either bully or victim) cited by C. Goodnow, "Bullying Is a Complex, Dangerous Game in Which Everyone's a Player," *Seattle Post-Intelligencer,* [http://www.seattle-pi.com/lifestyle/bull1at.shtml], Sept. 1, 1999.

Parry Aftab quotation on electronic bullying: A. Harmon, "Internet Gives Teenage Bullies Weapons to Wound from Afar," *New York Times,* Aug. 26, 2004, p. A1.

Vulnerability is the essential quality bullies look for in victims: P. Sheras with S. Tippins, *Your Child: Bully or Victim? Understanding and Ending Schoolyard Tyranny* (New York: Fireside, 2002), p. 60.

Learning to be assertive when faced with bullying leads to less targeting by bullies: J. Garbarino and E. deLara, *And Words Can Hurt Forever: How to Protect Adolescents from Bullying, Harassment, and Emotional Violence* (New York: Free Press, 2002), p. 146.

Insecure and anxious posture is more likely to cause kids to be victimized: S. Fried and P. Fried, *Bullies and Victims: Helping Your Child Through the Schoolyard Battlefield* (New York: Evans, 1996), p. 99.

Parents don't believe reports of bullying: S. Ziegler and M. Rosenstein-Manner, *Bullying at School: Toronto in an International Context* (Toronto: Toronto Board of Education, 1999), p. 22.

Kids can handle bullying better if they have one friend to confide in: A. D. Pellegrini and M. Bartini, "A Longitudinal Study of Bullying: Victimization and Peer Affiliation During the Transition from Primary School to Middle School," *American Educational Research Journal,* 2000, *37*(3), 699–725.

Twenty percent of kids in sixth through twelfth grade say they stay in a group to avoid harassment at school: K. Chandler, M. J. Nolin, and E. Davies, National Center for Education Statistics survey no. NCES 95-203 (Washington, D.C.: U.S. Department of Education, Office of Educational Research and Improvement), Oct. 1995, pp. 1–7.

Survey (43 percent of children afraid to use school bathrooms) cited by A. Mulrine, "Once Bullied, Now Bullies—with Guns," *U.S. News & World Report,* May 3, 1999, p. 24.

Research by the National Education Association quoted by S. Fried and P. Fried, *Bullies and Victims: Helping Your Child Through the Schoolyard Battlefield* (New York: Evans, 1996), p. xii.

Big part of success is assertive comeback delivery: S. Fried and P. Fried, *Bullies and Victims: Helping Your Child Through the Schoolyard Battlefield* (New York: Evans, 1996), p. 108.

Only one way to stop bullying: H. E. Marano, *"Why Doesn't Anybody Like Me?" A Guide to Raising Socially Confident Kids* (New York: Morrow, 1998), p. 163.

Research by D. Espelage citing teachers' ability to pick out only 10 percent of victims: P. Sheras with S. Tippins, *Your Child: Bully or Victim? Understanding and Ending Schoolyard Tyranny* (New York: Fireside, 2002), p. 64.

6—Cliques

Draw a cafeteria seating map to open discussion of cliques: C. C. Giannetti and M. Sagarese, *Cliques: 8 Steps to Help Your Child Survive the Social Jungle* (New York: Broadway Books, 2001), pp. 19–20.

Four social categories of peer status: P. A. Adler and P. Adler, *Peer Power: Preadolescent Culture and Identity* (Piscataway, N.J.: Rutgers University Press, 1998), pp. 38–55.

7—Clueless

Only 7 percent of messages are verbal: A. Mehrabian, *Silent Messages* (Belmont, Calif.: Wadsworth, 1987), as cited in M. P. Duke, S. Bowicki, and E. Martin, *Teaching Your Child the Language of Social Success* (Atlanta: Peachtree, 1996), p. 7.

Socially competent kids use eye contact and smiling: cited by M. Duke, S. Nowicki Jr., and E. A. Martin, *Teaching Your Child the Language of Social Success* (Atlanta: Peachtree, 1996), p. 5.

One out of ten children has significant nonverbal communication problems: cited by M. Duke, S. Nowicki Jr., and E. A. Martin, *Teaching Your Child the Language of Social Success* (Atlanta: Peachtree, 1996), p. vii.

8—Different

Mentors help children overcome life obstacles: E. Werner and R. Smith, *Vulnerable but Invincible: A Longitudinal Study of Resilient Children and Youth* (New York: McGraw-Hill, 1982).

Quality most attractive to peers is kindness: K. H. Rubin, *The Friendship Factor: Helping Our Children Navigate Their Social World—and Why It Matters for Their Success and Happiness* (New York: Viking Penguin, 2002), p. 192.

9—Doesn't Share

Turn-taking rudiments evident around two-and-a-half years of age: Z. Rubin, *Children's Friendships* (Cambridge, Mass.: Harvard University Press, 1980), pp. 16–17.

Aggressive behaviors decrease when children report instances of cooperation: T. Grieger, J. M. Kauffman, and R. M. Grieger, "Effects of Peer Reporting on Cooperative Play and Aggression of Kindergarten Children," *Journal of School Psychology,* 1976, *14,* 307–313.

Putting toys away increases sharing: F. Frankel, *Good Friends Are Hard to Find: Helping Your Child Find, Make and Keep Friends* (Los Angeles: Perspective, 1996), p. 104.

Viewing prosocial TV shows increases prosocial behaviors: N. Eisenberg and P. H. Mussen, *The Roots of Prosocial Behavior in Children* (Cambridge, Eng.: Cambridge University Press, 1989), p. 97.

Citation of T. Berry Brazelton on the need to teach sharing: Gannett News Service, "Doctor Urges Parents to Teach Kids to Share," *Desert Sun,* June 7, 2000.

10—Fights

Viewing violence increases aggression: cited by American Academy of Pediatrics, "Joint Statement on the Impact on Entertainment Violence on Children, Congressional Public Health Summit," [http://www.aap.org/advocacy/releases/jstmtevc. htm], July 26, 2000.

Televised violence contributes to as much as 15 percent of kids' aggressive behaviors: cited by the American Psychological Association, "Summary Report of the American Psychological Association Commission on Violence and Youth," in *Violence and Youth: Psychology's Response,* Vol. 1 (Washington, D.C.: American Psychological Association, 1993), quoted in J. Garbarino, *Lost Boys* (New York: Free Press, 1999), p. 198.

Students hitting out of anger: Josephson Institute of Ethics and CHARACTER COUNTS! Coalition, "1998 Report Card on the Ethics of American Youth," [www.josephsoninstitute. org/98-survey/violence/98survey.htm], Oct. 19, 1998.

11—Gossips

Fourth and fifth grades are when gossip becomes a conversational mainstay: L. Oppenheimer, "Get a Grip on Gossip," *Parenting,* May 2003, p. 207.

Gossip topics among girls: R. Wiseman, *Queen Bees and Wannabes: Helping Your Daughter Survive Cliques, Gossip, Boyfriends, and Other Realities of Adolescence* (New York: Three Rivers Press, 2002), pp. 123–124.

12—Hot Tempered

Rates of violent incidents kids view by age eighteen cited by R. Taffel, *Nurturing Good Children Now* (New York: Golden Books, 1999), p. 18.

Harm of yelling: L. Marshall, "Study Says Yelling at Children Harms Them Long Term," *Desert Sun,* Feb. 5, 2003.

13—Insensitive

Niceness and decency as likability and popularity factors among kids: K. H. Rubin, *The Friendship Factor: Helping Our Children*

Navigate Their Social World—and Why It Matters for Their Success and Happiness (New York: Viking Penguin, 2002), p. 192.

Kids most self-conscious and sensitive in fourth and fifth grades: F. Vitro of Texas Woman's University, cited by J. S. Freedman, *Easing the Teasing: Helping Your Child Cope with Name-Calling, Ridicule, and Verbal Bullying* (New York: McGraw-Hill, 2002), p. 14.

Parents who express disapproval toward insensitive actions: N. Eisenberg, *The Caring Child* (Cambridge, Mass.: Harvard University Press, 1992).

Ability to read nonverbal emotions is a sign of popularity and emotional stability: S. Nowicki and M. Duke, "A Measure of Nonverbal Social Processing Ability in Children Between the Ages of Six and Ten," paper presented at the American Psychological Society meeting (1989), cited by D. Goleman, *Emotional Intelligence: Why It Can Matter More Than IQ* (New York: Bantam Books, 1995), p. 97.

Fathers' impact on children's empathy: R. Koestner, C. Franz, and J. Weinberger, "The Family Origins of Empathy Concern: A Twenty-Six-Year Longitudinal Study," *Journal of Personality and Social Psychology,* 1990, *58,* 709–717.

Sensitivity a key friendship criterion in preteen years: K. H. Rubin, *The Friendship Factor: Helping Our Children Navigate Their Social World—and Why It Matters for Their Success and Happiness* (New York: Viking Penguin, 2002), pp. 124–125.

Factors that enhance sensitivity: S. A. Denham, *Emotional Development in Young Children* (New York: Guilford Press, 1998), pp. 34–39.

14—Jealous and Resentful

Overpossessiveness due to fear of rejection: N. M. Elman and E. Kennedy-Moore, *The Unwritten Rules of Friendship: Simple*

Strategies to Help Your Child Make Friends (New York: Little, Brown, 2003), p. 99.

Jealousy declines in teen years: K. H. Rubin, *The Friendship Factor: Helping Our Children Navigate Their Social World—and Why It Matters for Their Success and Happiness* (New York: Viking Penguin, 2002), p. 165.

Jealousy is the top reason for relational aggression: C. Dellasega and C. Nixon, *Girl Wars: 12 Strategies That Will End Female Bullying* (New York: Simon & Schuster, 2003), p. 83.

Link jealousy to low self-esteem: C. Dellasega and C. Nixon, *Girl Wars: 12 Strategies That Will End Female Bullying* (New York: Simon & Schuster, 2003), p. 85.

15—Left Out

All kids are rejected: cited by E. McCoy, *What to Do . . . When Kids Are Mean to Your Child: Real Solutions from Experts, Parents, and Kids* (Pleasantville, N.Y.: Reader's Digest, 1997), p. 19.

Watch for serious reactions to rejection: cited by E. McCoy, *What to Do . . . When Kids Are Mean to Your Child: Real Solutions from Experts, Parents, and Kids* (Pleasantville, N.Y.: Reader's Digest, 1997), p. 50.

Skills of bouncing back are teachable: R. Brooks and S. Goldstein, *Raising Resilient Children: Fostering Strength, Hope, and Optimism in Your Child* (New York: Contemporary Books, 2002).

Rejection really hurts: M. Fox, "A Snub Really Does Feel Like a Kick in the Gut," *USA Today,* Oct. 13, 2003, p. D7.

16—New Kid

One-fifth of all Americans move every year: cited by D. Conley, *The Pecking Order: Which Siblings Succeed and Why* (New York: Pantheon, 2004), p. 181.

17—Peer Pressure

Survey of 991 kids about peer pressure, cited by A. Goldstein, "Paging All Parents," *Time*, July 3, 2000, p. 47.

Hovering parents hinder kids' relationships: cited by D. R. Schaffer, *Developmental Psychology*, 5th ed. (Pacific Grove, Calif.: Brooks/Cole, 1999).

18—Shy

Learning coping skills helped 90 percent of anxious kids: cited by J. S. Dacey and L. B. Fiore, *Your Anxious Child* (San Francisco: Jossey-Bass, 2000), p. 2.

Well-liked kids make frequent eye contact: M. Duke, S. Nowicki, and E. A. Martin, *Teaching Your Child the Language of Social Success* (Atlanta: Peachtree, 1966), p. 57.

Confident, well-liked kids smile a lot: M. Duke, S. Nowicki, and E. A. Martin, *Teaching Your Child the Language of Social Success* (Atlanta: Peachtree, 1966), p. 57.

Labeling correlated to kids' becoming shy: P. G. Zimbardo and S. Radl, *The Shy Child: A Parent's Guide to Preventing and Overcoming Shyness from Infancy to Adulthood*, 2nd ed. (New York: Doubleday, 1999), pp. 19–20.

Loose supervision more successful in enhancing social success: D. R. Shaffer, *Developmental Psychology*, 5th ed. (Pacific Grove, Calif.: Brooks/Cole, 1999).

Pairing older, shyer children with younger kids: P. G. Zimbardo and S. Radl, *The Shy Child: A Parent's Guide to Preventing and Overcoming Shyness from Infancy to Adulthood*, 2nd ed. (New York: Doubleday, 1999).

One-on-one play dates are the best opportunities to build close friendships: F. Frankel, *Good Friends Are Hard to Find: Help Your Child Find, Make and Keep Friends* (Los Angeles: Perspective, 1996), p. 3.

Two in five people consider themselves shy: P. G. Zimbardo and S. Radl, *The Shy Child: A Parent's Guide to Preventing and Overcoming Shyness from Infancy to Adulthood*, 2nd ed. (New York: Doubleday, 1999).

19—Siblings

Preschoolers need reminders to think of others: cited C. E. Schaefer and T. F. DiGeronimo in *Ages and Stages: Tips and Techniques for Building Your Child's Social, Emotional, Interpersonal, and Cognitive Skills* (New York: Wiley, 2000), p. 163.

Cooperation learned through modeling: N. Eisenberg and P. H. Mussen, *The Roots of Prosocial Behavior in Children* (New York: Cambridge University Press, 1995), pp. 68–72.

Listing what you like most and least about each child: W. Sears and M. Sears, *The Discipline Book: How to Have a Better-Behaved Child from Birth to Age Ten* (New York: Little, Brown, 1995), p. 220.

Sibling jealousy peaks during ages five to eleven: research by A. Kowal, conducted on siblings age eleven to thirteen, cited by E. McGowan in "Thwarting Jealousy," *Columbia Missourian*, Feb. 19, 2003.

Research results on benefits of problem solving: cited by G. Spivak and M. B. Shure, *Raising a Thinking Child* (New York: Henry Holt, 1994).

20—Sleepovers

Sesame Street survey of parents (most kids feel ready to sleep over by age seven): cited by N. Kalish, "Decisions: Sleepover Start-Up," *Working Mother*, Dec.-Jan. 2004, p. 80.

21—Tattletale

Children's moral development: J. Piaget, *The Moral Judgment of the Child* (Old Tappan, N.J.: Macmillan, 1965).

Before doing harm to themselves or others, 75 percent of kids tell intentions: cited by K. Zarzor, *Facing the Schoolyard Bully: How to Raise an Assertive Child in an Aggressive World* (Buffalo, N.Y.: Firefly Books, 2000).

Survey (81 percent of teens willing to report threats) cited in *Time*, "For the Record," April 22, 2002, p. 18.

22—Teased

Top ten things eight- to thirteen-year-olds are teased about: J. S. Freedman, *Easing the Teasing: Helping Your Child Cope with Name-Calling, Ridicule, and Verbal Bullying* (New York: Mc-Graw-Hill, 2002), p. 15.

Brain responds to verbal abuse the same way it does to physical abuse: M. Fox, "A Snub Really Does Feel Like a Kick in the Gut," *USA Today*, Oct. 13, 2003, p. D7.

Finding (80 percent of kids' teasing is unfriendly) based on survey by T. R. Warm of 250 children and adolescents, cited by E. McCoy, *What to Do . . . When Kids Are Mean to Your Child: Real Solutions from Experts, Parents, and Kids* (Pleasantville, N.Y.: Reader's Digest, 1997), p. 21.

Teasing in middle school years takes on sexual connotation: J. S. Freedman, *Easing the Teasing: Helping Your Child Cope with Name-Calling, Ridicule, and Verbal Bullying* (New York: Mc-Graw-Hill, 2002), p. 15.

Kids need a repertoire of comeback strategies: S. Fried and P. Fried, *Bullies and Victims: Helping Your Child Through the Schoolyard Battlefield* (New York: Evans, 1996).

National Education Association report (160,000 kids skip school out of fear of bullying) cited by S. Fried and P. Fried, *Bullies and Victims: Helping Your Child Through the Schoolyard Battlefield* (New York: Evans, 1996).

23—Tiffs and Breakups

Parents underestimate the seriousness of friendship breakups: Z. Rubin, *Children's Friendships* (Cambridge, Mass.: Harvard University Press, 1980), p. 89.

Convey to kids that new friends will be found but can't replace a lost one: M. Brenton, "When Best Friends Part," *Parents,* May 1978, p. 45.

Kids need different friends at different stages of development: B. Spock, "How Children Make Friends," *Redbook,* Mar. 1975, p. 31.

Friendship tiffs and breakups are normal: C. E. Schaefer and T. F. DiGeronimo, *Ages and Stages: A Parent's Guide to Normal Childhood Development* (New York: Wiley, 2000), p. 191.

Kids age ten or eleven have a lot to learn about being friends: F. Frankel, *Good Friends Are Hard to Find: Help Your Child Find, Make and Keep Friends* (Los Angeles: Perspective, 1996), p. 141.

Signs that a friendship is cooling off: F. Frankel, *Good Friends Are Hard to Find: Help Your Child Find, Make and Keep Friends* (Los Angeles: Perspective, 1996), p. 147.

Three characteristics of good friends: K. H. Rubin, *The Friendship Factor: Helping Our Children Navigate Their Social World—and Why It Matters for Their Success and Happiness* (New York: Viking Penguin, 2002), pp. 37–38.

24—Too Competitive

Parental pledge of good conduct required in 163 cities: reported by S. Smith, "Is the Choice Sportsmanship or Death?" Knight-Ridder/Tribune Information Services, [www.youthdevelopment.org], July 23, 2000.

Athletic Footwear Association survey cited by D. J. Burnett, "Kids and Sports: What's a Parent to Do?" in J. Biederman and

L. Biederman (eds.), *Parent School* (New York: Evans, 2002), pp. 335–340.

25—Too Sensitive

Approximately 15 to 20 percent of kids are highly sensitive: E. Aron, *The Highly Sensitive Child: Helping Our Children Thrive When the World Overwhelms Them* (New York: Broadway, 2002).

Kids are most self-conscious and sensitive in fourth and fifth grades: F. Vitro of Texas Woman's University, cited by J. S. Freedman, *Easing the Teasing: Helping Your Child Cope with Name-Calling, Ridicule, and Verbal Bullying* (New York: McGraw-Hill, 2002), p. 14.

Research (children in six countries reveal that their number one area of distress, next to losing the security of their family, is humiliation) conducted by Kaoru Yamamoto of the University of Colorado, cited by E. McCoy, *What to Do . . . When Kids Are Mean to Your Child: Real Solutions from Experts, Parents, and Kids* (Pleasantville, N.Y.: Reader's Digest, 1997), p. 15.

About the Author

Michele Borba, Ed.D., is an internationally renowned educator who is recognized for her practical, solution-based strategies to strengthen children's behavior and social and moral development. A sought-after motivational speaker, she has presented workshops to over one million participants worldwide and has been an educational consultant to hundreds of schools.

Dr. Borba frequently appears as a guest expert on television and radio, including NPR talk shows, *Today, The Early Show, The View, Fox & Friends,* MSNBC's *Countdown, Vicki Gabereau,* and *Canada AM.* She has been interviewed in numerous publications, including *Redbook, Newsweek, U.S. News & World Report,* the *Chicago Tribune,* the *Los Angeles Times,* and the *New York Daily News.* She serves as the advisory board member for *Parents* magazine.

Dr. Borba's numerous awards include the National Educator Award, presented by the National Council of Self-Esteem. She is the award-winning author of nineteen books, including *Don't Give Me That Attitude!; No More Misbehavin':*

38 Difficult Behaviors and How to Stop Them; Building Moral Intelligence, cited by *Publisher's Weekly* as "among the most noteworthy of 2001"; *Parents* Do *Make a Difference,* selected by *Child* magazine as an "Outstanding Parent Book of 1999"; and *Esteem Builders,* used by over 1.5 million students worldwide. Her proposal to end school violence (SB1667) was signed into California law in 2002. She currently serves as a consultant for the U.S. Office of Education. She lives in Palm Springs, California, with her husband and has three sons.

To contact Dr. Borba regarding her work or her media availability, or to schedule a keynote or workshop for your organization, go to www.behaviormakeovers.com or www.moralintelligence.com.